A WAY WITH WORDS

A WAY WITH WORDS

*The Language of English
Renaissance Literature*

Gert Ronberg

Edward Arnold
A division of Hodder & Stoughton
LONDON NEW YORK MELBOURNE AUCKLAND

© 1992 Gert Ronberg

First published in Great Britain 1992

Distributed in the USA by Routledge, Chapman and Hall, Inc.
29 West 35th Street, New York, NY 10001

British Library Cataloguing in Publication Data

Ronberg, Gert
  Way with Words: Language of English
  Renaissance Literature
  I. Title
  428.009

ISBN 0-340-49307-0

Typeset in 11/12pt Times by Rowland Phototypesetting Ltd,
Bury St Edmunds, Suffolk.
Printed and bound in Great Britain for Edward Arnold, a division of
Hodder and Stoughton Limited, Mill Road, Dunton Green,
Sevenoaks, Kent TN13 2YA by Biddles Ltd, Guildford and
King's Lynn.

Contents

Acknowledgements

I wish to express my gratitude to my colleagues Derrick McClure, for reading the typescript of this book and making valuable suggestions, and Patricia Marshall, for her help in the realm of word processing.

G.R.

Phonetic Notation

A colon after a phonetic symbol indicates a long vowel, as in [i:].

Front Vowels

[i:]   as in *see*
[ɪ]   ,,   *sit*
[e:]   ,,   Scottish *say*, German *see*, French *né* (but long)
[e]   ,,   *set*
[ɛ:]   ,,   French *lèvre* or *rêve*
[æ]   ,,   *sat*
[a]   ,,   northern English or Scottish *sat*, French *chat*

Back vowels

[u:]   as in *zoo*
[ʊ]   ,,   *put*
[o:]   ,,   Scottish or German *so*, French *eau* (but long)
[ɔ:]   ,,   *saw*
[ɒ]   ,,   *got*
[ʌ]   ,,   *but*
[ɑ:]   ,,   *father*

Central vowels

[ɜ:]   as in *cur*
[ə]   ,,   *about* (first syllable), *father* (last syllable)

Diphthongs

[ɪə] as in *here*
[ɛə] ,, *there*
[ʊə] ,, *poor*
[əʊ] ,, *so*
[aɪ] ,, *find*
[aʊ] ,, *found*
[ɔɪ] ,, *boy*
[əɪ] ,, Scottish *find*
[ʊɪ] ,, *cooey* (but short)
[əu] ,, Scottish *found*

Consonants

[p] as the first sound in *pet*
[b] ,, *bet*
[t] ,, *tip*
[d] ,, *dip*
[k] ,, *cot*
[g] ,, *got*
[tʃ] ,, *cheap*
[dʒ] ,, *jeep*
[f] ,, *ferry*
[v] ,, *very*
[θ] ,, *thin*
[ð] ,, *then*
[s] ,, *sue*
[z] ,, *zoo*
[ʃ] ,, *shoe*
[ʒ] ,, *genre*
[h] ,, *hit*
[m] ,, *map*
[n] ,, *nap*
[ŋ] as the last sound in *sing*
[l] as the first sound in *lap*
[r] ,, *rap*
[j] ,, *yet*
[w] ,, *wet*

Introduction

The Renaissance began relatively late in Britain. In Italy it had started, according to most scholars, in the thirteenth century, and Dante (1265–1321), author of *The Divine Comedy*, is often referred to as a Renaissance man. So are, for instance, the painters Cimabue (*c*.1240–1302) and Giotto (*c*.1266–1337). In Britain the transitional period between the Middle Ages and the Renaissance is the fifteenth century. This was the time of the Scottish poets King James I (1394–1437) and Robert Henryson (1430–1506?); and another great Scot, William Dunbar (1465–1530), is just outside it in literary activity (he wrote his first great poem *The Thrissill and the Rois* in 1503). As regards prose the fifteenth century was also a time of some importance. Two of the finest writers, the first Renaissance or near-Renaissance authors to be quoted in this book, were translators: William Caxton (*c*.1421–1491) and Sir Thomas Malory, who died in 1471.

Caxton's main claim to fame is the setting up of his famous press at Westminster and thus introducing printing to Britain, which naturally had wide-reaching implications for the development and dissemination of literacy and literature. His style appears at its most distinctive in the interesting prefaces to his published translations, and it is clear that although his language is often simple and direct, he tried, and makes this explicit, to give the English language a further boost of dignity by attempting greater and more varied complexity of syntactic structure.

Malory was so much more than a mere translator. He was very individual in the way he selected from, and moulded, his sources; and often he would add matter of his own. Although in one sense his famous *Morte Darthur* is a skilfully arranged compilation of translated quotations, it is also a single literary creation of great spiritual unity. Equally important is the fact that *Morte Darthur* became the first prose work in English to form part of the average reader's reading matter now that printing was well established.

Another reason why this book considers the fifteenth century is a linguistic one. It was the time when the English vowel system was being changed to what was becoming in many respects its modern structure although, as we shall see in the first chapter, the modern stage was not reached during the Renaissance.

But it was the next century, the sixteenth, in which the Renaissance really came to make itself felt in Britain. The word Renaissance itself means 'rebirth' and refers to the rebirth of interest in, and study of, classical ideas and literature, to some extent as a reaction to the scholasticism of the Middle Ages. This renewed interest resulted in the generally European, anthropocentric, cultural current we call 'Humanism' (see p. 140), which was to influence deeply and pervasively the subject matter of Renaissance literature. The New Learning also manifested itself in considerable interest in the English language as worthy of close scrutiny. The sixteenth and seventeenth centuries abound with spelling reformers, phoneticians and grammarians, such as John Cheke, John Hart, William Bullokar, Richard Mulcaster, Alexander Gil and Robert Robinson; and some of these also made significant pronouncements on attitudes to language, especially in respect of vocabulary, for this was also an age when a huge influx of Latin and other foreign words took place.

The poetry of the Renaissance was very different from its medieval types. It became much more personally intense and less didactic. The famous *Tottel's Miscellany* appeared in 1557 with songs and sonnets by Sir Thomas Wyatt and Henry Howard, Earl of Surrey. It was Wyatt who introduced the sonnet form to England and ever since, whenever a poet has wished to make a short but emphatic declaration of personal feeling, he has more often than not gone for the sonnet as his vehicle. This poetic form of fourteen lines was modelled on the sonnets of the Italian-Renaissance poet Petrarch (1304–74), although the Petrarcan form was altered, mainly by Surrey, who changed the arrangement of the fourteen lines into three quatrains of four lines each, followed by a final couplet. He thus established what is generally referred to as the Shakespearean sonnet. Illustrative examples of Renaissance language will be taken from a succession of poets stretching from Wyatt via the great Elizabethans Spenser and Sidney and metaphysical poets such as Donne and Herbert to Milton, who can be said to be the last great poet in the Renaissance, humanist tradition.

The rhythm and prosody of Renaissance verse were also different from that of medieval times, mainly because of a very important linguistic development: the loss of final -*e* in words like *time* and *take*, which were now monosyllabic; in Chaucer's time they normally had two syllables. In any case, the fifteenth century had suffered a deterioration of metrical 'propriety'. Wyatt and his followers put that right, having, in a more cosmopolitan age, learnt much from the Italians in this respect.

As for prose, Sidney showed his command of the Renaissance high style (mostly), as seen in his romance *Arcadia*, but perhaps the greatest writer of courtly fiction was John Lyly, famous for his edifying prose work *Euphues*. Both he and Sidney were heavily influenced by classical models in matters of rhetorical balance and sentence structure, which by now had become quite different from that of the preceding century. Middle-style prose was effective in, for instance, the essays of Sir Francis Bacon, and later, towards the middle of the seventeenth century, in Sir Thomas Browne's *Religio Medici*, and non-courtly, didactic, but vivid, prose in a much plainer style by Phillip Stubbes' *Anatomy of Abuses* and the earlier Elizabethan Thomas Nashe's *Pierce Penniless his Supplication to the Devil*. A good example of diary literature is the diary of the Londoner, Henry Machyn. Popular Elizabethan fiction was continued by, amongst others, Thomas Deloney, in his *Jack of Newbury* and *The Gentle Craft*, which are both humorous narratives or novels portraying middle-class Elizabethan life, with graphic depictions of London scenes, and by the anonymous author of *The Pinder of Wakefield*, an often very funny narrative of 'the mad merry history of George a Greene, the lusty pinder of the north', as the author describes his work. (A pinder was an officer of a manor whose duty it was to impound stray beasts.)

The Renaissance literary genius manifested itself in the drama more than in any other genre, and throughout the pages that follow many illustrations have been taken from the great dramas of the time, stretching from Lyly's *Endimion* and Kyd's *Spanish Tragedy* via Marlowe and Shakespeare, Heywood and Tourneur to the racier works by Jonson. Most of the drama is in blank verse, i.e. verse without rhyme, especially in iambic pentameter, and introduced by Surrey in his translation of the *Aeneid*. It was also used with great flexibility and artistry by Milton in, for instance, *Paradise Lost* and *Samson Agonistes*.

It is the language of such writers that will be discussed in the pages that follow. The book does not pretend to be a close linguistic analysis of Renaissance English; it is a book primarily aimed at students of literature. It is my experience, after seventeen years of teaching Renaissance literature and language to undergraduates, that students need considerable help in attuning themselves to the linguistic habits and niceties of the period. All literature is language and the more we know about the latter, the better we are equipped to appreciate the former.

The first chapter describes the sounds and spellings of the period in so far as they are significant for literary appreciation, but also for the more practical purpose of enabling the reader to get accustomed to earlier spelling habits, which could otherwise 'interfere' with the reading. (My reasons for quoting both from modernized editions and from editions with the original spelling and punctuation have been set out on pp. 13 and 117.) Matters of prosody or versification have been only cursorily referred to. They are of such a complex and intricate nature that to do them any kind of justice, they would occupy a disproportionate amount of space, and they have been fully treated elsewhere in books such as G. Saintsbury's *A history of English prosody* and M. A. Bayfield's *A study of Shakespeare's versification*. The second chapter deals with vocabulary and meaning. Its relative brevity may surprise some people, but experience tells me that the areas where students need most help are those of syntax and rhetoric. Syntax works by stealth; it is often much less obvious in its effects compared to graphic imagery on the lexical level, for instance; and the long third chapter therefore describes those peculiarities of morpho-syntax that I find the most significant, viz. those of the verbs and the pronouns. (There are other morpho-syntactic problems of considerable significance, especially within the noun phrase, but space does not permit discussion of these. Some may also regret the absence of any treatment of prepositions, for instance.) Chapter four moves on to considerations of the Renaissance sentence, which is closely tied up with the punctuation practices of the period. This is an area where students most definitely want assistance, and it is surprising how often sentence structure is ignored, or treated very cursorily, in the many histories of the language on the market. The last chapter is devoted to rhetoric, whose importance must never be underestimated, but often is, in the appreciation of works from the greatest period of literature in the English language.

1

Sounds and Spellings

Rhymes

The Great Vowel Shift that took place roughly between the times of Chaucer and Shakespeare brought the sounds of Renaissance English considerably closer to ours. Whereas the sounds of Middle English would make it very difficult for us to understand Chaucer, should he suddenly materialize, we would probably not have too many problems conversing with Shakespeare, especially if we drew on the resources of present-day dialects, which often preserve sounds current in the sixteenth century but no longer normal in, say, the southern English of today. For instance, in the words *time* and *house* Shakespeare would have the diphthongs [əi] and [əu], which are still current in Scottish standard pronunciation but have become [aɪ] and [aʊ] in the southern standard. Chaucer, on the other hand, would pronounce those two words as if they were spelt *hoos* (still current in Scots dialects) and *teem*.

All the same, there were considerable differences between the sounds of the Renaissance and those of today. This is mainly due to the number of variant pronunciations current in the sixteenth century, both as regards the quality and the quantity of vowels. ('Quality' refers to the actual acoustics of the sound, 'quantity' to whether the sound was long or short.) Nothing reveals this more clearly than the rhymes of the period. Many of these look distinctly peculiar to us nowadays and have led students to regard them as half-rhymes or eye-rhymes only. I have even experienced students going into great detail, in their literary interpretations of certain poems, about the 'tensions of discord' produced by what they assumed to be false rhymes. In the following section we shall consider some of the most common Renaissance rhymes that look like rhymes no more:

1 *A* as in *have*. In the sixteenth century some words that now have a short vowel only, had variants (going back to Middle English) with a long vowel, so that *have*, for instance, could rhyme with words like *gave* and *crave* as in *The Faerie Queene* I.i.3; and in a rhyme like *sad:shade* (*A Midsummer Night's Dream* IV.i.94–5) and we do not know whether the -*a*- was short or long since either word could have a short as well as a long vowel.

2 *A* as in *swan*. It was not until the eighteenth century that a *w*-rounded a following -*a*, so rhymes like *are:war:far* (*The Faerie Queene* II.v.15ff) are perfectly genuine. Incidentally, the verb *are* had a long-vowel variant, as evidenced by the rhyme like *are:care* (Sidney, *Astrophel and Stella*, sonnet 34) and *spare:are* (Donne's *The Flea*).

3 *A* in *shall*. This word could have a stressed variant rhyming with *all*. Thus: *call:shall:all* in Wyatt's *A Paraphrase of the Penitential Psalms* 74ff.

4 *A* as in *haste*. Many words in -*aste* and -*ace* (-*ase*) had short variants, which explains e.g. *forecast:fast:haste* and *face:case:alas* in Wyatt's *A Paraphrase of the Penitential Psalms* 17ff and 34ff, respectively. This sound-value is behind the confusion of -*fast* with -*faced* in *shamefaced*, the original form of which is *shamefast* 'rooted in shame'. Note that the long vowel [ɑ:], which the southern standard normally has in words like *fast*, *grass*, is a post-Renaissance development before [s], [f], [ɵ] (i.e. before voiceless fricatives).

5 *Er* as in *serve* and *clerk*. During the transitional period between Middle and early Modern English the combination short *e+r* began to develop into *ar*: Middle English *fer* and *sterre* became early Modern English *far* and *star*. The trouble is that the sound-change never became general, mainly because of the tendency to retain the spelling *er* in French or Latin loanwords. If the *er* was retained, the pronunciation with an *e*-sound would be encouraged and normally win out in the end (finally giving us the Present-day English pronunciation we have in, say, *serve*), despite early variants with an *ar* pronunciation. But a few words with *er* still have, mainly in British English, the *ar* pronunciation, words like *clerk*, *Berkeley*, *Derby*. Occasionally an *er/ar* word was spelt with *ea*, e.g. *heart*, to keep it distinct from *hart* (though *hart* was found for both) and *heard* (with *ea* from *hear*).

In Renaissance English (and indeed some time afterwards) there was considerable vacillation. Thus when Wyatt rhymes *heart:convert:depart* (*A Paraphrase of the Penitential Psalms* 711ff), the middle word clearly has the *ar* pronunciation, because *depart* has original *ar*. So does *heard* in *Astrophel and Stella*, sonnet 34, in a rhyme with *marred*. The original Renaissance spellings were often *ar* where now *er* has been generalized: *darth* (for *dearth*), *marmaide*), (for *mermaide*), *clark* (cp. the modern name *Clark(e)*), etc.

6 EA as in sea. In the sixteenth and seventeenth centuries *ea*-words did not yet normally rhyme with *ee*-words: *sea* and *see* would, in good pronunciation of the time, sound quite different. *Sea* would have [e:], i.e. the vowel a Scotsman would use in the word *say* or a Frenchman in the word *né* (but pronounced long), whereas *see* would have the vowel it has today, i.e. [i:]. In Middle English the difference between the two vowels was ignored in spelling (they were both spelt *e* or *ee*); but in the late fifteenth century the *ea*-spelling was being introduced to show that the vowel it represented was different from the one represented by *ee*.

In the sixteenth century *ea*-words preserving the long [e:] would rarely rhyme with anything other than other *ea*-words. *Feature:nature* in, for instance, Spenser and Shakespeare may thus depend on *feature* being derived from the Middle English variant *faiture* (from French) (Dobson 1968, §115, note 3) since *ay*/*ai* had by then fallen together in sound with the long *a* (i.e. *sale* and *sail* could rhyme as they do today).

However, during the seventeenth century *ea* began to fall together with the long *a* (and, of course, *ai*/*ay*) so that, say, *seal:sale:sail* could rhyme, especially towards the end of the century, but we find e.g. *creature:Nature* in Herbert's *The Pulley* (unless *creature* could be pronounced with the vowels of *create*). It is likely that even Shakespeare knew of the kind of pronunciation that could rhyme *ea* with long *a*/*ai*. Thus, when Gloucester in his opening speech in *Richard III* bitterly refers to his deformity by being 'Cheated of feature by dissembling nature' (I.i.19), Shakespeare very likely intended to foreground Gloucester's pain through assonance and rhyme, i.e. *cheated* was meant to be pronounced with the same vowel as in *feature* and *nature*. Compare also his rhyme *play:sea* in *Henry VIII* III.i.9–10; and no doubt there is a pun on *grease* and *grace* in Dromio of Syracuse's remark 'Marry, sir, she's the kitchen wench, and all grease' in *The Comedy of Errors* III.ii.96–7.

It was not until the eighteenth century that *ea*-words began to rhyme regularly with *ee*-words, as in *sea:see*; but the old seventeenth-century identification of *ea* with a long *a* has lingered on in *break, great, steak*, which still rhyme with *brake, grate, stake*, and of course in the Irish pronunciation of names like *Reagan, Yeats, MacClean*; cp. also *Juno and the Paycock* (for *Peacock*) by the Irish playwright Sean O'Casey.

The quantity of the vowel also varied considerably. Sometimes the vowel could be short as in our *dead* or *breast*: *heath:Macbeth* (*Macbeth* I.i.6–7). The vacillation was particularly frequent in words ending in -*st*: When Samson in *Samson Agonistes* complains that he has been 'Put to the labor of a beast, debased / Lower than bondslave!' (37–8),

Milton intends us to hear an internal rhyme in *beast:debased*, where *beast* has a long vowel. But in Shakespeare's *beast:blessed* (*Venus and Adonis* 326ff) the word has a short vowel; and *sweat* in Spenser's *heat:sweat:eat* (infinitive) (*The Faerie Queene* I.iv.22) has a long one. In *release:press:cease* in sonnet 39 of *Astrophel and Stella* we do not know whether the vowel was short or long since all three words could be pronounced with either at the time.

7 *Ear* and *ere* as in *fear*, *bear*, *here*. An *-r* would often, at the end of the Middle English period, have an opening effect on the preceding long vowel [e:], turning it into [ɛ:], as in *fear* or *here* which in the sixteenth century very often had this vowel and therefore might rhyme with *fare* and *hare*. In fact, *here* and *hare* are used in a pun by Falstaff in *Henry IV*; see the chapter on Rhetoric, p. 164. This is the reason why words like *fear* and *year* came to be spelt with *ea* rather than *ee* in early Modern English. (In some cases there was no problem since the vowel had remained open [ɛ:] before *-r* since Middle English, as in *bear*, *swear*, *wear*.) But sometimes, as we can see from today's pronunciation of words like *fear*, *year* and *here*, the vowel [e:] was not thus affected and developed regularly to [i:] in the Great Vowel Shift. Had that been the most frequent pronunciation in the sixteenth and early seventeenth centuries in words like *fear*, *year*, *hear*, we should probably have had spellings like *feer*, *yeer*, *heer* today. The frequent early Modern English [ɛ:] in such words was responsible for very common rhymes like *bear:near* (*The Faerie Queene* II.viii.4); *near: bear:spear:rear* (*Astrophel and Stella*, sonnet 13); *fear:where* (Donne, *The Good-Morrow*).

8 *O* as in *hop*. At Shakespeare's time two pronunciations of the short *o* were current, viz. the one we have today in British English and one that fell together with short *a*. Occasionally the latter pronunciation provided rhymes like *crab:bob* in *A Midsummer Night's Dream* II.i.48–9, and *pap:hop* (ibid. V.i.293–4). Our doublets *strap/strop* (the latter = 'leather strap for sharpening razors') and *chap(s)/chop(s)* 'jaws' have arisen in the same way.

9 *O* in *one*, *none*, *gone* and *done*. The most frequent pronunciation of these words used the long vowel [o:], indicated by rhymes like *one: bone* (*Venus and Adonis* 293–4); *bone:gone* (ibid. 56–8); *none:bone* (*Timon of Athens* IV.iii.528–9); but short variants like today's were also current, though in the case of *(n)one* with the vowel of *con* rather than that of *bun*, as is still the case in northern English.

The vowel in *done* has a different origin and frequently retained its long vowel [u:] during the Renaissance, providing rhymes like *moon:done* in *Hamlet* III.ii.154–5. But *done* would also sometimes have the shortened vowel current today and rhyme with words like *begun*; even sometimes with the words above (*none, one*), in which case the shortened form of *done* must have gone back to Middle English.

10 O as in *love* and *prove*. In the sixteenth century the words *above*, *dove* and *love* could have either a short *u*-sound, as in *push* [ʊ], or a long one, as in *moon* [u:]. The same, for somewhat different historical reasons, applied to *move, prove* and *approve*. The short-long vowel vacillation persisted in the seventeenth century, when the short *u*-sound began to be unrounded and opened to the vowel of today's southern English *but* [ʌ] in the seventeenth century. Thus in the sixteenth century the extremely common rhymes *love:move: above:prove:dove* would typically be with either [ʊ] throughout or [u:], and with either [ʌ] or [u:] in the seventeenth. A glance at the index under *move, prove* in Wright (1905) shows that [ʌ] has survived in these words in dialects right into the twentieth century.

For similar reasons the word *come* could also have long [u:], as shown by Wyatt's rhyme *come:doom* (*A Paraphrase of the Penitential Psalms* 703–5).

11 OO as in *good* and *flood*. Words ending in -*ood* in Present-day English can have [ʌ] (as in *blood, flood*), [ʊ] (as in *good, hood*) or [u:] (as in *food, mood*). The first two short vowels derive from shortening: in the case of [ʌ] *before* the seventeenth-century unrounding (see 10 above); in the case of [ʊ] *after* it. The distribution of the three vowels involved much more variation in early Modern English. Thus *flood: good* was a perfectly normal rhyme, as was, say *food:stood* (which it still is in Scotland).

12 OI as in *joy* and *join*. In Middle English some of our *oi*-words had [ʊi], some [ɔi] like today, owing to their different origins in French. Thus *joy* would regularly have [ɔi] and *join* [ʊi]. When the early seventeenth-century unrounding of [ʊ] to [ʌ] was taking place (see 10 above), [ʊi] followed suit and became a diphthong that could rhyme with that of a word like *line*; cp. rhymes in e.g. Pope like *join:divine*. And Milton's *servile toil* in the passage from *Samson Agonistes*, discussed on pp. 188–90, was a rhyme.

Because of the possible coalescence of *oi* and *i-e* (as in *join:divine*), some words that were originally *i-e* later came to be spelt with *oi*. Our *boil* (= 'cyst') is a case in point, and so is *groin* (they really ought to be spelt *bile* and *grine*), which explains a rhyme like *swine:groin* in *Venus and Adonis* 1115.

It should also be mentioned that the evidence of sixteenth and seventeenth century phoneticians is that in the combination *kn-*, as in *knee* and *know*, the *k-* was still pronounced at that time; but in *gn-*, as in *gnat* and *gnaw*, the *g-* had often disappeared (Dobson 1968, §§417–8).

The Pronunciation of Certain Endings

1 The ending *-ed*. This was pronounced as a full syllable if the metre required it. Thus, in the following three lines (6, 10, 30) from Glou-cester's opening speech in *Richard III*, the ending must be syllabic for each line to emerge as an iambic pentameter of ten syllables:

Our bruised arms hung up for monuments
And now – instead of mounting barbed steeds
I am determined to prove a villain

For the pronunciation of the present tense endings *-es* and *-eth*, see pp. 53–4.

2 Endings such as *-iage, -tience, -tion, -tious*. These had one syllable (as now), but if the metre required it, they had two. In the following lines from Shakespeare these endings clearly require two syllables for each line to emerge as an iambic pentameter of ten syllables:

MERCUTIO: Making them women of good carriage
(*Romeo and Juliet* I.iv.94)

DUCHESS OF YORK: What means this scene of rude impatience?
(*Richard III* II.ii.38)

MAYOR: But to make open proclamation
(*1Henry VI* I.iv.70)

ANTHONY: For Brutus says he was ambitious
(*Julius Caesar* III.ii.87)

3 The ending *-y (-ie)*. This could be pronounced as today or with the full diphthong of the word *lie* according to necessities of rhyme, as in the following two lines from Donne's *Satyre: Of Religion*:

The mindes indeavours reach, and mysteries
Are like the Sunne, dazling, yet plaine to all eyes.
(87–8)

Those past, her nature, and name is chang'd; to be
Then humble to her is idolatrie.
(101–2)

4 The ending -*ure* in words like *venture* and *tenure*. The normal pronunciation of this, when it was not required to rhyme with words like *sure* and *dure*, was normally just [ər] rather than [jər], as shown by spellings like *venter* for *venture*, *tenor/tener* for *tenure*, and, conversely, *tenure* for *tenor* and *tuture* for *tutor*. (Kökeritz 1953, 271). *Enter:venture* is a rhyme in e.g. *Venus and Adonis* 626–8. Cp. also:

> FOOL: She that's a maid now, and laughs at my departure,
>   Shall not be a maid long, unless things be cut shorter.
> (*King Lear* I.v.49–50)

Early spellings like *forten* for *fortune* indicate a similar pronunciation habit.

A Note on Stress

We must first of all distinguish between prosodic stress and inherent stress. We use the term 'prosodic stress' when we refer to stress according to metrical requirements (in verse) or rhythm in general. The word *fifteen*, for instance, changes its stress for rhythmical reasons dependent on the position in the utterance. Thus, if *fifteen* is at the end of the utterance, we stress, in British English at least, the second syllable (unless we wish to make a contrast with, say, *fourteen*), as in *she's only fiftéén*; but if a stressed word follows fifteen, we stress the first syllable, as in *fífteen years*. Such rhythmical variation is not possible in words with inherent stress. One such example is *antique* in today's English. We stress the second syllable irrespective of whether we say *this is antíque* or *antíque plates*. (The only cases in which inherent stress can be said to vary are from one person to another or from one variety of English to another. Some people always say *cómparable*, some say *compárable*; and American English has *résearch* where British English has *reséarch*.)

The whole question of inherent stress and prosodic stress in early Modern English, especially in words from Latin or French, is a very complex one; see e.g. Kökeritz (1953, 332ff) and Danielsson (1948). We may illustrate prosodic stress variation according to the needs of rhyme and metre by Wyatt's *measure:treasure:not dure* (*A Paraphrase of the Penitential Psalms* 525ff), in which the stress must clearly be on the last syllable of the first two words. Similarly, in the same poem the noun *comfort* (114) must have second-syllable stress because of the rhyme with *resort* and *sort*. Such variation, but this time in a word not borrowed from Latin or French, can also be illustrated by the word *daylight* in two lines close to each other in *A Midsummer Night's Dream* III.iii:

DEMETRIUS: If ever I thy face by daylight see
(15)

HELENA: That I may back to Athens by daylight
(21)

The first instance has the stress, as it is today, on the first syllable; the next has it on the second (and *-light* rhymes with *night* two lines earlier). It is, however, the non-native words that are the greatest problem. Inherent stress and prosodic stress are generally identical, and we should regard this as a fundamental rule of sixteenth-century prosody also (Danielsson 1948, 440); but in some cases, the inherent stress was different from what it is today. Take the word *antique* 'ancient' from the Latin *anticus* or French *antique* which was spelt *antic(k)* in the sixteenth century. (This word should not be confused with *antic* 'grotesque', a borrowing from Italian *antico*.) As we have seen, *antique* has inherent stress on the second syllable in today's English but until *c*.1700 the stress was always on the first. For example:

FIRST PLAYER: Striking too short at Greeks. His ántique sword,
(*Hamlet* II.ii.471–2)

SALISBURY: In this the ántique and well-noted face
(*King John* IV.ii.21)

Similarly, the word *obscure* invariably has the stress on the first syllable in Shakespeare, as in:

KING RICHARD: A little, little grave, an óbscure grave
(*Richard II* III.iii.153)

Whereas *obdurate*, *aspect* and *advertise* are invariably stressed on the second syllable, such as:

CARDINAL: Anon expect him. But if she be obdúrate
(*Richard III* III.i.39)

LADY ANNE: Whose ugly and unnatural aspéct
(*Richard III* I.iii.23)

MESSENGER: As I by friends am well advértised
(*Richard III* IV.iv.430)

Note the syllabic value of *-ed* in the last example.

But in words of foreign origin prosodic stress in verse was much more flexible then than now (unless we allow for unusually irregular metre, which we must do in some cases). *Comrade* (from Spanish/

French), for instance, should be stressed on the second syllable in the first two examples below, but on the first syllable in the last:

POLONIUS: Of each new-hatched unfledged comráde. Beware
(*Hamlet* I.iii.65)

HOTSPUR: And his comrádes that daffed the world aside
(*1Henry IV* IV.i.96)

LEAR: To be a cómrade with the wolf and owl
(*King Lear* II.ii.382)

Kökeritz lists a huge number of such instances (1953, 392ff).

Spellings

Most students read editions of Renaissance literature in which spelling has been modernized, but sometimes there are excellent and useful editions either with the original or near-original spelling (although punctuation has been modernized in some); and certain works are available only in such editions. It is also important to bear in mind, as we shall see in the next chapter, that earlier spellings can be semantically significant; i.e. modernizing can result in distortion of meaning. It can also obscure rhymes, as shown by e.g. *appease:disease:counterpoise* in Wyatt's *A Paraphrase of the Penitential Psalms* (lines 66ff) in the edition by Rebholz: *poise* had a common Middle English and Renaissance variant *peise* or *pese* (ultimately going back to a different French variant), and *counterpese* is what we find in the original Egerton Manuscript 2711 (together with *disese* and *apese*).

For these various reasons it seems appropriate to say a little about Renaissance spelling; and so as to keep the student reminded of it, several quotations in this book have been taken from editions preserving the old spellings, though all citations from drama, Milton and a few other texts have been taken from modernized editions, unless otherwise specified.

Following the decline of Latin and French for official use, English was reintroduced in the 1430s for the writing of official documents. This gave impetus to the adoption of a standard spelling system in contrast to the huge variation that had prevailed in Middle English. Once printing, introduced to Britain by William Caxton in 1476, was fully under way, the standard was consolidated even further; but it was not until the beginning of the eighteenth century that systematization of spelling had resulted in a 'look' very similar to today's, although even then some older habits remained, such as final -*ck* and -*ll* in unstressed endings, as in *musick, publick, musicall* and *generall*.

However, before that look was achieved, there were considerable differences between Renaissance spelling and today's. One of these was the tolerance of variant spellings of the same word. In the words of Vallins 'it is, indeed, ironical that the only element in the modern language which is rigidly fixed is spelling. We still have a certain latitude in pronunciation, grammar, syntax, and even idiom. But spelling, except in a very few words . . . , leaves us no choice at all.' (1965, 71). Well, that was not the picture in the fifteenth, sixteenth, and to some extent the seventeenth centuries, when a word could be spelt in two, and sometimes more than two, ways even within the same paragraph: *idolatry/idolatrie, doth/dooth, heere/here, with/wyth, heart/hart, forbidden/forbiden*. A final *-e*, which had ceased to be pronounced by the end of the Middle English period, was often added to words in the earliest printed books as a 'filler' to create neat margins since the technique for the adjustment of spacing both within words and between them was, as yet, undeveloped. Many a *pot* became a *potte* that way.

In Middle English *-gh* was pronounced in words like *light* and *thought*. (It had the sound of Scottish or German *-ch* in words like *loch* or *ach*.) But once it had ceased to be pronounced, the *-gh* got into words where it was etymologically unjustified. We frequently come across fifteenth and sixteenth-century spellings like *waight* for *wait* and *despight* for *despite*. Most of these anomalies were removed during the seventeenth century, but we still have *delight* and *sprightly*, which ought to be *delite* and *spritely*. Presumably *delight* got its spelling by erroneous association with *light*; and *spright-* is the same word as *sprite* (in e.g. *watersprite*), which is simply a variant of *spirit*.

As already mentioned in the section on rhyme above (6), *ea* was introduced in early Modern English to signal a vowel different from the one in *ee*-words (*sea* vs *see*); but it took some time to become regular, and we often see spellings like *leef* and *leues* for *leaf* and *leaves*, especially early in our period, for instance in Caxton and Malory.

The distribution of the letters *i/j* and *u/v* was unlike ours. Right up until the eighteenth century *j* was considered a variant of *i*, and *v* a variant of *u*. The *j* was generally confined to finishing off a Roman numeral, as in *iij* for 3. Elsewhere *i* was used where we now have *j*, as in *ioy* or *Iack*. As for *u* and *v*, a *u* was used for both the vowel and consonant in the middle of a word, as in *but* and *loue*, whereas *v* was only used in initial position, as in *vp* and *valley*. The letter *s* also had the variant ſ, used initially and within a word, as in ſ*peake and* gueſſe. Many editors who otherwise preserve the original spellings in their editions print *i, j, u, v* according to modern usage and *s* for ſ.

Mention should also be made of *y* for *th*, especially in the definite article (*ye* for *the*). When people wish to provide their establishment with a vague flavour of old tradition, they still give them names like

Ye Olde Tea Shoppe. This *y* for *th*, which could save the compositor one letter type in a very frequent word, was used because of its similarity to the Middle English þ, which had the same sound-value.

Italics were often used for names, and so was an initial capital letter, just like today. But owing to the influence of Continental books initial capitals also became common during the seventeenth century in other words, especially those that were considered important in the text. This habit, which was at its height around the time of Dryden, was on the wane from the mid-eighteenth century.

As a mark of the possessive the apostrophe did not become fully established until the second half of the seventeenth century in the case of the possessive singular (*the boy's home*) and not until the early eighteenth in the case of the plural (*the boys' home*), although *it's* for *its* and the possessive apostrophe in names ending in a vowel were regular in, for instance, those of Shakespeare's plays of which Ralph Crane had provided fair copies for the printers (Salmon 1986, lv). When it was used, the apostrophe would normally show that a syllable was not to be pronounced, as in forms like *'tis* for *it is*, *for't* for *for it*, *did'st* for *didest*, *smooth'd* for *smoothed* (alternatively *smoothd*, *smoothde*), but normally *Ile* for our *I'll*.

We shall end this chapter with a phonetic transcription of a short extract from Shakespeare to show how it might have been pronounced about 1600. Those unfamiliar with phonetic notation can refer to the list of symbols preceding this chapter. The passage is *Romeo and Juliet* II.i.43–56, and will first be given in the spelling of the First Folio of 1623 (*s* has been substituted for the long variant ſ):

ROMEO He ieasts at Scarres that neuer felt a wound,
But soft, what light through yonder window breaks?
It is the East, and *Iuliet* is the Sunne,
Arise faire Sun and kill the enuious Moone,
Who is already sicke and pale with griefe,
That thou her Maid art far more faire then she:
Be not her Maid since she is enuious,
Her Vestal liuery is but sicke and greene,
And none but fooles do weare it, cast it off:
It is my Lady, O it is my Loue, O that she knew she were,
She speakes, yet she sayes nothing, what of that?
Her eye discourses, I will answere it:
I am too bold 'tis not to me she speakes:

hi: dʒeːsts ət skarz ðət nevər felt ə wɔund
bʊt sɒft hwat lɔit ɵruː jɒndər wɪndoː breːks
ɪt ɪz ði eːst ənd dʒuːlɪət ɪz ðə sʊn
əraiz fɛːr sʊn ənd kɪl ði envɪəs muːn
huː ɪz ɔːlreːdɪ sɪk ənd pɛːl wɪð griːf
ðət ðəu hər mɛːd art far moːr fɛːr ðən ʃiː

bi: nɒt hər mɛːd sɪns ʃiː ɪz envɪəs
hər vestəl lɪvrɪ ɪz bʊt sɪk ənd griːn
ənd noːn bʊt fuːlz duː wɛːr ɪt kast ɪt ɒf
ɪt ɪz məi lɛːdɪ oː ɪt ɪz məi lʊv oː ðat ʃiː knjuː ʃiː wɛːr
ʃiː speːks jet ʃiː sɛːz noːθɪŋg hwat əv ðat
hər əi dɪskuːrsɪz əi wɪl ansər ɪt
əi am tuː boːld tɪz nɒt tʊ miː ʃiː speːks

2

Vocabulary and Meaning

Increase in the Vocabulary

A major reason why Renaissance literature was so different from the literatures of previous ages was the enormous increase in the vocabulary. The power of the press, established in the fifteenth century, was enormous throughout Europe. This in tandem with the great European Humanist movement resurrecting classical works from ancient Rome and Greece saw to the rapid spreading of foreign influences. The new words that were introduced could now become consolidated in multiple copies available to a much larger section of the population than previously.

During this period nationalism was an important cultural current in England, and although Latin was the most significant language of learning at the time, there was an increasing feeling that it was high time English was tried out, as it were, much more frequently for purposes other than common-core uses. After all, Chaucer and Gower, and their immediate followers, such as Lydgate and Hoccleve, had paved the way in using English as a literary medium of great power, and in dialects close to the standard about to take shape. The increased importance of London in the later Middle Ages as a centre of administration and culture and the loosened ties with France had brought about augmented feelings of national pride and considerable prestige of English as a dignified language (though not in every quarter, as we shall see in a moment). The Chancellor's address at the opening of Parliament had reverted from French to English in 1362; and so had the language of the law courts in the same year. It was also in the 1360s that English came to be seen as a worthy medium of instruction in the grammar schools, though Latin retained a central place. Although many academic works were still being written in Latin, they also now began to appear in English; but because Latin was still by many considered to be *the* language towards whose perfection

English ought to aspire, an enormous number of Latin loan words (and imitation of Latin syntax) entered English during the Renaissance period. The New Learning had to find new words for the many new concepts that were introduced, and the fresh developments in areas like philosophy, politics, religion and studies of the mind were there to be followed by literate people in much greater numbers than ever before. Ben Jonson's Volpone relishes the scientific and pseudo-scientific jargon with which he dazzles and confuses his surroundings:

> 'To fortify the most indigest, and crude stomach, aye, were it of one, that (through extreme weakness) vomited blood, applying only a warm napkin to the place, after the unction, and fricace; for the *vertigine*, in the head, putting but a drop into your nostrils, likewise, behind the ears; a most sovereign and approved remedy: the *mal-caduco*, cramps, convulsions, paralyses, epilepsies, *tremor-cordia*, retired-nerves, ill vapours of the spleen, stoppings of the liver, the stone, the strangury, *hernia ventosa, iliaca passio*; stops a *disenteria* immediately; easeth the torsion of the small guts; and cures *melancolia hypocondriaca*, being taken and applied according to my printed receipt. (*Pointing to his bill and his glass*) For this is the physician, this the medicine; this counsels, this cures; this gives the direction, this works the effect: and (in sum) both together may be termed an abstract of the theoric and practice in the Aesculapian art. Twill cost you eight crowns. And, Zan Fritada, pray thee sing a verse, extempore, in honour of it.'
>
> (*Volpone* II.ii.93ff)

The Latin words are of course the most learnedly impressive in that passage. Of Volpone's other medical terms, *convulsion, epilepsy, fricace* 'friction, rubbing', *nerve* and *paralysis* are all sixteenth-century loans from Latin or French (*epilepsy* and *paralysis* being ultimately from Greek). It may also surprise some that *practice, retire* and *term* (as a verb = 'to phrase') were not recorded until the sixteenth century, when they were borrowed from French; nor was the Latin loan *extempore*. Other post-medieval (fifteenth-century) words are *abstract* (the noun), *extreme, fortify, napkin* and *torsion*, all from French. And the word *spleen*, although Middle English as a term for the gland, became in Shakespeare for the first time a popular metaphor for various states of mind, such as 'whim', 'courage' or 'gaiety'. The technical compound *retired-nerves* 'contracted sinews?' may be a Jonsonian coinage since this is the only instance in the *Oxford English Dictionary*.

The Renaissance was also an age of exploration, with people being exposed to linguistic influences from most of the inhabited world and resulting in a huge influx of many foreign words. Between 1500 and 1650 we obtained new words like *apparatus, area, caesura, census, decorum, genius, series* from Latin; *fanfare, genteel, machine, promenade, rôle, scene, sirrah* (so common in Renaissance drama) from French; *carnival, gambol, scope* from Italian; *comrade, don* (the title),

sherry from Spanish; *cannibal*, *cockroach*, *negro* from America (ultimately from Spanish); *dock*, *frolic*, *waggon* from Dutch, and thou-
sands of others from these (especially Latin and French) and other
sources.

The importation of Latinate words and adaptations of them during
the Renaissance were favoured by many people, but because the
number of such new words was so extraordinarily large, others began
to complain about them, mainly because they considered a good deal
of the loans unnecessary and because, in their view, they disfigured
the English language. Many of the loans and adaptations died an early
death; for example, by the end of the sixteenth century, *commorse*
'pity' and *ingent* 'immense'; and by the end of the seventeenth century
illecebrous 'attractive' and *anacephalize*, from Greek, introduced by
somebody evidently not satisfied with *recapitulate* from Latin, had also
disappeared. But many that must have looked equally strange at the
time, have remained and now look perfectly familiar, such as *antique*,
celebrate and *contemplate*. In general this resulted in English being
furnished with a very large number of synonyms (words identical or
similar in meaning), a process that had begun in earnest with the many
French words entering Middle English after the Norman Conquest.
This had important stylistic implications for literature since the
Latinate words would often convey a relatively lofty tone compared
to those from the Anglo-Saxon wordstock or those that had long since
become naturalized, such as *suffer* and *joy*, which had been borrowed
in medieval times from French. We can all respond to the different
stylistic nuances of pairs (in which the native word comes first) like
friendliness/amity, *brotherly/fraternal* and *truthful/veracious*. Donne's
stylistic exploitation of such contrasts in the synonomic pairs *suffering/
passion* and *doing/action* is discussed in the last chapter on p. 180; and
when Macbeth says:

> Will all great Neptune's ocean wash this blood
> Clean from my hand? No, this my hand will rather
> The multitudinous seas incarnadine,
> Making the green one red.
>
> (*Macbeth* II.ii.58ff)

we immediately experience the effect of the contrast between *multitudinous seas* and *the green one* and that between *incarnadine* and *red*.
The first instance of *multitudinous* in the *Oxford English Dictionary* is
this one. *Incarnadine* was first recorded in 1591 as a colour adjective
or noun for 'flesh-coloured' (from Latin *caro*, *carnis* 'flesh'). Here
Shakespeare creates a verb and exploits the flesh etymology to make
it mean 'stain with blood'. The cosmic offence that Macbeth has committed against nature or the natural order by killing a man who was
king by divine right is conveyed by the Latinate words, whereas the

native monosyllables *green* and *red* punch the point home, effecting a gut reaction.

Later in our period Milton's use of Latinate vocabulary, together with his Latinate syntax, could also be powerful: 'Who can extenuate thee?' cry the heavenly audience after one of God's speeches in *Paradise Lost* (I.645), i.e. 'lessen thee'. Sometimes he uses words from learnedly scientific registers with special effect; for example, after the apple of the Tree of Knowledge had been tasted:

> These changes in the heav'ns, though slow, produced
> Like change on sea and land, sideral blast,
> Vapor, and mist, and exhalation hot,
> Corrupt and pestilent.
>
> *(Paradise Lost X.692ff)*

and when describing Satan's flight through God's universe:

> Thither his course he bends
> Through the calm firmament (but up or down,
> By center, or eccentric, hard to tell,
> Or longitude) . . .
>
> *(Paradise Lost III.573ff)*

Especially the words *sideral* 'produced by the influence of the stars' and *eccentric* (*by eccentric* meaning 'away from the centre') are striking, but appropriate because their scientific connotations emphasize the mathematical precision and perfection of God's creation. When Milton uses *eccentric*, he never employs it in the normal modern sense of 'odd' or 'capricious'; see e.g. *Paradise Lost* V.623 and VIII.83, where the senses are equally scientific. The modern sense did not appear until about a century after the word was introduced in the 1550s. Milton's Latinate words would often retain their Latin meaning even though they had become current in their modern senses. Consider this description of Satan:

> He above the rest
> In shape and gesture proudly eminent
> Stood like a tower
>
> *(Paradise Lost I.589–91)*

The original Latin meaning of *eminent* was 'protruding' and this is the main sense here, boosted by the strong physicality of *stood* in line-initial position. It is Satan's enormous size that Milton, above all, wishes to convey, although the modern metaphorical connotation is not absent. In the following lines from a passage about the dazed angels having just been hurled down from the celestial regions:

Abject and lost lay these, covering the flood,
Under amazement of their hideous change.
　　　　　　　　　(*Paradise Lost* I.312–3)

abject (with stress on the second syllable) has as much the literal sense
of 'cast down' as the metaphorical one of 'downcast'. Milton no doubt
also wanted us to be aware of the literal senses of *ruin* and *perdition*
in:

　　Him the Almighty Power
Hurled headlong flaming from th'ethereal sky
With hideous ruin and combustion down
To bottomless perdition
　　　　　　　　　(*Paradise Lost* I.44ff)

coming as they do from Latin *ruere* 'to fall' and *perdere* 'to drop, lose'.
The violence of the physical falling is at least as prominent as the idea
of spiritual damnation.

Not everybody was in favour of introducing foreign words and a
controversy, often referred to as the 'inkhorn controversy', sprang up
between those for and those against. One of the latter was the poet
Samuel Daniel. In his *Defense of Rhyme* (1602 or 1603) he replied to
Thomas Campion's *Art of English Poesy*, maintaining that the English
language was fit for rhymed verse:

> And I cannot but wonder at the strange presumption of some men, that
> dare so audaciously aduenter [venture] to introduce any whatsoeuer
> forraine wordes, be they neuer so strange, and of themselues, as it were,
> without a Parliament, without any consent or allowance, establish them
> as Free-denizens in our language. But this is a Character of that per-
> petuall reuolution which wee see to be in all things that neuer remaine
> the same: and wee must heerein be content to submit our selues to the
> law of time, which in a few yeeres wil make al that for which we now
> contend *Nothing*.
> 　　　　　　　　　(Cited in Pennanen 1951, 31)

Thus there were people who advocated the use of native resources to
express lexical needs, rather than relying on Latinate words to do so.
John Cheke, a sixteenth-century Greek scholar, went so far as to
suggest and use words like *washing* for 'baptism', *hundreder* for 'cen-
turion' and *uprising* for 'resurrection', the last one still going strong in
the sense of 'insurrection' rather than 'resurrection'. And in his poetry
Spenser strove for a tone harking back to medieval times. In his
preface to *The Shepheardes Calender*, E.K. (probably Edward Kirke,
a friend of Spenser's) comments on Spenser's Chaucerian or Middle
English-inspired archaisms and their stylistic significance:

> . . . hauing the sound of those auncient Poetes still ringing in his eares, he mought [must] needes in singing hit out some of theyr tunes. But whether he vseth them by such casualtye and custome, or of set purpose and choyse, as thinking them fittest for such rusticall rudenesse of shepheards, eyther for that [because] theyr rough sounde would make his rymes more ragged and rustical, or els because such olde and obsolete wordes are most vsed of country folke, sure I think, and think I think not amisse, that they bring great grace and, as one would say, auctoritie to the verse.
>
> (416–7)

Those familiar with Chaucer will recognize words like *algate* 'always', *eld* 'old age', *hent* 'seize', *soote* 'sweet', *underfong* 'receive', *yfere* 'together', all in Spenser and some in imitators of his, such as Michael Drayton. 'When archaisms and dialect words are found in 17th century English poets (English as opposed to Scots), they are usually imitated from Spenser, not taken directly from medieval literature or regional speech; sometimes they occur in whole phrases closely modelled on those in Spenser's poetry' (Barber 1976, 99). The tone of such archaic words in Spenser is boosted by his occasional archaic grammatical endings like *-n* in the plural of verbs (*doen* 'do', *bringen* 'bring') and nouns (*eyne* 'eyes', *foen* 'foes').

The Renaissance delight in English as a literary language is particularly apparent in the dramatists, above all Shakespeare:

> The sheer quantity of Shakespeare's contribution to the word-stock is astonishing . . . it can be shown that for the years he was active as a dramatist (1590–1610), he contributed approximately 10 per cent of the new words and meanings accreting to the language. His total vocabulary is variously estimated at between 20,000 and over 30,000 words (as against 8,000 for Milton).
>
> (Hughes 1988, 110)

The lexical creativity can be seen in, for instance, the Elizabethan dramatists' fondness for creating striking compound adjectives and for using one word-class for another. Shakespeare was the undisputed master here. Consider the evocative and startling effects of the compound adjectives in the following lines:

BUCKINGHAM: A care-crazed mother to a many sons
  A beauty-waning and distressed widow
(*Richard III* III.vii.174–5)

STANLEY: Of bloody strokes and mortal-sharing war
(*Richard III* V.v.43)

Some editions have *mortal-staring*, which is equally effective.

ARIEL: Jove's lightning, the precursors
   O'th' dreadful thunderclaps, more momentary
   And sight-outrunning were not.

                               (*The Tempest* I.ii.202–4)

IRIS: I met her deity
   Cutting the clouds towards Paphos, and her son
   Dove-drawn with her.

                               (*The Tempest* IV.i.92–4)

CLEOPATRA: Now from head to foot
   I am marble-constant.

                  (*Antony and Cleopatra* V.ii.235–6)

As for using one word-class for another, often called 'conversion', this
became much more frequent after the loss of grammatical endings like
-e and *-en* by the end of the Middle English period, so that there was
no difference in grammatical form between, say, the infinitive of a
verb and a noun. That is why conversion is so frequent in English
compared to other European languages. We can easily use a word like
carpet not only as a noun but also as a verb (*he carpeted the whole
house*). This grammatical possibility was exploited very imaginatively
by Renaissance writers, especially the dramatists, and was known as
anthimeria in the many books on rhetoric at the time; cp. examples
like:

POMPEY: Julius Caesar,
   Who at Phillipi the good Brutus ghosted
                (*Antony and Cleopatra* II.vi.12–13)

KING CLAUDIUS: For goodness, growing to a plurisy
   Dies in his own too much.
                (*Hamlet* IV. vii. 100–1, in the extra
                Second Quarto lines (p. 690 in the
                edition by Wells *et. al.*))

and Milton's *imparadised* and *pillow* as a verb (see *anthimeria* on
pp. 148–9.
   Jonson typically employs conversion in more popular language; cp.
his racy *stare-about* for 'on-looker' in:

NIGHTINGALE: Yea, under the gallows, at executions,
   They stick not the stare-abouts' purses to take.
                (*Bartholomew Fair* III. v.115–6)

(*stick not* meaning 'do not hesitate'). Equally racy is Leatherhead's
use of *pestilence* as an emphatic adverb in the same play:

The Fair's pestilence dead, methinks
(II.ii.i)

'Conversion' also sometimes refers to changing the syntactical properties of a word. *Journey*, for instance, had already been converted from
noun to verb in medieval times, but then it was always intransitive,
i.e. could not take an object. It could do so occasionally during the
Renaissance in the sense of 'traverse', but the transitive use in the
following example from Marlowe, is wholly new (the first instance in
the *Oxford English Dictionary*):

> TAMBURLAINE: But as for you, viceroy, you shall have bits,
>   And, harness'd like my horses, draw my coach . . .
>   . . . you know I shall have occasion shortly to journey you.
>   (*2Tamburlaine* III.v.103–4 and 114–5)

The word may have originally been technical (i.e. 'take (a horse)
through a journey' or 'ride'). Here Tamburlaine uses it haughtily and
aggressively as a vivid metaphor similar to our 'take you through your
paces'.

Popular Vocabulary

It is often difficult for us to comprehend the slang or colloquialisms of
the period, and there is no doubt that a modern audience at Renaissance plays are unaware of many stylistic nuances and cultural implications of the more popular words in early Modern English. Take, for
instance, the famous *Hamlet* crux involving the word *handsaw*, which
has puzzled editors for ages:

> HAMLET: I am but mad north-north-west; when the wind is southerly,
>   I know a hawk from a handsaw.
>   (II.ii.380–81)

Amongst the commentators on this, Hulme (1962, 54–61) is particularly convincing. She shows how the Elizabethans would have got this
pun at once because they knew that a hawk could mean not only a
falcon but also a tool for carrying bricks (a so-called hod). This goes
with -*saw*. But there is, in this part of the word, a pun on the technical
term *sore* in falconry, which was then much more popular as a sport
than it is now. It referred to a young hawk that had not yet moulted.
And, as we know, hawks or falcons sit on the hand of its trainer. It is
virtually impossible for a modern audience to understand such cultural
allusions. And who would get the implications of these lines of the
Queen in *Richard II?*:

So, Green, thou art the midwife to my woe,
And Bolingbroke my sorrow's dismal heir.
Now hath my soul brought forth her prodigy,
And I, a gasping new-delivered mother,
have woe to woe, sorrow to sorrow joined.

(II.ii.62ff)

The specific reference to a midwife and birth (*new-delivered mother*) in the Queen's metaphor makes it highly likely that Shakespeare intended his audience to get the pun of *soul/sole* here: *sole* 'the bottom of something' was a slang word at the time meaning 'arse' (Rubinstein 1989). *Prodigy* did not get its favourable connotations until the second half of the seventeenth century; at Shakespeare's time it meant 'something abnormal, unnatural or monstrous', therefore not born the normal way from the womb but from the *sole*. The Queen is expressing her extreme disgust, mixed with sorrow, at the turn of events.

At a recent performance of *Richard III* a friend asked me during the interval: 'Who is this Mrs Shore that keeps cropping up?'. I informed him that she was Jane Shore, the wife of a London citizen and Edward IV's mistress, but also found it significant to add that *shore* – according to Rubinstein (1989; see under *shore*) – was a term for a whore (with which it rhymes) because Shoreditch was to Shakespeare's London what King's Cross is to ours: a favourite haunt for ladies of the night. What kind of place Shoreditch was is clear from, for instance, Thomas Nashe's *Pierce Penniless his Supplication to the Devil*, which has a section in which he condemns lechery (referring unflatteringly to some great ladies of the past):

> Lais, Cleopatra, Helen – if our clime hath any such, noble Lord Warden of the witches and jugglers, I commend them with the rest of our unclean sisters in Shoreditch, the Spital, Southwark, Westminster, and Turnbull Street to the protection of your Portership, hoping you will speedily carry them to hell, there to keep open house for all young devils that come, and not let our air be contaminated with their sixpenny damnation any longer.

(68)

Shakespeare's audience would therefore be sensitive to an unflattering innuendo in Clarence's remark:

> By heaven, I think there is no man secure
> But the Queen's kindred, and night-walking heralds
> That trudge betwixt the King and Mrs Shore.

(*Richard III* I.i.71–3)

made explicit in Gloucester's 'And this is Edward's wife, that monstrous witch, / Consorted with that harlot, strumpet Shore' (III.iv. 70–1).

But there is help at hand for us, both in the many carefully annotated editions available and in the *Oxford English Dictionary*. For Shakespeare in particular, Hulme (1962), for instance, is a good follow-up, also on the less decent language, which Partridge (1968) and Rubinstein (1989) specialize in. And, for instance, Jonson's popular vocabulary, which is immense, has been discussed in detail by Pennanen (1951).

Meaning

All students and general readers of Renaissance literature have been baffled by passages containing not only obsolete words but also perfectly ordinary-looking ones (as we have already seen), the reason for their bewilderment being the different sense(s) current in earlier times. A student of mine got very confused by what appeared to her to be plainly contradictory in the following lines of Queen Elizabeth in *Richard III*:

> Give me no help in lamentation.
> I am not barren to bring forth complaints.
> All springs reduce their currents to mine eyes,
> That I, being governed by the wat'ry moon,
> May send forth plenteous tears to drown the world.
> (II.ii.66ff)

'If the springs *reduce* their currents', she understandably asked, 'how can they provide her with ''plenteous tears''?'. She did not know that *reduce* originally meant 'bring back', and that that was a much more frequent sense in early Modern English than the later 'to reduce in numbers'. In fact, the general sense of to 'lessen' does not become current until the eighteenth century. Once this had been explained to her, the student had no difficulty with Henry VII's lines towards the end of the same play: 'Abate the edge of traitors, gracious Lord, / That would reduce these bloody days again' (V.viii.35–6). To stay with *Richard III*: three words in III.vii. provide good examples of these 'false friends'. When Buckingham tries, in his best politic manner, to convince the Mayor and the other bystanders of Gloucester's suitability for kingship by pretending to persuade him to accept 'this proffered benefit of dignity', he does not of course imply sarcasm when he says: 'we know your tenderness of heart / And gentle, kind, effeminate remorse' (III.vii.200–1). In the sixteenth century *effeminate* need not have negative connotations, but could be a synonym of *tender*. A little earlier Buckingham gently pretends publicly to take issue with Gloucester's pretended and elaborate reasons for not accepting the throne by calling them *nice* and *trivial* (165), which looks like something of a paradox to us until we remember that the most common meaning of *nice* in the sixteenth and seventeenth centuries was 'fastidious', as in Milton's 'to taste / Think not I shall be nice' (*Paradise Lost* V.432–3). And when Buckingham publicly 'did infer your lineaments' (12) in respect of Gloucester's noble birth, he neither deduced nor implied them (the two meanings of *infer* today); he simply reported or alleged them.

We have already seen how Milton frequently employs his Latinate words in their original senses. In the following quotation a certain word, not particularly Latinate in appearance, at first glance looks wholly inappropriate in Adam's description of paradisiacal idyll:

> To-morrow ere fresh morning streak the east
> With first approach of light, we must be ris'n,
> And at our pleasant labor, to reform
> Yon flow'ry arbors, yonder alleys green,
> Our walk at noon, with branches overgrown,
> That mock our scant manuring . . .
>
> (*Paradise Lost* IV.623ff)

The 'certain' word is of course the last one, which at Milton's time simply meant 'cultivate'. It is unfortunate if, here, heaps of dung present themselves to our mind's eye. Another instance from the same work illustrates an even more dangerous 'false friend':

> Thus Eve her night
> Related, and thus Adam answered sad
>
> (V.93–4)

The dream that Eve has just related was the one about the Temptation, no less. Adam's reaction is not one of sadness but one of fear: 'nor can I like / This uncouth dream, of evil sprung, I fear', as he says three lines further on. A perfectly normal meaning of *sad* in early Modern English was 'serious, with a heavy mind', and this is the sense the word has here.

It is thus clear that word-meaning is not constant; it is extremely volatile and changes are taking place all the time, a recent change being one referred to above, viz. *infer* in the sense of 'imply' rather than 'deduce'. One rather obvious, but very significant, reason for semantic change is change of circumstance in one way or another. Cultural and social changes result in new objects and new concepts, and the language, in the way it adjusts to the expression of these, will reflect such developments. We sometimes borrow from other languages the way the Renaissance did, though not on the same scale, in our need for expressing new concepts: *glasnost*, a recent loan from Russian, has, in the wake of the liberalization of certain eastern countries, become useful to denote a special kind of openness in cultural relations. But more often than not, an old word is given new senses, as in the case of *car*, which goes back to Latin; but we do not imagine Caesar and Augustus behind the wheel of a Lamborghini.

A less obvious example is the word *science*, which used to denote 'knowledge in general'; and that is the normal sense in Renaissance English, as in:

> DUKE: Of government the properties to unfold
>   Would seem in me t'affect speech and discourse,
>   Since I am put to know that your own science
>   Exceeds in that the lists of all advice
>   My strength can give you.
>   (*Measure For Measure* I.i.3–7)

It is not until later, after the post-Renaissance consolidation of scientific principles, that the word changed its meaning.

A cultural area of enormous significance for literature is that of church and religion. This becomes obvious in the reading of especially medieval and much Renaissance literature, written when faith was central to people's lives in ways difficult for many of us to comprehend today. In the words of Jonathan Sachs in his 1990 Reith Lecture on BBC Radio 3, printed in *The Listener*, 22 November 1990:

> For the greater part of human history, religion has been seen as the foundation of morality. In Dostoevsky's words: if God did not exist, all would be permitted. But this belief must seem to us now decidedly strange. Whether or not we believe in God, we inhabit a culture in which religious teachings are marginal to many people's moral choices. When did we last hear, in a television discussion or a newspaper editorial, the simple assertion that something was wrong because God or religious doctrine said so? Even a religious leader who said this would nowadays be branded a fundamentalist. Our moral language has effectively been secularised. Religion enters our conversations obliquely and with embarrassment. Yet society survives. The world continues uninterrupted on its course. What is hard for us to understand is how anyone could have thought otherwise.

Yes indeed; it is hard. It is difficult for us to attune ourselves to the force, power and meaning of many religious or ethical words in the literature of earlier ages. As pointed out by Hughes (1988, 32ff), the seven deadly sins have undergone considerable amelioration, i.e. their connotations have become less negative and pejorative. It seems that a good sex life is impossible in today's western world without multiple orgasms, clitoral stimulation, extensive foreplay etc.; in short, without what amounts to the satisfaction of what used to be one of the seven, viz. *lust*, which is now celebrated in literature, and other forms of art, rather than condemned. The word has certainly lost much of its deeply serious connotation of sin and evil in its reference to sex. There is not necessarily anything wrong with that. All I am trying to point out here is that attitudes have changed. No longer do we, as in the Middle Ages and, to some extent, in the Renaissance, conceive of the seven deadly sins as spirits of evil, or even demons in animal shapes, forever ready to lead man astray, corrupt him and poison his soul.

Take the word *sin* itself. For many people the once deep-rooted meaning of 'transgression of the divine law and an offence against God' has been diluted to 'naughty': *eating that creamcake was positively sinful.* The first instance in the *Oxford English Dictionary* of this ameliorated sense is very late (1863) in the history of this ancient word, and even then the nineteenth-century writer felt that he had to enclose it in inverted commas to indicate a not as yet fully established use: *he considered it 'sinful' to expend 10/6 on a bottle of any wine.* Since the word has become so innocuous in most contexts, a modern reader may find it hard to be sensitive to its use in a poem like the following by Donne, in which the old powerful connotations of transgression accompanied by fear are essential for a true appreciation of the tone and depth of feeling:

> Wilt thou forgive that sinne where I begunne,
>   Which is my sin, though it were done before?
> Wilt thou forgive those sinnes through which I runne,
>   And doe them still: though still I doe deplore?
>   When thou hast done, thou has not done,
>   For, I have more.
>
> Wilt thou forgive that sinne by which I wonne
>   Others to sinne? and, made my sinne their doore?
> Wilt thou forgive that sinne which I did shunne
>   A yeare, or two: but wallowed in, a score?
>   When thou hast done, thou hast not done,
>   For, I have more.
>
> I have a sinne of feare, that when I have spunne
>   My last thred, I shall perish on the shore;
> Sweare by thy selfe, that at my death thy Sunne
>   Shall shine as it shines now, and heretofore;
>   And, having done that, Thou hast done,
>   I have no more.
>
>   (*A Hymne to God the Father*)

It is also important to bear in mind while reading earlier texts that a word which now belongs to a certain language register might have been typical of a different one in bygone days. *Coax* and *clever*, for instance, were considered 'low' words, pertaining to slang or a very colloquial register, in the sixteenth and seventeenth centuries. Thomas

Browne (the author of *Religio Medici*) described the latter as being among the 'words of no general reception in England'; now both are part and parcel of the central common-core wordstock. A similar route has been taken by *dwindle*, a highly unusual (and probably at the time still thought of as dialectal) and therefore subtly nuanced word in Elizabethan English, first recorded in Shakespeare. To us it is perfectly ordinary though of restricted use (mainly with light or resources); but to the Elizabethan the word was evocatively powerful, as when used by the First Witch in *Macbeth*, its strangeness at the time suiting to perfection the odd register of the weird sisters:

> Sleep shall neither night nor day
> Hang upon his penthouse lid.
> He shall live a man forbid.
> Weary sennights nine times nine
> Shall he dwindle, peak and pine.
>
> (I.iii.18ff)

Oldcastle (Falstaff) uses the word quaintly selfmockingly in *1Henry IV* when he says to Russell (Bardolph):

> Russell, am I not fallen away vilely since this last action? Do I not bate? Do I not dwindle? Why, my skin hangs about me like an old lady's loose gown.
>
> (III.iii.1–3)

Conversely, the word *silly* is now marked as colloquially pejorative; but in Renaissance English it was a 'serious' word meaning 'poor, helpless, pitiful'. It had a spelling variant *seely* and because of the considerable danger of misunderstanding, some editors print that spelling, as in:

> Thoughts tending to content flatter themselves
> That they are not the first of fortune's slaves,
> Nor shall not be the last – like seely beggars,
> Who, sitting in the stocks, refuge their shame
> That many have, and other must, set there
>
> (*Richard II* V.v.23ff)

Amazement, to take another example of register change, is, like *dwindle*, first recorded in Shakespeare (though *amazed* is older). It belonged to the high-style register, but does so no more, and denoted a state of mental paralysis through bewildered shock. We are supposed to understand how profoundly the shipwreck at the beginning of *The Tempest* must have affected Miranda when Prospero tells her:

PROSPERO: Be collected.
  No more amazement. Tell your piteous heart
  There's no harm done.
MIRANDA: O woe the day!
                             (I.ii.13–15)

And Milton gives us a powerful illustration of the semantic force of
this word in *Paradise Lost*, when the angels following Satan in their
enforced exile from heaven lay

                 covering the flood,
  Under amazement of their hideous change.
                         (I.312–3)

The angels are more than surprised! They are in deep shock, and this
is supported by *hideous*, which does not refer to their looks but to
their mental state. It here has the original sense of 'horrifyingly and
agonizingly distressing'.

    The instances of register change mentioned so far have been through
time, from one language era to another; they have been *diachronic*
register changes. Borrowing from one current register into another in
a given period (*synchronic* register switching) can be highly effective,
and is a not uncommon feature of modern poetry. The poetry of
Donne, and that of other metaphysical poets, sometimes makes use
of register switching in extended metaphor, as when in one of his
sonnets he employs at the start the register of the smithy to express
his recalcitrance in mending his ways:

    Batter my heart, three person'd God; for, you
    As yet but knocke, breathe, shine, and seeke to mend;
    That I may rise, and stand, o'erthrow mee, and bend
    Your force, to breake, blowe, burn and make me new.

Shakespeare's sonnet 87 is about the loss of love, as is no 73, discussed
on pp. 186–7. But whereas the latter sonnet employs essentially plain
Anglo-Saxon words, resulting in elementally direct and heartfelt simplicity in the treatment of loss of love through death, no 87 'discusses'
the theme more obliquely by drawing a parallel between it and finan-
cial/legal transactions in the use of words that are typical, though
not always confined to, that register; words such as *dear, possessing,
estimate, charter, worth, releasing, bonds, determinate, granting, riches,
gift, patent, misprision, judgement*. Part of the success of this 'conceit'
poem lies in the consistent, weblike spread of the distancing register
throughout the sonnet. Even the first (and here important) word *farewell* carries the ambiguity or double-levelled meanings essential to the
poem, since *farewell* in the sixteenth century also served as a legal
term for a payment on quitting a tenancy:

> Farewell – thou art too dear for my possessing,
> And like enough thou know'st thy estimate.
> The charter of thy worth gives thee releasing;
> My bonds in thee are all determinate.
> For how do I hold thee but by thy granting,
> And for that riches where is my deserving?
> The cause of this fair gift in me is wanting,
> And so my patent back again is swerving.
> Thyself thou gav'st, thy own worth then not knowing,
> Or me to whom thou gav'st it else mistaking;
> So thy great gift, upon misprision growing,
> Comes home again, on better judgement making.
> Thus have I had thee as a dream doth flatter:
> In sleep a king, but waking no such matter.

Two of the most important processes of semantic change are through 'semantic restriction' and 'semantic extension', and if we are not constantly aware of such processes having operated between the Renaissance and today, bad misconceptions may be the result. Semantic restriction is a change through which a word develops certain specializing semantic features, resulting in a less general meaning; compare *science* above (p. 28) and *human / humane* below. Consider the following lines from *As You Like It*:

> ROSALIND: . . . your brother and my sister no sooner met but they
> looked; no sooner looked but they loved; no sooner loved but
> they sighed; no sooner sighed but they asked one another the
> reason; no sooner knew the reason but they sought the remedy;
> and in these degrees have they made a pair of stairs to marriage,
> which they will climb incontinent, or else be incontinent before
> marriage.
>
> (V.ii.31ff)

At Shakespeare's time *incontinent* normally meant two things: (1) 'at once' and (2) 'wanting in self-restraint' and he typically puns on both. Due to later semantic restriction we got the sense 'unable to retain natural evacuations', as the *Oxford English Dictionary* delicately puts it; and this meaning might lead the unwary to a ludicrous misreading of Shakespeare, investing his text with a sense that would never have occurred to him. Similarly, when Valtemand tells Claudius in *Hamlet* of the King of Norway's *age, and impotence* (II.ii.66), he is not referring to the King's waning sexual powers. The first example in the *Oxford English Dictionary* of this later and narrower meaning is from 1655. This should alert us to exercising great care when we wish to employ the word in its original sense, which is not quite dead yet.

The opposite of semantic restriction is 'semantic extension' whereby, by losing one or more specializing features, the meaning is generalized.

A word that is in the process of semantic extension at the moment is *anticipate*, which used to mean 'foresee and forestall'. Now it is used much more in the more general sense of 'expect', the idea of forestalling having almost been lost; so we must be careful not to misread a line like Macbeth's: 'Time, thou anticipat'st my dread exploits' (*Macbeth* IV.i.160).

A more subtle, but important, extension can be seen in a semantic spread from subjectivism to the inclusion of objectivism, i.e. from a sense denoting a person's feeling about something to a sense denoting the *object* of that feeling. An example will, I hope, make the distinction clear: the original meaning of *abomination* was a subjective one (and is still current) i.e. 'detestation' or 'disgust', as in *most people regard child abuse with abomination*. The word then extended or 'objectivized' its meaning so that it could refer to the abominable *act* as well, as in *child abuse is an abomination*. It is this subjective/objective *polysemy* (i.e. one form, more than one meaning) that enables King Richard to equivocate so magnificently on the word *care* (in the great deposition scene in *Richard II* IV.i.185ff), discussed on pp. 163–4. See also *courtesy / curtsy* below.

The next illustrations of semantic extension are of words that have been extended by figurative transference, i.e. they have come to be used metaphorically as well as literally. We are all aware that many words can be used in a transferred sense beside the literal one, as when a disliked person is called a *toad*, for instance. Some of these metaphors are now so common that we no longer think of them as such. A phrase like *the foot of the mountain* has lost all vividness, but the first time the transference took place, the image was probably considered strikingly creative. Nor do we think of the word *flour* as a metaphor any longer; but once it had the effect of one, being an extension of *flower* as in *the flower of the wheat*, i.e. the best part of the wheat (not the chaff); cp. *the flower of manhood* and other similar extensions. Thus *flour* and *flower* were originally the same word, and they were still not distinguished in Samuel Johnson's Dictionary of 1755. The insistence on separate spellings came about when the extension had gone so far that *flour* had lost all association with *flower* in people's consciousness; i.e. one was not thought of as a metaphor of the other. Johnson does distinguish *metal* and *mettle*, though, but in the century before him these two words were conceptualized as one and therefore not distinguished in spelling. Either could be spelt *metal* or *mettle* (or *mettel, metelle, mettaill* – there were even more variants, but not according to sense). If we do not realize that what we now know as *mettle* was originally a metaphorical extension of what we know as *metal*, and a 'live' metaphor in the sixteenth century, we are likely not to appreciate the powerful wordplay when Macbeth says to his fiendlike queen:

> Bring forth men-children only,
> For thy undaunted mettle should compose
> Nothing but males.
>
> (I.vii.72–4)

Macbeth puns on *metal* and *mails* 'coats of mail'. In addition to the
sense of *undaunted mettle* 'untamed spirit', seen as being particularly
suitable for producing male children, Macbeth also conjures up for us,
by inviting us to note the literal sense of *metal*, the image of Lady
Macbeth's nature as sufficiently steely for producing *mails*. Because
mettle was still comprehended as a metaphor when the play was first
performed, the wordplay was clear to an Elizabethan audience.

Human and humane and *courtesy* and *curtsy* are further examples
of words that were earlier thought of as one word for each pair, though
they were not in a literal vs metaphorical relationship. *Humane* arose
through semantic restriction from the addition of the specializing feature of compassion or kindness to *human* which means 'characteristic
of man'; and once the restriction had reached a certain point (not
until the eighteenth century) *humane* came to be comprehended as a
separate word, resulting in differentiation of spelling (and stress). But
when Bacon, in the original spelling, writes of truth and the knowledge
of it as *the Soveraigne Good of humane Nature* in his essay *Of Truth*
(p. 8), he obviously means 'human nature'.

Curtsy arose by the objectivizing process described above: *courtesy*
was originally subjective and was used to describe 'a courteous state of
mind' (a meaning still current); then by objectivizing extension it came
to mean (1) 'act of courtesy' and (2) 'little bow' or 'respectful lowering
of the body'. When the word was used in sense (2), it ended up by being
thought of as a different word invariably spelt *curtsy*; but no matter what
the sense, there was no differentiation in spelling according to meaning
in Renaissance times. It can therefore sometimes be hard for an editor
of Renaissance texts to decide which sense is meant or which is the more
prominent if both are meant. Take this instance from *The Merchant Of
Venice*, where Shylock says of Antonio:

> . . . a beggar, that was used to come so smug upon the mart. He was
> wont to call me usurer: let him look to his bond. He was wont to lend
> money for a Christian courtesy: let him look to his bond.
>
> (III.i.42ff)

As we can see Wells *et al.* print *courtesy* and thus probably take the
word in the sense of 'act of generosity'. But I would not be surprised
if the Elizabethan Shylock made a little bow here (curtsies were not
confined to women) in scornful imitation of Antonio approaching him.

For further discussion of such semantically relevant spelling problems, see e.g. Wells (1979, 10–13) and Salmon (1986).

3

Forms and Usage: Verbs and Pronouns

Verbs

The Renaissance verb was in its syntactic behaviour often different from ours, which may cause some bewilderment to readers not accustomed to this. As an introductory illustrative example we may take the 'verbal noun' or the 'gerund', which ends in *-ing* (and should therefore not be confused with the 'present participle', for which see 1.2 below). The term 'verbal noun' implies that synctactically it can function as both a noun and a verb. Its noun-like properties can be seen in its ability to be a subject (*smoking is bad for you*) or an object (*she hates smoking*) or the complement of a prepositional phrase (*she is against smoking*); its verb-like characteristics come out in its ability to *take* an object (*smoking two cigars is quite enough*) or be modified by an adverb (*smoking excessively is bad for you*). Because of its noun-like behaviour, the verbal noun can be preceded by the definite article: if it is, it cannot take an object but must be followed by an *of*-phrase instead; if it is not, it can take an object but not an *of*-phrase; compare *the timing of his remarks was unfortunate* with *timing your remarks well is very important*. However, this rigid rule was not a grammatical rule at all during the Renaissance, as we can see from the following two examples:

> . . . it was no hurt to trust downe ones hand, but to get out impossible, without great tearing of the hand to peeces
>
> (*The Pinder of Wakefield* 41)

> CORDELIA: What can man's wisdom
>   In the restoring his bereaved sense
>
> (*King Lear* IV.iii.8–9)

We would now have to say *without greatly tearing the hand to pieces* and *in restoring his bereaved sense*; but a conflation, as it were, of the two structures was perfectly good Renaissance grammar.

1 Tense and Aspect. Unlike many tongues Germanic languages, of which English is one, have only two tenses by *inflection*, viz 'present' and 'past'. In the history of English, or any other Germanic language, there has never been any way of marking *inflectionally* the 'future' or the 'perfect' or the 'pluperfect'. These have come, in the centuries from Old English to Modern English, to be expressed with increasing frequency by means of auxiliaries accompanying main verbs, i.e. by complex verb phrases, as in *I shall try* (future), *I have tried* (present perfect), *I had tried* (past perfect).

In the terms 'present perfect' and 'past perfect', 'present' and 'past' refer to *tense*, 'perfect' to one of the three *aspects*. The other two are the 'progressive' (i.e. *be* + the present participle), as in e.g. *I am trying* (present progressive), *I was trying* (past progressive), and the 'simple' aspect, as in e.g. *I try* (present simple), *I tried* (past simple).

1.2 The Simple vs the Progressive Aspect. Nowadays we use the progressive aspect very frequently to express ongoing, normally temporary, events in the present, past or future:

> He is trying to get the car to start.
> He was trying to get the car to start when Lisa arrived.
> While I am marking essays, you'll be looking after the baby.

The student of Renaissance writing must not expect such frequent use of the progressive. This aspect has become particularly common in recent times, but the Renaissance made much less use of it. The danger for the modern reader is that if he does not bear that in mind, he may misunderstand the tone, or even the meaning, of a passage. The progressive is relatively *marked*, the simple aspect relatively *unmarked*, during the Renaissance period, and the difference in meaning between them did not become clear-cut until after the beginning of the eighteenth century. Thus a sentence like *I read* in a Renaissance writer can mean either 'I read' or 'I am reading', i.e. it is the context that will show whether the meaning is one of habit, as in *I read for an hour every evening*, or one of continuous action, as in *Be quiet, I am reading*. In the following quotation from *Hamlet* Polonius is not enquiring about Hamlet's reading habits, but about what he is reading when Polonius speaks to him:

> POLONIUS: . . . What do you read, my lord?
> HAMLET: Words, words, words.
> POLONIUS: What is the matter, my lord?
> HAMLET: Between who?
> POLONIUS: I mean the matter you read, my lord.

(II.ii.193ff)

Similarly, *walk* is used for *are walking* in the following speech by Hero at the start of Act III.i of *Much Ado About Nothing*:

> HERO: Good Margaret, run thee to the parlour.
> There shalt thou find my cousin Beatrice
> Proposing with the Prince and Claudio.
> Whisper her ear, and tell her I and Ursula
> Walk in the orchard, and our whole discourse
> Is all of her.

During the Renaissance the progressive, when it was used, was often, as in Middle English, with verbs of motion, as in these examples from Shakespeare:

> KING HENRY: Good my lord,
> You are full of heavenly stuff, and bear the inventory
> Of your best graces in your mind, the which
> You were now running o'er.
> (Henry VIII III.ii.137ff)

> GADSHILL: Case ye, case ye, on with your visors! There's money of the
> King's coming down the hill; 'tis going to the King's exchequer.
> SIR JOHN: You lie, ye rogue, 'tis going to the King's tavern.
> (1Henry IV II.ii.52ff)

> LEONATO: The revellers are entering, brother. Make good room.
> (Much Ado About Nothing II.i.76)

or these from Spenser's *Faerie Queene*:

> A Gentle Knight was pricking on the plaine
> (I.i.1)

> But *Timias* him lightly ouerhent,
> Right as he entring was into the flood
> (III.v.25)

> So now she had bene wandring two whole yeares
> (VI.vii.38)

The last type, combining the progressive with the perfective aspect, which is perfectly normal in today's English, was much less common in Renaissance English, and would therefore be particularly marked stylistically.

With non-motion verbs the progressive is less usual and therefore stylistically marked:

> OPHELIA: My lord, as I was sewing in my chamber . . .
> (Hamlet II.i.78)

VICEROY: What help can be expected at her hands
   Whose foot is standing on a rolling stone,
   And mind more mutable than fickle winds?
                        (*The Spanish Tragedy* I.iii.28–30)

In this example *standing* is close to being a participial adjective, qualifying *foot* the way *mutable* qualifies *mind*.

MENENIUS: When you are hearing a matter between party and party,
   if you chance to be pinched with the colic, you make faces like
   mummers . . .
                        (*Coriolanus* II.i.71ff)

i.e. 'are listening to'. Another instance, with the verb *seek*, from Thomas Deloney's *The Gentle Craft* 172:

. . . therefore when they should be seeking of vs in *Fleetstreet*, we would be seeking out the Coast of *Florida*.

The last example illustrates the use of the progressive infinitive after an auxiliary. Compared to its high frequency in today's English, this construction was uncommon during the Renaissance:

CARDINAL WOLSEY: For your great graces
   Heaped upon me, poor undeserver, I
   Can nothing render but allegiant thanks,
   My prayers to heaven for you, my loyalty,
   Which ever has and ever shall be growing,
   Till death, that winter, kill it.
                        (*Henry VIII* III.ii.175ff)

Shall be growing would catch the attention of a Renaissance audience in a way that is difficult for a modern listener to imagine, now that constructions like *I'll be seeing you* are so commonplace. For further discussion of *shall/ will* + progressive infinitive, see 8.5. (p. 70) below.

1.3 The Simple vs Perfective Aspect. In present-day English the present perfect is used for past actions or events that are closely associated with, or have some relevance for, the present time, as in:

She has read an enormous number of books (i.e. she is very well-read)
Have you heard the news this morning? (it is still morning)

But if the action or event is firmly set in the past without the close association with the present, the simple past is used:

Did you hear the news this morning? (said in the afternoon or evening)

This difference in meaning between the simple past and the present perfective is now well-established. There are a few exceptions. Thus in statements or exclamations reflecting excitement or emotion, especially with the strong adverb *never*, the simple past may be used: *I never saw the like!* (cp. *I have never seen her before*); and American English will sometimes have the simple past where British English prefers the present perfect: '*Do you want some stew?*' – '*No thanks, I already ate.*'

In Middle and Renaissance English, however, the distinction between the two was less clear-cut. We find not infrequently the present perfect where we should now use the simple past, and *vice versa*. In the following example today's English would have the simple past because of the conjunction *whiles* referring to the time of Borachio's speech, which has finished:

> CLAUDIO: I have drunk poison whiles he uttered it.
>
> (*Much Ado About Nothing* V.i.238)

and in the next example it seems not to matter which of the two verb forms is used; Malory uses both where we would use the simple past only (in the context *hath wounded* refers to the action in the past rather than to a now wounded man):

> as he wolde have rescowed his lady, sir Bleoberis overthrewe hym and sore hath wounded hym.
>
> (*Morte Darthur* 397)

Conversely, we should use the present perfective in the following instance:

> KENT: You spoke not with her since?
>
> (*King Lear*, Quarto text, sc. 17, 36)

> KING HARRY: I was not angry since I came to France
>   Until this instant.
>
> (*Henry V* IV.vii.53–4)

and the past perfective (pluperfect) *had thrown* for Spenser's past tense *did throw* in:

> A louely Ladie rode him faire beside,
> Vpon a lowly Asse more white then snow,
> Yet she much whiter, but the same did hide
> Vnder a vele, that wimpled was full low,
> And ouer all a blacke stole she did throw,
> As one that inly mournd . . .
>
> (*The Faerie Queene* I.i.4)

As in Middle English the perfective of verbs of motion was often constructed with *be* instead of, as now, with *have*:

> So whan the duke and his wyf were comyn unto the kynge . . .
>
> (Malory, *Morte Darthur* 7)

A survival of this can be seen in *he is gone* as opposed to *he has gone*. Stylistically the choice available during the Renaissance between *have* and *be* in such cases could be important in that emphasis on the state (*be*) rather than the action (*have*) could be conveyed more subtly then than it can today:

EDMOND: The wheel is come full circle.

(*King Lear* V.iii.165)

Completeness of state rather than completion of action is conveyed by *is* here. Similarly:

CASSIUS: My life is run his compass

(*Julius Caesar* V.iii.25)

2 Mood: the Subjunctive vs the Indicative. As opposed to the indicative mood, which stresses the factual, the subjunctive implies the non-factual, such as wish, hope, possibility and the like. The present subjunctive is identical in form with the infinitive in all persons, i.e. there are no endings in the second and third persons singular: *thou see, he see* as opposed to the indicative *thou seest, he seeth/sees*. Note that the form *be* is not confined to the subjunctive in the plural; it frequently survives from Middle English as an indicative (beside *are*) in early Modern English and is particularly common in *there be*. (*Be* for *are* is still current in dialects.) In the following two examples *be* and *been*, the latter confined to the early part of our period, are both indicatives:

There be two points that never move but firmly keep their place
(Wyatt, *Iopas's Song* 18 (p. 217))

But they been corrupt, simple and pure, unmixed
(ibid. 29)

The past subjunctive is marked in form in the first and third persons singular of *to be*, which are both *were*. In the second person singular, i.e. with *thou*, we sometimes find *wert* beside *were*.

In main clauses the subjunctive is today confined to the present tense and to fixed expressions of hoping or wishing, as in:

God save the Queen!
Long live the King!
Heaven be praised!
God be with you.
Heaven/God forbid that . . .

The subjunctive was very frequent in Middle English but it was during that period that auxiliaries began to appropriate the meaning of the subjunctive. Besides a sentence like *It is strange he sit there all day*, it now became possible also to say *It is strange he should sit there all day*. During the Renaissance the use of auxiliaries gained ground at the expense of the subjunctive, but the latter was still much more common than it is today. In some cases we do not even use an auxiliary to make up for the loss of the subjunctive, but just employ the indicative. Thus it was normal in Middle and early Modern English to say e.g. *I shall stay until she come home*, indicating through the use of the subjunctive *come* the relative uncertainty of the arrival home. Now the indicative *comes* has taken over. Variant modern constructions are sometimes dependent on style or variety of English:

a It is important that he be told about this (present subjunctive).
b It is important that he should be told about this (auxiliary).
c It is important that he is told about this (present indicative).

The first of these variants is particularly formal and is more common in American English than in British English, which prefers (b) or the less formal third sentence with the verb in the indicative. The corresponding Renaissance version would naturally have the subjunctive in such an instance; and it is important that today's readers of early Modern English texts do not read inappropriate, lofty or formal tones into sentences containing subjunctives where we would not use them.

2.1 The Subjunctive in Main Clauses. During the Renaissance the subjunctive was much more frequent than today in main clauses. It was not confined to set expressions and would therefore sometimes take the modern student by surprise or prove confusing:

ORCANES: Come banquet and carouse with us a while,
    And then depart we to our territories.
    (*2 Tamburlaine* I.ii.88–9)

i.e. 'let us depart'.

JENKIN: Every man agree to have it as Nick says.
    (*A Woman Killed With Kindness* I.ii.45)

i.e. 'let every man agree'.

Other examples, expressing wish:

ZABINA: Such good success happen to Bajazeth!
    (*1 Tamburlaine* III.iii.116)

NESTOR: He is not emulous, as Achilles is.
ULYSSES: Know the whole world he is as valiant –
    (*Troilus and Cressida* II.iii.228–9)

QUEEN MARGARET: No sleep close up that deadly eye of thine
> (*Richard III* I.iii.222)

This subjunctive of wish can sometimes be found also in relative clauses:

SIR CHARLES: There's music in this sympathy, it carries
Consort, and expectation of much joy,
Which God bestow on you . . .
> (*A Woman Killed With Kindness* I.i. 69–71)

i.e. 'and may God bestow it on you'.

The past subjunctive in main clauses sometimes occurred in *be* (as a main verb) or *have* (as an auxiliary). These past subjunctives correspond to *would* + infinitive in Present English. Here are first some instances with *were*:

it were grete joye unto us all and hit [if it] myghte please the kynge to make her his queene
> (Malory, *Morte Darthur* 9)

DON PEDRO: She were an excellent wife for Benedick.
> (*Much Ado About Nothing* II.i. 329)

Ah Ladie (said he) shame were to reuoke
The forward footing for an hidden shade
> (*The Faerie Queene* I.i.12)

And were her vertue like her beautie bright,
She were as faire as any vnder skie
> (*The Faerie Queene* IV.viii.49)

In this last example, the subjunctive *were* occurs first in the subordinate clause (i.e. 'and if her virtue were . . .'), then in the main clause ('she would be as fair . . .'). Needless to say, in those cases where there would be no contrast between indicative and subjunctive *were*, i.e. the plural, the danger of misreading is particularly acute:

VICEROY: O, wherefore went I not to war myself?
The cause was mine; I might have died for both:
My years were mellow, his but young and green;
My death were natural, but his was forced.
> (*The Spanish Tragedy* I.iii.39ff)

The Viceroy, who thinks his son has died in a war he (the Viceroy) did not himself join, is emphasizing the contrast between what was (indicative) and what might have been (subjunctive). This is clear in *my death were* (subjunctive – 'would have been') vs *his was* (indicative), but it is less clear that *were* in the preceding line is equally a subjunctive because the indicative would also be *were* and is understood in *his* [were] *but young and green*. The Viceroy means 'Had I gone to war myself, my years would have been mellow': the two lines are syntactically and rhetorically parallel.

This use of *were* survived for a long time (still found very occasionally in the twentieth century, as in *it were a shame*), and was still normal at Milton's time;

> To bow and sue for grace
> With suppliant knee, and deify his power
> Who from the terror of his arm so late
> Doubted his empire, that were low indeed,
> That were an ignominy and shame beneath
> This downfall
>
>   (*Paradise Lost* I.i.111ff)

It is important to realize that *had* in an example like the following (Lucio's aside to Isabella) is a subjunctive, i.e. 'would have':

ANGELO: How, bribe me?
ISABELLA: Ay, with such gifts that heaven shall share with you.
LUCIO: (*aside to Isabella*) You had marred all else.
                               (*Measure for Measure* II.ii.150–2)

Other examples with the auxiliary *had* – 'would have':

BARABAS: One dram of powder more had made all sure
                                   (*The Jew of Malta* V.i.24)

KING RICHARD: Let's whip these stragglers o'er the seas again, . . .
   Who – but for dreaming on this fond exploit –
   For want of means, poor rats, had hanged themselves.
                                 (*Richard III* V.vi.57ff)

2.2 The Subjunctive in Subordinate Clauses. In early Modern English the subjunctive was used much more extensively than today in subordinate clauses expressing non-facts:

SIR FRANCIS: I'll rise into my saddle ere the sun
Rise from his bed.
                              (*A Woman Killed With Kindness* I.i.110–11)

> . . . that forbidden tree, whose mortal taste
> Brought death into the world, and all our woe,
> With loss of Eden, till one greater Man
> Restore us, and regain the blissful seat
>
> (*Paradise Lost* I.i.2ff)

Here Heywood and Milton use the subjunctives *rise, restore* and *regain* because the temporal *ere* and *till*-clauses imply as yet unfulfilled events. Similarly, in Deloney's *The Gentle Craft* (76):

> Long and tedious hath the winter of my woes beene, which with nipping care hath blasted the beauty of my youthfull delight, which is like neuer again to flourish, except the bright Sunshine of thy fauour doe renew the same . . .

We can see in this example that *except* must mean 'unless' because of the subjunctive *doe* rather than the factual indicative *does*.

Sometimes we find the indicative used in the same type of clause in which a subjunctive is often found. The reason for this may simply be, in some instances, the increasing tendency for the indicative to replace the subjunctive, as it has done now in so many cases; but often the reason can be seen to be more subtle: when the subjunctive is used, it is frequently because the speaker is less certain than in those instances where the indicative is employed in the same type of clause. Take the following pairs of examples:

> MARGARET: I hope it be
> Only some natural passion make her sick.
>
> (*The Massacre at Paris* I.iii.17–18)

> DESDEMONA: I hope my noble lord esteems me honest.
>
> (*Othello* IV.ii.67)

Queen Margaret is expressing the hope, by no means certain, that her mother-in-law is not seriously ill (Her uncertainty is well-founded as the Old Queen of Navarre dies three lines later.) On the other hand, Desdemona's use of the indicative shows that she takes Othello's esteem for granted. She finds it almost impossible to imagine herself being considered unfaithful by anybody, least of all her husband. Her sentence is equivalent to: 'My noble lord esteems me honest, I hope.'

> For he is one the truest knight aliue,
> Though conquered now he lie on lowly land
>
> (*The Faerie Queene* I.iii.37)

> And though good lucke prolonged hath thy date,
> Yet death then, would the like mishaps forestall
>
> (*The Faerie Queene* I.ix.45)

Certainty is stressed in the second example by the concession being equivalent to an admitted fact (i.e. 'though, as we have seen, good luck has prolonged thy date') but not in the first ('though he may be lying there conquered, he is one of the truest . . .').

> CALLAPINE: And never will we sunder camps and arms
> Before himself or his be conquered.
>
> > (*2 Tamburlaine* V.ii.52–3)

> KING EDWARD: Yet stay a while; forbear thy bloody hand,
> And let me see the stroke before it comes
>
> > (*Edward the Second* V.v.77–8)

Edward's pleading is with his murderer, but he shows by his use of the indicative *comes* that he knows his death is imminent and inevitable; cp. Arundel's lines in the same play (II.v.36ff):

> ARUNDEL: His majesty, hearing that you had taken Gaveston,
> Entreateth you by me, yet but he may
> See him before he dies.

Bearing in mind that temporal clauses beginning with *before* normally have the subjunctive in Marlowe, an indicative like *dies* is important. We must be careful not to take it for granted just because only the indicative is possible nowadays. Arundel is here indicating the certainty (his own and/or Edward's) that Gaveston will not escape death. A similar difference between the subjunctive and indicative often shows itself in *if*-clauses:

> QUEEN ISABELLA: Ah, Mortimer, the king my son hath news
> His father's dead, and we have murder'd him!
> YOUNGER MORTIMER: What if he have? The king is yet a child.
>
> > (*Edward the Second* V.vi.15ff)

> LIGHTBORN: If you mistrust me, I'll be gone, my lord.
> KING EDWARD: No, no; for, if thou mean'st to murder me,
> Thou wilt return again; and therefore stay.
>
> > (*Edward the Second* V.v.100–1)

Mortimer's subjunctive makes light of Isabella's worry. Edward's indicative *mean'st* shows once again his certainty that Lightborn will kill him.

> REGAN: If, sir, perchance
> She have restrained the riots of your followers,

> 'Tis on such ground and to such wholesome end
> As clears her from all blame.
>
> > (*King Lear* II.ii.314ff)

> BASTARD: (*to King Philip*) An if thou hast the mettle of a king,
> Being wronged as we are by this peevish town,
> Turn thou the mouth of thy artillery,
> As we will ours, against these saucy walls
>
> > (*King John* II.i.401ff)

By using the subjunctive Regan is saying with feigned politeness to her father that *even if* Gonerill has done this, then . . . ; whereas the Bastard is telling the King to show his mettle, taking it for granted that he has some.

M. R. Ridley, the editor of the Arden edition of Shakespeare's *Antony and Cleopatra* (based on the edition of 1906 by R. H. Case) prints a speech by Cleopatra as follows:

> Cut my lace, Charmian, come,
> But let it be, I am quickly ill, and well,
> So Antony loves.
>
> > (*Antony and Cleopatra* I.iii.71–73)

and tells us in a footnote that *I . . . loves* means 'I am no sooner ill than well again, provided Antony loves.' This interpretation is unlikely in view of the indicative *loves*. If *so* meant 'provided', it would almost certainly have been followed by the subjunctive in Renaissance English, as in the following examples from elsewhere in Shakespeare:

> KATHERINE: I prithee, go and get me some repast.
> I care not what, so it be wholesome food.
>
> > (*The Taming of the Shrew* IV.iii.15–16)

> ROSALIND: Will you hear the letter?
> SILVIUS: So please you, for I never heard it yet
>
> > (*As You Like It* IV.iii.37–8)

i.e. 'if it may please you'. Similarly in e.g. Marlowe: 'So he be safe, he cares not what becomes / Of king or country' (*The Massacre at Paris* IV.ii.42–3). Thus it is much more probable that *so* in Cleopatra's speech is an adverb of manner so that the clause means 'thus Antony loves', i.e. 'Antony's love comes and goes in the same way'. This interpretation also seems to be behind the Wells and Taylor punctuation (and that of several other editors):

> Cut my lace, Charmian, come.
> But let it be. I am quickly ill and well;
> So Antony loves.

3 Voice: the Passive vs the Active. The passive consists of a form of *be* + the past participle, as in *she was admired*, as opposed to the active *he admired her*. It is a feature of the history of English that ever since Old English the passive has become more and more common. In earlier English active forms would often imply passive meaning, and even today such instances are not all that rare. Thus the following promise figured recently on the wrapper of a type of loaf: '*Eats Well – Keeps Well*, where *eats* can only be understood passively; cp. *this garment washes well* and *she photographs well*, which does not mean that she is good at taking pictures but that she looks good in them.

Although the passive was certainly found in Old English, the Anglo-Saxons preferred an active construction with the indefinite pronoun *man*, corresponding to German *man* or French *on*, as in *man ofsloh hine* 'somebody slew him', i.e. 'he was killed'. This type of construction remains common in Middle English but *man* had died out by the beginning of the early Modern English period. The pronoun *one* (boosted by the French word *on*) came to replace it, but only to a very limited extent. By Shakespeare's time the passive was certainly used more extensively than in Middle English, but it was not as common as it is today, and there were certain forms of the verb that simply did not occur in the passive but do so today.

Take a sentence like *I was given a book*. This is now a perfectly normal use of the passive, where in the corresponding active sentence the *I* would become the indirect object *me*: *Somebody gave me a book*. *I was given* is therefore an instance of what we call the 'indirect passive'. This was unknown in Old English and was exceedingly rare in Middle English which preferred the direct passive (i.e. a passive whose subject would be the direct object in the active version), as in *a book was given me* or *me was given a book*, or an active equivalent with *man* or another pronoun. The indirect passive had still not become fully established by Shakespeare's time; it was still marked as an unusual choice. We must bear this in mind when the Priest says in *Hamlet* (V.i.226) about the dead Ophelia:

Yet here she is allowed her virgin rites

The normal passive version then would have been *yet her virgin rites are allowed her here*, which would be unusual today. By choosing the indirect passive, Shakespeare made the line stand out with a beauty of emphasis that is all but lost to a reader not attuned to the language of the period. Marlowe did the same when Baldock, after King Edward is taken away, turns to his friend Spenser and says:

> We are depriv'd the sunshine of our life
>
> (*Edward the Second* IV.vi.106)

Similarly, the passive infinitive (*to be admired*) was relatively uncommon in early Modern English, which preferred an active infinitive with passive sense – a construction that has survived in some cases in Present-day English, as in *I am to blame* or *the truth is not to seek here*:

> BASTARD: Now by this light, were I to get again,
>   Madam, I would not wish a better father
>
> (*King John* I.i.259–60)

i.e. 'to be begotten again'. Similarly *to trust* could equal 'to be trusted' in Shakespeare's famous sonnet 129 ('Th'expense of spirit in a waste of shame'):

>   lust
> Is perjured, murd'rous, bloody, full of blame,
> Savage, extreme, rude, cruel, not to trust

Thus Autolycus's remark in *The Winter's Tale* (IV.iv.792ff):

> But what talk we of these traitorly rascals, whose miseries are to be smiled at, their offences being so capital?

coming as it does after a gruesome list of tortures, is likely to have drawn considerable attention to itself in the early seventeenth century, as may Sidney's in the sixteenth:

> Yet thinking warre never to be accepted, untill it be offred by the hand of necessitie . . .
>
> (*Arcadia* 149)

unless we consider *accepted* an adjective i.e. 'acceptable', rather than a verb. But gradually the passive infinitive gained ground influenced, no doubt, by the Latin passive infinitive.

As for the passive progressive (*the meal is being eaten*), this form was totally unknown in early Modern English and only started to be used around 1800; even then it was strongly frowned upon by many. Until that time the active had been used with passive sense (as in *the meal was eating*) and instances of this survive in today's English: *the film is still showing* / *the book is still printing*; but now the passive progressive is normal. It can therefore be very hard for the modern student to understand straightaway Cressida's remark in *Troilus and Cressida* (I.ii.282):

> Women are angels, wooing

which means that women are angels when they are being wooed.

The following two examples from Spenser's *Faerie Queene* are further instances of the active infinitive used passively:

> In sumptuous bed she made him to be layd,
> And all the while his wounds were dressing, by him stayd.
>
> (II.xi.49)

i.e. 'were being dressed'.

> there was for to be heard
> The tryall of a great and weightie case,
> Which on both sides was then debating hard
>
> (V.ix.36)

i.e. 'was being debated'.

4 Impersonal Verbs. This is the normal term for verbs in the third person which have either no personal subject or the subject *it*, as in *it does not become you*. A typical Middle English example would be (*it*) *me liketh*, i.e. 'it pleases me' or 'I like (it)', surviving into the Renaissance:

SHERIFF: Sir, will you go?
SIR CHARLES: Even where it likes you best.
(*A Woman Killed With Kindness* I.iii.109)

Impersonal verbs were very common in the Old and Middle English periods: the object was originally in the dative case (as in e.g. German *es gefällt dem König* meaning literally 'it is pleasing to the king'). Since the case ending used to signal clearly the syntactic function (dative implies indirect object), word order was flexible and the dative could occupy initial position in the sentence. This was, and is, the typical position of the subject, which was in the nominative case. But during the Middle English period the case endings of nouns merged so that there was no difference between the endings of the nominative (subject), accusative (direct object) and dative (indirect object). By Shakespeare's time the original nominative pronoun *ye* was being replaced by the object form *you*, now universal in Standard English. Clauses like *if the king like* and *if you like* would in Middle English have *like* as an impersonal subjunctive (no subject) and *the king* or *you* as the dative (indirect object) i.e. 'if (it) be pleasing to the king/you'. But once the endings had been eroded or had merged, *the king* and *you* (which by 1600, remember, could be the subject as well as the object form) came to be taken as the subject because of the initial position. The result was that *like* changed from being an impersonal verb to a personal one, a process that started in the fourteenth century.

Similarly *me thinks* or *methinks* (literally 'it seems to me'), so common during the Renaissance, has now become *I think* or been replaced by another impersonal verb: *it seems to me.*

However, the change from impersonal to personal had not fully taken place by Shakespeare's time. Throughout the sixteenth century and for some considerable time afterwards, the old impersonal idiom survived in many cases and can sometimes give the modern reader difficulties. In Spenser's *The Faerie Queene*, for instance, there is considerable vacillation between impersonal and personal constructions with verbs like *chance, list* 'please', *need, please, seem*: it is clear, even bearing in mind that Spenser could sometimes be grammatically as well as lexically archaic, that the sixteenth century was a strongly transitional time in this respect:

> At last him chaunst to meete vpon the way
> A faithlesse Sarazin all arm'd to point
>
> (I.ii.12)

but: At length they chaunst to meet vpon the way
> An aged Sire, in long blacke weedes yclad
>
> (I.i.29)

> And when her listed, she could fawne and flatter
> (VI.vi.42)

but: And when she list poure out her larger spright [spirit],
> She would commaund the hastie Sunne to stay
>
> (I.x.20)

> Him needeth sure a golden pen I weene
> (IV.v..12)

but: All that I need I haue
>
> (II.vii.39)

> I will, if please you it discure [reveal], assay,
> To ease you of that ill
>
> (II.ix.42)

but: Take what thou please
>
> (II.vii.18)

> Him seem'd his feet did fly, and in their speed delight.
> (VI.iv.19)

but: He seemed breathlesse, hartlesse, faint, and wan
> (II.vi.41)

A few examples from Marlowe:

SIR JOHN: Will you go with your friends,
  And shake off all our fortunes equally?
PRINCE EDWARD: So pleaseth the queen my mother, me it likes.
                        (*Edward the Second* IV.ii.21–3)

In Prince Edward's line *pleaseth* is probably personal, and is indicative:
'thus the queen, my mother, pleases'; but *likes* is clearly impersonal,
as it is in I.iv.357 of the same play:

KING EDWARD: . . . if that lofty office like thee not

but Marlowe also uses the personal variant: 'I like not this relenting
mood in Edmund' (ibid. IV.v.47), 'You'll like it better' (*The Jew
or Malta* II.iii.67). The personal construction with *like* is particularly
common in the first person.
   Shakespearean instances include:

BUCKINGHAM: Meseemeth good that, with some little train,
  Forthwith from Ludlow the young Prince be fet [fetched]
                        (*Richard III* II.ii.108–9)

LORD HASTINGS: There's some conceit or other likes him well,
  When that he bids good morrow with such spirit.
                        (*Richard III* III.iv.49–50)

Note in that example also the omission of the relative *that* or *which*
after *other*.

DIOMEDES: I do not like this fooling.
TROILUS: (*aside*) Nor I, by Pluto – but that that likes not you
  Pleases me best.
                        (*Troilus and Cressida* V.ii.104–6)

Diomedes uses a personal *like* whereas Troilus uses the verb imper-
sonally, parallel with *pleases*.
   It is quite possible that the impersonal *list* is deliberately archaic in
Spenser, where it is common, since Shakespeare only has the personal
construction with this verb (normally in the form *list* rather than *listeth*,
the contraction going back as far as Old English):

NORFOLK: The King-Cardinal,
  That blind priest, like the eldest son of fortune,
  Turns what he list.
                        (*Henry VIII* II.ii.19–21)

MISTRESS QUICKLY: Do what she will; say what she will; take all, pay
all; go to bed when she list; rise when she list; all is as she will.
(*The Merry Wives of Windsor* II.ii.114–16)

5 Reflexive Verbs. Today a reflexive verb takes a pronoun ending in
-*self* or, in the plural, -*selves*, as in *I/we wash myself/ourselves*. The
verb is called 'reflexive' because the pronoun refers to the subject.
This construction was also current during the Renaissance, but so was
verb + personal pronoun, i.e. *me, him, it, us* etc instead of *myself,
himself, itself, ourselves* etc. Because many of these verb constructions
can now take -*self* forms only or have become non-reflexive, i.e. have
dropped the pronoun altogether, the Renaissance variants can often
look strange to the modern student and sometimes cause difficulties:

See how my soul doth fret it to the bones
(Wyatt, *A Paraphrase of the Penitential Psalms* 122)

i.e. 'fret itself'. Consider the following instance from *The Massacre at
Paris*, in which Catherine says to Navarre:

You see we love you well,
That link you in marriage with our daughter here
(I.i.13–14)

A reader not used to the sixteenth-century reflexive verb + personal
pronoun construction may take the relative pronoun *that* to refer to
we. But it is much more likely to refer to the preceding *you*, thus
making the second *you* reflexive, i.e. 'you who link yourself . . .'

Such reflexive verbs were very common in the sixteenth and, to a
slightly lesser extent, in the seventeenth centuries. Here is another
instance from Marlowe's *The Jew of Malta*: 'then, let every man / Provide him' (I.i.173–4). Shakespeare: 'To all the host of heaven I complain
me' (*The Rape of Lucrece* 598); 'Your highness shall repose you at the
Tower' (*Richard III* III.i.65). Spenser was particularly fond of reflexive
verb + personal pronoun, so much so that it seems a deliberate attempt
at archaism: 'So well she sped her', i.e. 'succeeded' (IV.vii.31); 'To
Vna back he cast him to retire', i.e. 'planned' (III.v.41); 'I me resolu'd
the vtmost end to proue' (IV.vii.16), 'He rested him a while' (III.v.41),
'She . . . / . . . her bowd / Vpon her knee' (VI.vi.31).

6 Strong and Weak Verbs. A weak verb is a verb that adds -*(e)d* in
the past tense and past participle, like *love – loved – has loved, kiss –
kissed – has kissed*. A strong verb normally does not add an ending,
except sometimes -*en* in the past participle, but often changes its vowel
or diphthong in the past tense and/or past participle, like *sing – sang
– sung* or *write – wrote – written*.
Old English had over three hundred strong verbs; present-day Eng-

lish has only around sixty. The gradual loss of most strong verbs took place because the weak verbs form an open-ended class, i.e. almost any new verb entering the language will automatically become weak. Thus the weak pattern has been, and still is, the dominant one and consequently many strong verbs have conformed to it and become weak. Quite a few strong verbs developed weak variants in Middle English, but it was during the early Modern English period that the movement from strong to weak was at is height, the principal reason for this being the effects of the considerable sound-changes that took place at that time. These changes resulted in the blurring of many strong-verb vowel constrasts between the present and past. All the same, many verbs, now weak, retained strong or irregular variants during the Renaissance, e.g. the past tenses *holp, clomb* for *helped, climbed*, and the archaic *yede* for *went* in early texts: 'And I like deaf and dumb forth my way yede' (Wyatt, *A Paraphrase of the Penitential Psalms* 372). In cases where the verbs have remained strong, their vowel contrasts were often different in early Modern English. For instance, we find in Renaissance texts past participles like *wrote, strove, rode, drove, arose, took* for today's *written, striven, ridden, driven, arisen, taken*. Since some of these participles, e.g. *wrote* and *took*, have survived in some varieties of non-Standard English, the unwary reader may, consciously or unconsciously, regard such forms as substandard also in Renaissance texts. This would be a grave mistake since it could lead to misunderstanding the tone or style.

The past tense of verbs like *bear, break, speak* now have -*o*- (*bore, broke, spoke*) from the past participle (*born, broken, spoken*); but in early Modern English, variants that had developed regularly from Middle English past tense forms were still normal in the sixteenth century: *bare, brake, spake*; they were in fact the unmarked forms (-*o*- being marked) and it is important that today's readers of sixteenth century texts do not regard such forms as solemnly archaic, with a vague flavour of the biblical *spake*, although this may be behind Milton's preference for *spake* and *bespake* in *Paradise Lost*. For by 1600 things were changing fast, mainly because the Great Vowel Shift that took place between Chaucer and Shakespeare had by now changed the old -*a*- vowel of the past tense from [a:] to [ɛ:], which did not provide sufficient contrast with the vowel of the present tense of these verbs. Shakespeare, for instance, already preferred the new -*o*- to the old -*a*- in such verbs, although he uses both.

7 The Endings of the Present Tense Indicative. The only endings in the present indicative were almost universally in the second and third persons singular. In the second person it was normally -*st* (less commonly -*s*), as in *thou makest (thou makes)*. In the third it could be either -*(e)s* or -*(e)th*, the latter being the older form. In the prose literature of the first half of the sixteenth century -*(e)th* was almost universal, and this was also preferred later in the century by writers of artistic or serious prose, such as Lyly (e.g. in *Euphues*), Sidney (e.g. in *Arcadia*) or Spenser (e.g. in *The Present State of Ireland*). In these writers the -*(e)th* ending is likely to have been a conservative feature, judging by, for instance, Queen Elizabeth's preference for -*(e)s* in her letters, and the clear preponderance of the same ending in the prose of dramatists (e.g. Shakespeare and Heywood). In other words, we can be fairly sure that -*(e)s* had become the normal *spoken* ending of the third person singular by the second half of the sixteenth century, if not earlier, except perhaps in the common monosyllables *hath* and *doth*. The following example is typical:

> JENKIN: My master hath given me a coat here, but he takes pains
> himself to brush it . . .
> *(A Woman Killed With Kindness* II.i.98–100)

In poetry matters were different in the distribution of third person singular -*(e)th* and -*(e)s*. The reason for this is that, apart from monosyllables like *quoth, hath, doth,* -*(e)th* would provide a syllable, -*(e)s* would not (unless it followed a sibilant; see below). Thus *mistaketh* had three syllables, *mistakes* only two. The convenience of this for fitting metres with the correct number of syllables is obvious, and we must therefore not conclude (as we might in prose) that -*(e)th* is more serious or solemn than -*(e)s*. Even Spenser, who is consciously archaic in *The Faerie Queene*, exploits this possibility of syllabic variation, thus abandoning, by not preferring – *(e)th* to -*(e)s*, the possibility of dignified archaism in this inflection. When the verb stem ended in a sibilant, the addition of -*(e)s* would, of course, also provide an extra syllable: both *pleaseth* and *pleases* have two. It is interesting to note that sixteenth-century poets generally prefer the -*eth* variant in such cases. The reason for this must be due to the fact that it was considered a more appropriate and dignified ending for poetic use.

Although Spenser did not use -*(e)th* for the sake of archaism, preferring the metrical convenience of variation with -*(e)s*, he did sometimes exploit the old Middle English plural ending -*en* as an archaism in, for instance, *The Faerie Queene*, as in *they marchen* (I.iv.37) and *they binden* (I.v.29). Although this ending also provided him with an extra syllable, it had become extinct by Spenser's time.

A plural ending in -*(e)s*, still current today in certain non-standard varieties, was sometimes found but it was rare outside rhyming positions (Queen Elizabeth I used it occasionally in her letters): 'Whiles I threat, he lives. / Words to the heat of deeds too cold breath gives' (*Macbeth* II.i.60–1).

8 The Auxiliaries. Auxiliaries are verbs that modify other (main) verbs, such as *may* or *shall* in *she may go* and *we shall see*. They are potential traps for the modern reader: their familiarity of form makes us sometimes overlook or disregard certain kinds of meaning or usage typical of Renaissance English but untypical or even obsolete today. This section will focus on such danger spots and highlight features like relative frequency and syntactical and semantic differences.

We shall start with the auxiliary *do* which, more than any other auxiliary, is characteristic in many of its functions of early Modern English as compared with both Middle English and English after 1700.

8.1 *Do*. One of the most notable features of early Modern English was the development and functions of *do* as an auxiliary. Nowadays we use it for questions, negations and emphasis:

Do you smoke?
I don't smoke.
I *do* smoke.

These functions were also there during the Renaissance, but their distribution was considerably different from today's and they were not the only uses of auxiliary *do* in the fifteenth, sixteenth and seventeenth centuries. But before we take a close look at *do* in Renaissance literature, we shall briefly consider its development into a 'periphrastic auxiliary', i.e. an auxiliary without any inherent meaning, which is essentially an early Modern English departure. There have been several theories about this, but the most authoritative still remains the one put forward by Ellegård (1953). He derives the semantically empty periphrastic use from an early causative function. Take the following lines from Chaucer's *Pardoner's Tale*:

Men wolde seyn that we were theves stronge,
And for oure owene tresor doon us honge.

(789–90)

The meaning is 'People would say that we were hardened thieves and cause us to be hanged (or have us hanged) for our own treasure', i.e. *do* is here a causative verb, i.e. 'cause, have, make, get' or the like. According to Ellegård it is this causative *do* that is behind the periphrastic one. How, then, did it lose its causative element?

There are certain verbs, says Ellegård, that contain, beside their basic meaning, an implicit sense of causality. If I say *the king built a castle*, nobody would think he built it with his own hands; *built* means 'caused to be built' here. Imagine then a Middle English sentence with a causative *do* and such an implicitly causative verb, e.g. *the king did bylde a castel*. This would first mean *the king caused a castle to be built*; but because there already is an implicit element of causality in the main verb *build*, the causative element in *do* would not really be needed; it would be redundant. It was in this way, according to Ellegård, that *do* developed into a purely periphrastic auxiliary. The first instances appeared around 1400; then it gradually gained ground during the fifteenth century, and accelerated considerably in the sixteenth. The result was that periphrastic *do* attached itself by analogy to all sorts of verbs, i.e. not necessarily verbs with an implicit causative element. Thus *he did hit her* came to be, in the large majority of cases, the equivalent of *he hit her* in Renaissance texts. Some fifteenth and early sixteenth-century writers, notably Caxton, were so fond of this extra *do* that they used it twice, as in *he did do show me*, i.e. 'he showed me'.

We no longer use causative *do* except very occasionally in the fossilized and archaic *do somebody to wit* 'make somebody know, inform somebody'. Other verbs have usurped its function, verbs like *make* and *get*, as in *he made me try it* or *I got him to help me*. Shakespeare no longer uses *do* in the causative sense, but it was found occasionally in the early part of our period:

> The blind master whom I have served so long,
> Grudging to hear that he did hear her say,
> Made her own weapon do her finger bleed
>
> (Wyatt, Epigram 41)

Whereas *did* in the second line is periphrastic, *do* in the third is causative, i.e. 'made her own weapon cause her finger to bleed'. In Spenser *do somebody to die* was still common, mainly as a stylistic archaism:

> O hold thy mortall hand for Ladies sake,
> Hold for my sake, and do him not to dye
>
> (*The Faerie Queene* I.vii.14)

and in e.g. I.viii.18, I.ix.54, II.v.12, II.vi.39, II.viii.18, 45.

A factor that contributed to the popularity or upsurge of periphrastic *do* in early Modern English was the Great Vowel Shift, after which present vs past tense vowel contrasts in some strong verbs had got neutralized or at least were no longer very clear. In such cases *did* was a handy way of signalling the past tense. The preference for *did eat* to *ate* in, for instance, the King James Bible is thought to be due to such a sound development. Similarly, the ambiguous *they cut* would often, if the reference was to the past, be turned into *they did cut*. The extra syllable could of course be exploited metrically, or rhyming factors might decide whether *do*-periphrasis was employed or not:

> A louely Ladie rode him faire beside,
> Vpon a lowly Asse more white then snow,
> Yet she much whiter, but the same did hide

Vnder a vele, that wimpled was full low,
And ouer all a blacke stole she did throw,
As one that inly mournd: so was she sad,
And heauie sat vpon her palfrey slow:
Seemed in heart some hidden care she had,
And by her in a line a milke white lambe she lad.

(The Faerie Queene I.i.4)

Did in lines 3 and 5 is there for both metre and rhyme. In the last line it is absent for precisely the same reasons.

It is important for the modern reader to realize at once that during the Renaissance the auxiliary *do* normally would not imply the kind of emphasis it has in affirmative clauses today (*I DID cut it!*). It may do so, as when Winifred says to Sir Hugh:

I doe meane to try you better before I trust you

(The Gentle Craft 74)

or when Benedick in *Much Ado About Nothing* tries to convince Beatrice that he believes her tears and a little later that he really loves her:

BENEDICK: Surely I do believe your fair cousin is wronged.
(IV.i.262)

BENEDICK: I do love nothing in the world so well as you.
(IV.i.269)

Since those lines are prose, *do* is not needed for metrical reasons, and the best interpretation is an emphatic one. But some instances are highly ambiguous:

the deuke lyghtly avoyded his horse and dressed his shylde and drew his swerde, and bade sir gareth alyght and fyght with hym. So he dud alyght, and they dud grete batayle togedyrs . . .

(Morte Darthur vol.1.356)

Does *he dud alyght* mean 'he *did* alight/he decided to alight' or is it completely unemphatic i.e. 'he alighted'? We cannot be sure. But normally careful reading of the context will take us in the right direction.

In negative and interrogative clauses *do* was by no means regular in Renaissance English. Shakespeare (and others) would sometimes use it in such cases, sometimes not. If an interrogative clause is signalled by a question word such as *who, what, why, how*, then *do* is less common, though by no means rare, in dramatic texts. The reverse is true of other interrogative clauses, unless the verb is a common monosyllabic one such as *know, say, mean*. In negations clauses without *do* predominate, especially if the main verb is *know, like* or *doubt*;

and this is still the case even in Milton's prose. But if the clause is both interrogative and negative, *do* is preferred. This is clear even in poetry that frequently avoids *do* in questions and negations. For instance, in Spenser's *Faerie Queene* there is a clear preference for *do*-less interrogative clauses and negative clauses: 'And liues yet Amyas?' (IV.viii.63); 'It fell not all to ground' (I.i.54); but as soon as the clause becomes a blend of these two varieties, *do*-periphrasis prevails: 'what doest not thou know?' (III.iii.21); 'Doth not your handmayds life at your foot lie?' (V.v.31).

The following typical and less typical instances (the latter prefaced with 'but') are mostly from drama, and they have been taken from prose passages so as to eliminate metrical considerations:

OLIVER: Now, sir, what make you here?
(*As You Like It* I.i.27)

ROSALIND: What did he when thou sawest him? What said he? How looked he? Wherein went he? What makes he here? Did he ask for me? Where remains he? How parted he with thee?
(*As You Like It.* III.ii.215ff)

ABIGAIL: Why, how, now, Ithamore! Why laugh'st thou so?
(*The Jew of Malta* III.iii.4)

BELLAMIRA: And didst thou deliver my letter?
(*The Jew of Malta.* IV.ii.4)

ITHAMORE: Say'st thou me so?
(*The Jew of Malta* IV.iv.2)

JENKIN: . . . if you like not that, put it to the musicians.
(*A Woman Killed With Kindness* I.ii.51–2)

. . . when he who praises, by showing that such his actual persuasion is of whom he writes, can demonstrate that he flatters not
(*Aeropagitica* 152)

JENKIN: O Slime, O Brickbat, do not you know that comparisons are odious?
(*A Woman Killed With Kindness* I.ii.19–20)

but: SLENDER: Why do your dogs bark so?
(*The Merry Wives of Windsor* I.i.267)

but: MISTRESS FORD What doth he think of us?
(*The Merry Wives of Windsor.* II.i.80)

but: WAGNER . . . although I do not doubt but to see you both hanged
the next session.

(Doctor Faustus I.ii.23–4)

but: . . . whom I so extolled I did not flatter

(Aeropagitica 153)

It is also worth reminding ourselves that the contractions *don't* and
didn't were not used in writing. Whether *do not/did not* were sometimes pronounced like *don't/didn't* is uncertain but likely in view of
the fact that in negative questions prose speeches prefer the word
order *do not* + subject (cp *do not you know* in the example from *A
Woman Killed With Kindness* above), whereas verse speeches tend to
have *do* + subject + *not*. In Present-day written English the contracted
form is in stylistic variation with the more formal (or emphatic) *do not/
did not*. The absence of (written) *don't/didn't* in Renaissance literature
might leave the naive reader with a sense of unintended formality. A
Scot is less likely to fall into that trap since he would prefer e.g. *did
you not see him?* to *didn't you see him?*

But it is the affirmative clauses that pose the main problem for the
modern student. In very general terms we can say that the more *do* is
used in these, the less colloquial the style, whether this be drama or
non-dramatic prose. In the latter, affirmative *do* (as we shall call *do*
in affirmative clauses) was particularly favoured in the sixteenth century when a tone of solemnity was aimed at. Sidney's *Arcadia* and
Deloney's *The Gentle Craft* do not make particularly great use of
periphrastic *do* except in passages like the ones below, where it is
important for the modern reader to appreciate the role of *do*: it is
there to lend a distinctly solemn tone to the language. This may sometimes be ironic, as in the second example:

But at length taking the occasion of his owne weeping, he thus did speake
to *Euarchus*. Let not my teares most worthely renowmed prince make my
presence unpleasant . . . geve me leave excellent *Euarchus* to say, I am
but the representer of all the late florishing *Arcadia*, which now with mine
eyes doth weepe, with my toong doth complaine, with my knees doth lay
it selfe at your feete . . . Imagine, vouchsafe to imagine most wise and
good King, that heere is before your eyes, the pittifull spectacle of a most
dolorously ending tragedie: wherein I do but play the part, of all the newe
miserable province, which being spoiled of their guide, doth lye like a ship
without a Pilot . . . *Arcadia* finding her selfe in these desolate tearmes,
doth speake, and I speake for her, to thee not vainly puissant Prince, that
since now she is not only robbed of the naturall support of her Lord, but
so sodainly robbed, that she hath not breathing time to stande for her
safetie: so unfortunately, that it doth appall their mindes, though they had
leisure: and so mischevously, that it doth exceede both the sodainnes and
infortunatenes of it . . .

(Arcadia 153–4)

Conquering and most imperious Loue, hauing seized on the heart of
young Sir *Hugh*, all his wits were set on worke, how for to compasse
the loue of the faire Virgin *Winifred*, whose disdain was the chiefe cause
of his care, hauing receiued many infinite sorrows for her sake: but as a
streame of water being stopt, ouerfloweth the bank, so smothered desire
doth burst out into a great flame of fire, which made this male-contented
Louer to seeke some meanes to appease the strife of his contentious
thoughts, whereupon he began to encourage himselfe.

(*The Gentle Craft* 73)

There is normally no problem when affirmative *do* appears in verse
with a main verb together with another main verb without *do* in the
same sentence. In such cases, *do* is nearly always there for metrical
reasons only, as in *did starve* vs *gave* in the following lines from Shakespeare:

BOYET: Be now as prodigal of all dear grace
    As nature was in making graces dear
    When she did starve the general world beside
    And prodigally gave them all to you.

(*Love's Labour's Lost* II.i.9ff)

But there can sometimes be doubt as to whether, in such cases, the
do-periphrasis is emphatic or purely metrical, as in:

TROILUS: O Pandarus! I tell thee, Pandarus,
    When I do tell thee 'There my hopes lie drowned',
    Reply not in how many fathoms deep
    They lie endrenched.

(*Troilus and Cressida* I.i.48ff)

Prose examples can be particularly difficult:

EVANS: Shall I tell you a lie? I do despise a liar as I do despise one
    that is false, or as I despise one that is not true.

(*The Merry Wives of Windsor* I.i.62–4)

It is probable, but by no means certain, that *do despise* is here more
emphatic than *despise*. There is no need to regard Evans' instance as
idiosyncratic (he is Welsh) in *this* respect, as there are other similar
examples by native speakers.

Affirmative *do* could also carry a kind of emphasis alien to it today
and therefore easily missed. Consider the following example from *The
Tempest* (I.i.12–13), in which the boatswain tells his passengers (in
prose) to go below deck or they will be shipwrecked:

You mar our labour. Keep your cabins; you do assist the storm.

This *do* carries an explanatory and, at the same time, reprimanding
tone, which we would have to convey by other means today: 'Can't

you see you're assisting the storm?' The difference between this and our use of a castigating, affirmative *do* is that nowadays it would imply general behaviour, as in 'you do get on my nerves'. The *Tempest* example refers to a single instance of behaviour only; and it is by no means certain that *do* was even stressed: the longer verb phrase might in itself be enough to carry the reprimand.

In verse affirmative *do* is by no means always a simple metrical filler. Its use can be so marked that other explanations are called for. Thus it may not infrequently reflect the excited or emotional state of speakers in their attempt to convince – not in any stubbornly or queru-lously protesting manner (which would have implied a stress on *do* like today's emphatic one) – whoever they are speaking to of the 'truth' of something incredible or supernatural. The effect in Renaissance drama is subtle, often with an element of awe in the face of Nature's mysteries, as in *Julius Caesar* in the scene where Calpurnia is trying desperately to prevent her husband from leaving the house:

> Horses do neigh, and dying men did groan,
> And ghosts did shriek and squeal about the streets.
> (II.ii.23–4)

When Caesar a little later tells Decius that he is not going out because

> Calpurnia here, my wife, stays me at home.
> She dreamt tonight she saw my statue,
> Which like a fountain with an hundred spouts
> Did run pure blood; and many lusty Romans
> Came smiling and did bathe their hands in it.
> (II.ii.75ff)

his use of *do* indicates that either he believes his wife or wishes to tell Decius that she is absolutely serious and that it would therefore be discourteous or inconsiderate to her if he ventured forth. The same kind of portentous effect is conveyed in a speech by Hastings in *Richard III* III.iv.80ff:

> Woe, woe for England! Not a whit for me,
> For I, too fond, might have prevented this.
> Stanley did dream the boar did raze our helms,
> But I did scorn it and disdain to fly.
> Three times today my footcloth horse did stumble,
> And started when he looked upon the Tower,
> As loath to bear me to the slaughterhouse.

Towards the end of the seventeenth century auxiliary *do* could no longer be used for such stylistic purposes. By then it had been regu-lated largely in accordance with the practice we observe today, i.e. it died out in unemphatic affirmative clauses and became obligatory in questions (including negative ones) and negations, unless of course another auxiliary was used instead. Thus a sixteenth and early seventeenth-century sentence like *do we know the cause?* is stylistically different from a late seventeenth-century one of exactly the same wording. During the Renaissance there was a choice; *know we the cause?* was an alternative. Shakespeare could exploit such subtleties, Dryden could not.

8.2 Can/Could. As an auxiliary during the Renaissance, *can* meant roughly what it means today: *can you swim?* ('know how to'), *I can/ could see nothing* (ability), *can/could this be true?* (possibility). But it was not used for permission, as in *can I have a sweet?* In such cases Renaissance English would use *may*.

In Old and Middle English *can* was, apart from being an auxiliary, also a main verb meaning 'know' or 'know how to'; cp. other Germanic languages: *kannst du Englisch?* (German) / *kan du engelsk?* (Danish) meaning 'do you know English?', and Chaucer's Miller:

I can a noble tale for the nones [for the occasion]
(*The Miller's Prologue* 3126)

This usage soon became rare after the medieval period. Spenser may be using it as a conscious archaism:

Seemeth thy flocke thy counsell can
(*The Shepheardes Calender*, February, 77)

For well it seem'd, that whilome he had beene
Some goodly person, and of gentle race,
That could his good to all
(*The Faerie Queene* VI.v.36)

The hermit is here described as a man who knew what is good for everybody. We also occasionally find this main-verb usage in other writers. Here are four instances, three from Shakespeare and one from Marlowe:

Let the priest in surplice white
That defunctive music can,
Be the death-divining swan
(*The Phoenix and Turtle* 13–15)

CORDELIA: What can man's wisdom
In the restoring his bereaved sense
(*King Lear* IV.iii.8–9)

KING CLAUDIUS: I've seen myself, and served against, the French,
And they can well on horseback
(*Hamlet* IV.vii.69–70)

LEICESTER: What cannot gallant Mortimer with the queen?
(*Edward the Second* IV.vi.50)

In the third example *can* means 'know how to' rather than just 'know', and in the fourth it means 'be able to do'

The following instance is ambiguous:

DORSET: The sum of all I can, I have disclosed.
(*Richard III* II.iv.45)

Can may be a main verb such as 'know', or an auxiliary with its infinitive understood: 'all I can disclose I have disclosed'.

8.3 May/Might. This auxiliary could be used the way it is today, as in *may I come?* (permission), *this may/might be true* (possibility). The possibility sense includes those instances in which *may* replaces a subjunctive: *may the best man win* (main clause) / *buy him some new clothes so that he may look his best* (subordinate clause). As we have seen, in such cases the subjunctive was, as opposed to today's usage, a frequent alternative.

One difference from today's usage includes the frequent negative *may not* to indicate prohibition. Today we prefer *must not* because *may not* (except immediately after a request with *may*) tends to refer to possibility:

AENEAS: I may not dure [endure] this female drudgery.
(*Dido, Queen of Carthage* IV.iii.55)

Aeneas says that he *must* not succumb to Dido.

The original sense of *may* was 'be able to'. *Can* has now ousted this meaning, but it was still current in early Modern English. It is therefore important that we do not confuse this *may* with present-day usage. When Faustus asks Mephistopheles:

But may I raise such spirits when I please?
(*Doctor Faustus* I.v.85)

he is not asking for permission to raise the spirits; he is asking whether he will be able to. Instances from Shakespeare:

BASSANIO: May you stead me?
(*The Merchant of Venice* I.iii.7)

Bassanio is asking Shylock if he is able to help him with a loan?

OBERON: But I might see young Cupid's fiery shaft
Quenched in the chaste beams of the wat'ry moon
(*A Midsummer Night's Dream* II.i.161–2)

i.e. Oberon says he was definitely able to see the shaft, not that it might be a possibility.

Might had an old variant *mought*, used by Spenser as an archaism (but he also uses *might*):

> So sound he slept, that nought mought him awake.
>
> > (*The Faerie Queene* I.i.42)

It is rare after the first half of the sixteenth century. In Marlowe's *Dido, Queen of Carthage*, Aeneas's use of *mought* in the following lines contributes to the grandeur of his utterance and contrasts with Iarbas's *might* in a more mundane wish:

> AENEAS: And mought I live to see him sack rich Thebes
>   And load his spear with Grecian princes' heads,
>   Then would I wish me with Anchises' tomb,
>   And dead to honour that hath brought me up.
> IARBAS: (*aside*) And might I live to see thee shipp'd away,
>   And hoist aloft on Neptune's hideous hills
>
> > (III.iii.42ff)

8.4 Must. This was like today essentially an auxiliary of necessity, as in *I must go* or of deduction: *you must be mad*. However, it is important to realize that as an auxiliary of necessity it had a strong competitor in *shall*, which was much more common in that sense than it is today (see *shall* under 8.5. below). Today's competitor is *have to*.

Must was also used as an auxiliary of the future where today we would prefer *is to be*, i.e. in cases where we wish to imply what is in store for us. Thus early Modern English would tend to have *this must not be* (or *this shall not be*) for *this is not to be*. It is obvious that such usage can easily lead to misunderstanding. When Thersites, in *Troilus and Cressida*, says of Ajax that:

> He must fight singly tomorrow with Hector
>
> > (III.iii.240)

he is not saying that he *needs* to fight with Hector, but that he is due to fight him. Similarly, when Cassandra says in the same play that

> Troy must not be
>
> > (II.ii.108)

she is regretfully predicting a sad outcome.

The original present tense of *must* was *mote* and this form was still in use in the early part of the sixteenth century. It was frequently used as a past tense, having got confused with *mought*, a variant of *might*; see above. Spenser's usage used to be typical but was no longer so by his time, and he uses *mote* as a deliberate archaism:

And you Sir knight, whose name mote I request, [meaning 'must',
    present]
Of grace do me vnto his cabin guide.

(The Faerie Queene I.ix.32)

At last their wayes so fell, that they mote part [i.e. 'had to']

(The Faerie Queene III.iii.62)

O how, said he, mote I that well out find [– 'can']

(The Faerie Queene I.ii.43)

. . . that mote ye please [i.e. 'may']
Well to accept

(The Faerie Queene I.iii.29)

He by a priuie Posterne tooke his flight,
That of no enuious eyes he mote be spyde. [meaning 'might, could']

(The Faerie Queene I.v.52)

8.5 Shall/Should and Will/Would. Early Modern English usage differed considerably from ours. Modern students tend to pay far too little heed to how Renaissance writers employed these auxiliaries and to the connotations they might carry.

In the second and third persons *shall* and *should* were particularly frequent as an auxiliary of obligation or necessity. The obligation or necessity might be indicative of pre-arrangement by agents other than the speaker (and we must take great care not to confuse this sense of past tense *should* with *should* meaning 'ought to' (*you should not smoke so much*), which was of course also current):

DON JOHN: It is so. The Count Claudio shall marry the daughter of
    Leonato.

(Much Ado About Nothing II.ii.1)

i.e. 'it has been arranged that Claudio is to marry Hero'. Similarly, in the past tense, when Borachio says:

overheard me confessing to this man how . . . you disgraced her when
you should marry her.

(Much Ado About Nothing V.i.227–31)

We would have said *when you were (supposed) to marry her* or *when you were engaged to be married to her*. And when Page says to Shallow in *The Merry Wives of Windsor*:

I warrant you, he's the man should fight with him.

(III.i.64)

he is not saying that Caius is the man who ought to fight Evans but that he is the one who *is supposed to* fight with him. This use of *shall/should* is very restricted in today's English and occurs in the present tense only, especially in legal and bureaucratic language referring to the decree of a law or statute, as in *the committee shall consist of no more than six members*, and in plot summaries: 'It is contrived that Benedick shall overhear the Prince and Claudio speak of the secret love of Beatrice for him.'

Connected with this use of the *shall* of obligation is one, alien to us today, where the auxiliary implies that the speaker thinks something will have to take place or is bound to happen:

> BASSANIO: Graziano speaks an infinite deal of nothing, more than any
>   man in all Venice. His reasons are as two grains of wheat hid in two
>   bushels of chaff: you shall seek all day ere you find them
>   (*The Merchant of Venice* I.i.114ff)

In that example *shall* is equivalent to 'will have to'. Similarly:

> GREMIO: A bridegroom, say you? 'Tis a groom indeed –
>   A grumbling groom, and that the girl shall find.
>   (*The Taming of the Shrew* III.iii.25–6)

i.e. 'will find out, I'm sure' or 'is bound to find out'. And:

> DON PEDRO: I will teach you how to humour your cousin that she shall
>   fall in love with Benedick, and I, with your two helps, will so practise
>   on Benedick that, in despite of his quick wit and his queasy
>   stomach, he shall fall in love with Beatrice.
>   (*Much Ado About Nothing* II.i.355ff)

i.e. 'so that she/he is bound to fall in love'.

When the obligation ensues from the speaker's firm determination, typically in plans, promises, threats, or commands, *shall* in the second and third persons was exceedingly common in Renaissance English. Nowadays this usage is distinctly restricted and uncommon: *you/he shall get your/his money*; *you/he shall smart for this*; *you shall do as I say*. We prefer *will*, which includes the contraction *'ll*, or, in the case of commands, we prefer *must*. Not so in early Modern English, when *shall* was normal:

> 'Now make you redy,' said Merlyn. 'This nyght ye shalle lye with
> Igrayne in the castel of Tyntigayll. And ye shalle be lyke the duke her
> husband, Ulfyus shal be lyke syre Brastias, a knyghte of the dukes, and
> I will be lyke a knyghte that hyghte [is called] syr Jordanus . . .'
>   (*Morte Darthur* 9)

Merlin, the magician, tells King Uther of his plans. Note that he uses *will* in the first person. This carries, instead of the ring of prophecy implied by his *shall*, a tone of intention: 'and I am going to be . . .' Other instances of *shall* showing speaker-determined obligation:

PEDRINGANO: But how shall Serberine be there, my lord?

(*The Spanish Tragedy* III.ii.87)

i.e. 'how can we arrange for Serberine to be there?'

> Nay, nay (quoth she) your first word shall stand: after three months come to me a gaine, and then you shall know my mind to the full, and so good Sir *Hugh* be gone: but if I doe euer heare from thee, or see thee betwixt this time and the time prefixed, I will for euer hereafter blot thy name out of my booke of Remembrances . . .
>
> (*The Gentle Craft* 74)

Once again we note first-person *will* of intention or volition contrasting with second-person *shall*, here indicating a promise, as it does in the third person in:

DRUGGER: I pray you, speak for me to Master Doctor.
FACE: He shall do anything.

(*The Alchemist* I.iii.20–1)

Face promises or guarantees that Subtle will do anything for Drugger. The next two examples show threat:

> Therefore by Termagaunt thou shalt be dead
>
> (*The Faerie Queene* II.viii.30)

BAJAZETH: By Mahomet my kinsman's sepulchre,
   And by the holy Alcoran I swear,
   He shall be made a chaste and lustless eunuch,
   And in my sarell [serail, harem] tend my concubines;
   And all his captains, that thus stoutly stand,
   Shall draw the chariot of my emperess,
   Whom I have brought to see their overthrow!
TAMBURLAINE: By this my sword that conquer'd Persia,
   Thy fall shall make me famous through the world!
   I will not tell thee how I'll handle thee,
   But every common soldier of my camp
   Shall smile to see thy miserable state.

(*1Tamburlaine* III.iii.75ff)

The next two are commands:

LOUIS THE DAUPHIN: Your grace shall pardon me: I will not back.

(*King John* V.ii.78)

i.e. 'must' or 'will have to'.

> STEPHEN: I protest –
> EDWARD KNOWELL: No, no, you shall not protest, coz.
> *(Every Man In His Humour* I.iii.79–80)

i.e. 'mustn't'. The following example from *3Henry VI* shows clearly that the *shall* of obligation issuing from the speaker's determination is stronger than *must*:

> KING EDWARD: What danger or what sorrow can befall thee
> So long as Edward is thy constant friend,
> And their true sovereign, whom they must obey?
> Nay, whom they shall obey, and love thee too –
> (IV.i.75ff)

As an auxiliary of the future (as in *I shall be in Rome by this time next year*), *shall* was common in the first person. So it is today, though it tends to be marked as relatively formal compared with *will* or *'ll* which are now more frequent (but *will* or *'ll* would often imply stronger volition in Renaissance English; see discussion of *will* below):

> CUPID: I shall one day be a man,
> And better able unto other arms.
> *(Dido, Queen of Carthage* III.iii.35–6)

> SILENCE: We shall all follow, cousin.
> *(2Henry IV* III.i.34)

Compare first-person *will* and *shall* in:

> BENEDICK: . . . I will live a bachelor
> DON PEDRO: I shall see thee ere I die look pale with love.
> *(Much Ado About Nothing* I.i.230–1)

Benedick says 'I intend to', but Don Pedro says 'the time will come when . . .'

But unlike today *shall* was also a very frequent futuric auxiliary in the second and third persons. In Present-day English *shall* in the second and third persons is very restricted and implies threat, promise or command. This, as we have seen, it could also imply during the Renaissance. It is therefore very important for us nowadays to attune ourselves to the much *wider* and variegated use of *shall* in early Modern English. Examples of *shall* as a futuric auxiliary in the second and third persons:

> er the galewis [gallows] can be made redy it shal be nyght
> *(Reynard the Fox* 31)

it shalbe well to knowe, how the poore and princely prisoners, passed this tedious night.

(Arcadia 159)

We would now use *will* in such cases and in:

I am overthrowne in my selfe, who shall raise mee?

(Arcadia 10)

i.e. 'what man is there who can raise me?'. Had Sidney written *who will raise me?* the question would be less of a rhetorical one, more a request ('is there nobody who can please raise me?'). Compare *shall* and *will* in:

IAGO: She gives it out that you shall marry her.
    Do you intend it?

(Othello IV.i.115–6)

BAPTISTA: But thus, I trust, you will not marry her.
    (The Taming of the Shrew III.ii.115)

In Baptista's line *will* implies volition or intention. This is absent from *shall* in Iago's speech, where it is an auxiliary of the future, possibly with a notion of pre-arrangement (i.e. 'will be marrying her' or 'are to marry her'). Hence any idea of intention or volition must be stated or asked separately: *Do you intend it?*.

DON PEDRO: Well, as time shall try. 'In time the savage bull doth bear the yoke.'

(Much Ado About Nothing I.i.243–4)

DON LEONATO: Well then, go you into hell?
BEATRICE: No, but to the gate, and there will the devil meet me . . .
    (Much Ado About Nothing II.i.37–9)

Don Pedro refers to the arrangement by 'fate' in a proverb. Beatrice is saying that she is convinced the devil will be there.

When *will* does not imply volition (see below), i.e. when it is more futuric than modal, it nevertheless contrasts with *shall* as a futuric auxiliary in that the latter, even as a futuric auxiliary, often retains the connotation that the future event is in some way planned or will necessarily follow or happen, whereas with *will* there is less objective certainty or no implication of plan. If there is any kind of prediction, it is much less speaker-determined or fate-determined than with *shall* and is often couched in a personal expression of belief, fear, hope or persuasion. Thus a sentence like *right shall prevail* would imply that the speaker is determined to see that it does, *or* that it is what fate has in store for us, whereas *right will prevail* is more of a hope or a belief, sometimes uttered to encourage or comfort somebody:

JENKIN: I believe it will fall to thy lot.
(A Woman Killed With Kindness II.i.89)

ANTIPHOLUS OF EPHESUS: Perchance I will be there as soon as you.
(The Comedy of Errors IV.i.39)

ANTONY: We will yet do well.
(Antony and Cleopatra III.xiii.190)

YOUNGER SPENSER: I doubt it not, my lord; right will prevail.
(Edward the Second III.iii.5)

FAUSTUS: The stars move still, time runs, the clock will strike.
The devil will come, and Faustus must be damned.
(Doctor Faustus V.ii.153–4)

ARTHUR: O, this will make my mother die with grief.
(King John III.iii.5)

It follows from these observations on futuric *shall* and *will* that they were not *purely* futuric: an element of obligation of some kind, even if it is only a note of pre-arrangement, is present in the most weakly modal instances of *shall*, and we have also seen how the speaker's attitude is apt to colour the meaning of *will*. This may be the reason for the recent popularity of *shall/will* combined with the progressive (*we shall be taking*), a construction we feel carries less modality and is therefore more purely futuric. It was very unusual, and therefore highly marked stylistically, in early Modern English (see 1.2. above) and was not then, unlike today, used to avoid modality in *shall* and *will*. Samuels (1972, 57) discusses today's problem well:

> . . . the forms usually regarded as pure 'colourless' future (*I shall leave, I will leave, I'll leave, I'm going to leave*) all in fact carry some degree of modal nuance. The periphrasis *shall/will be leaving*, on the other hand, is well known for its 'actualising' or 'visualising' function: especially when it is used with non-durative verbs, it focusses more attention on the action of the lexical verb *(be) leaving* and less on the auxiliaries *shall/will*. It is therefore becoming more and more used as a colourless future without overtones of intention, wish, resignation or the like, and irrespective of whether the context demands a marked aspectual form.

Will frequently carries a strong, modal sense of volition, desire or intention. This sense tends to be much stronger in Renaissance English, especially in the second and third persons, than it is today and often corresponds not to our *will* but to verbs like *want to, wish to, would like, intend to, be going to*:

> . . . seeing that my good will is thus vnkindly requited, I will altogether abhor the sight of women, and I will seek the world throughout, but I will find out some blessed plot, where no kind of such corrupt cattell do breed.

> (*The Gentle Craft* 77)

> FAUSTUS: I will renounce this magic and repent.
> (*Doctor Faustus* II.i.11)

> PRINCE HARRY: Now, sirs; (*to Gadshill*) by'r lady, you fought fair . . .
>   You are lions too – you ran away upon instinct, you will not
>   touch the true prince; no, fie!
> (*Henry IV* II.v.301ff)

> DOL: You'll bring your head within a cockscomb, will you?
> (*The Alchemist* I.i.115)

> YOUNGER SPENSER: Ah, traitors! Will they still display their pride?
> (*Edward the Second* III.ii.175)

> AJAX: I'll let his humour's blood.
> AGAMEMNON: (*aside*) He will be the physician that should be the patient.
> (*Troilus and Cressida* II.iii.209–10)

i.e. 'he'd like to be . . .'. *Will* = 'intend', but without a main verb, was also current:

> BASTARD: Old Time the clock-setter, that bald sexton Time,
>   Is it as he will? – Well then, France shall rue.
> (*King John* III.i.250–1)

This *will* must not be confused with the main verb *will* 'request' or 'enjoin', which has a different origin from the auxiliary and, in its capacity as an original main verb, takes *-s* in the third person singular and *-ed* in the past tense:

> MISTRESS FRANKFORD: . . . he wills you, as you prize his love,
>   Or hold in estimation his kind friendship,
>   To make bold in his absence, and command
>   Even as himself were present in the house.
> (*A Woman Killed With Kindness* II.iii.75)

> George . . . willed him without any more trouble to deliuer it
> (*The Pinder of Wakefield* 42)

The Middle English negative form of auxiliary *will* was *nill*, surviving only in *willy-nilly*, i.e. 'will he, nill he'. It was used occasionally in Renaissance English:

> HORATIO: I nill refuse this heavy doleful charge
> (*The Spanish Tragedy* I.iv.7)

i.e. 'I won't'.

Volitional past tense *would* 'wanted to, wished to' was, like today, common in negative clauses (*he wouldn't talk to me*), but uncommon in affirmative ones (and obsolete today) presumably because it could be too easily confused with the conditional. In the following speech from *2Henry VI* the first instance is typical, the second is not:

> QUEEN MARGARET: Yet Aeolus would not be a murderer,
>   But left that hateful office unto thee.
>   The pretty vaulting sea refused to drown me,
>   Knowing that thou wouldst have me drowned on shore
>   With tears as salt as sea through thy unkindness.
>
> (III.ii.92ff)

i.e. 'Aeolus did not want to' and 'thou wanted to'.

On the other hand, *would* was very frequent in early Modern English on its own (i.e. not modifying a main verb) = 'wish', sometimes without a preceding pronoun. This is an old subjunctive survival:

> ROSALIND: The little strength I have, I would it were with you.
> (*As You Like It* I.ii.182)

> KNOWELL: Nay, would ourselves were not the first, even parents,
>   That did destroy the hopes in our own children
>   (*Every Man In His Humour* II.v.14–15)

Without a subject this *would* still survives, as in *would another keeper had been in goal!*, but is now more marked and much less frequent than during the Renaissance.

Like today *will* was also used to emphasize natural, inherent ability, capacity, inclination or characteristic behaviour rather than the future, as in *cork will float on water / John will sit playing with a matchbox for hours / boys will be boys*:

> Then (replyed Griffith) you are as much troubled in loue, as a Goat in an ague, and as blind as a Flie in October, that will stand still while a man cuts of his head . . .
> (*The Gentle Craft* 75)

Tarselius (1968) has shown convincingly how this use of *will* is a conspicuous feature of Francis Bacon's essay style. It is almost as if he continually wishes to distance himself by implying universal truths rather than personal opinions:

> A wise Man will make more Opportunities then [than] he findes.
> (*Of Ceremonies and Respects* 159)

> It appeareth in nothing more, that *Atheisme* is rather in the *Lip*, then in the *Heart* of Man, then by this; That *Atheists* will ever be talking of that their Opinion, as if they fainted in it [distrusted it], within themselves . . .
> (*Of Atheisme* 52)

> A man, that hath no vertue in himselfe, ever *envieth* Vertue in others, For mens Mindes, will either feed upon their owne Good, or upon others Evill; And who wanteth the one, wil prey upon the other; And who so is out of Hope to attaine to anothers Vertue, will seeke to come at even hand, by Depressing an others Fortune.
> (*Of Envy* 27)

Should, like futuric *shall*, was unlike today very common in the second and third persons in the main clause of conditional sentences. Since we now prefer *would* we must be careful, especially if there is no immediately preceding or following subordinate clause of hypothesis (as in Ulysses' speech below), not to confuse this *should* with the *should* meaning 'ought to':

> NERISSA: . . . you should refuse to perform your father's
> will if you should refuse to accept him
> (*The Merchant of Venice* I.ii.90–1)

i.e. 'would refuse'. (Notice also, in this example, *should* 'were to' in the *subordinate* clause. Such a *should* would be regular today only in hypothetical clauses without a conjunction (*should you see him, ask him to call*). In *if*-clauses in the second and third persons it is restricted and implies that the condition is rather unlikely (cp. *if you should see him, ask him to call* and *if you see him, ask him to call*), but *should* in such clauses was much more frequent in Renaissance English and thus did not carry as strong a tone of unlikelihood as it does today.) In the next example the condition is more loosely attached, not in a subordinate *if*-clause but in a separate clause (*Take but . . .*):

> ULYSSES: Take but degree away, untune that string,
> And hark what discord follows. Each thing meets
> In mere oppugnancy. The bounded waters
> Should lift their bosoms higher than the shores
> And make a sop of all this solid globe;

> Strength should be lord of imbecility,
> And the rude son should strike his father dead.
> > (*Troilus and Cressida* I.iii.109ff)

i.e. 'if you take away degree (meaning rank or hierarchy), then the waters *would* lift . . .'

For subjunctive *had*, i.e. 'would have', see 2.2 (Subjunctive) above.

In early Modern English *should* would often denote logical deduction much in the way that *must* does so today, or be roughly equivalent to 'seem to be'. This is a sense not available to *should* in Present-day English and is potentially confusing to the modern reader:

> AENEAS: Where am I now? These should be Carthage walls.
> > (*Dido, Queen of Carthage* II.i.1)

i.e. 'must be'.

> KING EDWARD: Father, thy face should harbour no deceit.
> > (*Edward the Second* IV.vi.8)

i.e. 'thy face does not seem to harbour any deceit'.

> HERMIA: It cannot be but thou hast murdered him.
> So should a murderer look – so dead, so grim.
> > (*A Midsummer Night's Dream* III.ii.56–7)

i.e. 'so must a murderer look'. And when Bianca goes on about the handkerchief Cassio has given her, Othello deduces:

> By heaven, that should be my handkerchief.
> > (*Othello* IV.i.155)

i.e. 'must be'.

> BOBADIL: By his discourse, he should eat nothing but hay.
> > (*Every Man In His Humour* I.v.81–2)

i.e. 'his only diet must be hay'.

8.6 With Verbs of Motion. In common with other Germanic languages today, a verb of motion was often omitted after an auxiliary in early Modern English (as it sometimes still is in Scots, as in *I'll away and look for it*):

> GUARD: You may not in, my lord.
> > (*Edward the Second* II.ii.137)

> BISHOP OF COVENTRY: . . . thou shalt back to France.
> > (*Edward The Second* I.i.185)

SHALLOW: Peradventure I will with ye to the court.

> (*2Henry IV* III.ii.292)

SIR JOHN: I must a dozen mile tonight.

> (*2Henry IV* III.ii.287)

and even sometimes after *be*:

COUNTESS: Towards Florence is he?

> (*All's Well That Ends Well* III.ii.68)

Pronouns

9 You and Thou. Late Middle English typically had the following distribution of the second person personal pronoun:

	Singular	Plural
As subject	*thou/ye*	*ye*
As object	*thee/you*	*you*

As early as the late thirteenth century the plural *ye/you*, influenced by the use of French *vous*, began to be employed as a polite singular. This was an important step in the history of our language since now for the first time *ye/you* could contrast in the *singular* with *thou/thee*, just like French *vous* vs *tu*.

During the early part of the Renaissance, *ye* was still normally used for the subject, *you* for the object. It is unusual to find in an early like Wyatt a line like:

In him your glory alway set you must

> (*A Paraphrase of the Penitential Psalms* 291)

where the object form *you* has been used for the subject. But it was not long before *you* began to be used also as the subject form, probably because of its similarity in spelling and pronunciation to *thou*: both had *-ou* and in early Modern English a fully stressed *you* could, in one kind of pronunciation, have the same diphthong as *thou*, i.e. they could rhyme. Conversely, *ye* came to be used also as object because of its similarity to *thee* and is common even in the archaic *Faerie Queene*, as in I.i.52: 'Why Dame (quoth he) what hath ye thus dismayd? / What frayes ye, that were wont to comfort me affrayd?' It could also be useful in rhyme, as in the couplet of Shakespeare's sonnet 111: 'Pity me then, dear friend, and I assure ye / Even that your pity is enough to cure me.' Thus the early Modern English distribution was as follows:

	Singular	Plural
As subject	*thou/you/ye*	*you/ye*
As object	*thee/you/ye*	*you/ye*

Thee used outside the object position was mainly confined to imperative phrases like *fare thee well*. Because of his fondness for archaism, Spenser has *ye* as subject (both singular and plural) more often than, say, Shakespeare. In *The Faerie Queene*, when subject *you* and *ye* are used in close proximity, there seems to be a stylistic difference in that *you* is apparently the more emphatic of the two:

> But you, faire Sir, be not herewith dismaid,
> But constant keepe the way, in which ye stand.
> > (II.ix.8)

> What be you wofull Dame, which thus lament,
> And for what cause declare, so mote ye not repent.
> > (VI.iv.27)

In the sixteenth and early seventeenth centuries, singular *you* (and of course *ye*) was employed by inferiors to superiors, e.g. children to parents, servants to masters, ordinary men to noblemen; and *thou/thee* were used in the reverse manner, but also when addressing God because of the wish for intimacy.

Thou was also the form that people from the lower classes would use among each other, like the murderers Black Will and Shakebag in *Arden of Feversham*:

> SHAKEBAG: Come, Will, see thy tools be in a readiness!
>   Is not thy powder dank, or will thy flint strike fire?
> WILL: Then ask me if my nose be on my face,
>   Or whether my tongue be frozen in my mouth.
>   Zounds, here's a coil!
>   You were best swear me on the intergatories [on oath]
>   How many pistols I have took in hand.
>   . . .
>   I pray thee, Shakebag, let this answer thee,
>   That I have took more purses in this down
>   Than e'er thou handled'st pistols in thy life.
> > (III.vi.1ff)

Since Will and Shakebag always address each other with *thou*, the *you* in Will's fourth line shows that he is addressing that particular remark not only to Shakebag but also to Greene, who is present; it is plural, not singular.

The upper classes preferred *you* (except in certain intimate or emotional situations; see below), even amongst close relatives, as in Heywood's *A Woman Killed with Kindness*, where Sir Francis Acton is Master Frankford's brother-in-law:

SIR FRANCIS: By your leave, sister – by your husband's leave,
  I should have said – the hand that but this day
  Was given you in the church I'll borrow: sound!
  This marriage music hoists me from the ground.
FRANKFORD: Ay, you may caper, you are light and free
                            (I.i.6ff)

But occasionally other factors as to the choice between *you* and *thou* may come into play:

His Lady sad to see his sore constraint,
Cride out, Now now Sir knight, shew what ye bee,
Add faith vnto your force, and be not faint:
Strangle her, else she sure will strangle thee.
              (*The Faerie Queene* I.i.19)

It seems that the change from *ye/your* to *thee* is because the latter could be more emphatic (Sugden 1936, 28). It is no use arguing that the rhyme is the reason. If so, Spenser could have chosen *ye*, which he uses often enough in the object position.

However, in the great majority of cases the choice between *you* and *thou* depended on attitude. In addition to the general attitudinal pattern outlined above, people from all classes could switch from *you* to *thou* for emotional reasons. Thus a furious person might say *thou* even to his superior; and members of the higher social classes, where *you* would be the normal unmarked form, might address each other with *thou* to signal intimacy, affection, playfulness or anger. In the following passage from the anonymous *The Pinder of Wakefield* a pickpocket (*cutpurse*) is trying to rob George (the principal character). But the latter, having anticipated the robbery, has sown sharp fishing hooks on to the lining of his pockets, so when the pickpocket strikes, he cannot extract his hand from George's pocket. Note how George addresses the cutpurse with *thou* when they are alone together, and then switches to *you* when their squabble has become public (I have italicized *thou/thy* and *you* in this passage):

  . . . at last *George* seemed to take notice; saying, what the Diuell aylest *thou*, art *thou* mad. Oh my hand, my hand, good Master, quoth the Cutpurse; what the Diuell doth *thy* hand in my pocket? quoth *George* . . . People thronged after to see this new Comedy . . . *George* perceiuing such a multitude stood still, and desired them to make a stand for a while, and they should all see him release him presently: With that the people all stood still, and *George* walkt along with his prize, certifying

him hee had lost a purse the day before . . . and therefore willed him
without any more trouble to deliuer it: . . .*you* fared so well yesterday
that made *you* bee so ready in the same place to day. Come, come,
quoth *George, you* must re-deliuer . . .

(42)

At the beginning of Deloney's novel *Jacke of Newberie* the eponymous
hero is secretary to a woman recently widowed and therefore on the
look-out for a new husband. She tells Jack about her suitors, 'crauing
his opinion'. Jack asks her for their names and professions. The widow,
who is attracted to Jack, decides to go into details about the matter of
the suitors, which creates a situation of some intimacy. She first
addresses Jack with a polite *you*, to indicate, although he is her
employee, her respect for him (she has also put him in charge of her
servants), but then switches to *thou* as she asks him to come and sit
down next to her. Since she began with *you*, this *thou* is quite different
from the one she would employ for her other lower-status employees.
Far from indicating a superior attitude, her switch to *thou* is flattering
to Jack: it immediately signals intimacy and confidentiality, flirtation
even. Jack (John) respectfully addresses his employer with *you*
throughout, and speaks first:

> I pray you let me intreat you to know their names that be your
> sutors, and of what profession they be.
>   Marry *Iohn* (sayth she) that you shall, and I pray thee take a
> cushion and sit downe by me.
>   Dame (quoth he) I thanke you: but there is no reason I should sit
> on a cushion till I haue deserued it.
>   If thou hast not thou mightest haue done (said she): but some
> Souldiers neuer finde fauour.
>   *Iohn* replied, that maketh me indeed to want fauour: for I neuer
> durst try maydens because they seeme coy, nor wiues for feare of
> their husbands, nor widowes doubting their disdainfulnes.
>   Tush *Iohn* (quoth she) . . . it may seeme immodesty in me to
> bewray my louers secrets: yet seeing thy discretion, and being
> perswaded of thy secrecy, I will shew thee . . .

(5)

Compare also the following two songs by Wyatt:

(1)   Though I cannot your cruelty constrain
         For my goodwill to favour me again,
         Though my true and faithful love
         Have no power your heart to move,
              Yet rue upon my pain.

         Though I your thrall must evermore remain
         And for your sake my liberty restrain,
         The greatest grace that I do crave

Is that ye would vouchsafe
      To rue upon my pain.

Though I have not deserved to obtain
So high reward, but thus to serve in vain,
Though I shall have no redress,
Yet of right ye can no less
      But rue upon my pain.

But I see well that your high disdain
Will no wise grant that I shall more attain.
Yet ye must grant at the least
This my poor and small request:
      Rejoice not at my pain.
                (no. 106)

(2)   What rage is this? What furor of what kind?
What pow'r, what plague doth weary thus my mind?
Within my bones to rankle is assigned
      What poison pleasant sweet?

Lo, see mine eyes swell with continual tears.
The body still away sleepless it wears.
My food nothing my fainting strength repairs
      Nor doth my limbs sustain.

In deep wide wound the deadly stroke doth turn,
To cured scar that never shall return.
Go to, triumph, rejoice thy goodly turn.
      Thy friend thou dost oppress.

Oppress thou dost, and hast of him no cure,
Nor yet my plaint no pity can procure.
Fierce tiger fell, hard rock without recure,
      Cruel rebel to love!

Once may thou love, never be loved again:
So love thou still and not thy love obtain.
So wrathful Love with spites of just disdain
      May threat thy cruel heart.
                (no. 117)

Both are poems addressed to a disdainful lady, and in both the speaker
is begging for mercy. But they are quite different in tone. The first is
more distant in its formal succession of concessive *though*-clauses,
which contrast with the desperate, short interrogative outbursts that
begin the second poem. These are followed by emotionally wrought
imperatives 'Lo, see mine eyes swell. . . / Go to, triumph, rejoice' in
the second and third stanzas, together with references to acute physical
suffering. The vocabulary is also much more intense in the second
poem, and is sometimes couched in violent exclamation: 'Fierce tiger

fell, hard rock without recure / Cruel rebel to love!'. It is this desperate intensity that precludes the use of *you (ye)* here. Emotional turmoil directed towards another person creates its own intimacy, and occasions the use of *thou*.

It is thus of the greatest importance to pay close attention to switches between *you* and *thou* in Renaissance literature if one wants to appreciate significant shifts in emotional and attitudinal nuance. By way of illustrating the extraordinary variation in such matters, we shall now take a close look at the second-person pronouns in four passages from Shakespeare. It is important to read the passages in full since the change of pronoun is dependent on the continually fluctuating relationships between the characters. We shall start with a short passage from *Troilus and Cressida* (II.i.78ff), involving Achilles, Ajax and Patroclus and the querulous and deformed character Thersites. Ajax and Thersites are having a quarrel:

> THERSITES: I say, this Ajax –
> ACHILLES: Nay, good Ajax.
> THERSITES: Has not so much wit –
> ACHILLES: (*to Ajax*) Nay, I must hold you.
> 5 THERSITES: As will stop the eye of Helen's needle, for whom he
> comes to fight.
> ACHILLES: Peace, fool.
> THERSITES: I would have peace and quietness, but the fool will
> not. He, there, that he, look you there.
> 10 AJAX: O thou damned cur I shall –
> ACHILLES: (*to Ajax*) Will you set your wit to a fool's?
> THERSITES: No, I warrant you, for a fool's will shame it.
> PATROCLUS: Good words, Thersites.
> ACHILLES: What's the quarrel?
> 15 AJAX: I bade the vile owl go learn me the tenor of the
> proclamation, and he rails upon me.
> THERSITES: I serve thee not.
> AJAX: Well, go to, go to.
> THERSITES: I serve here voluntary.
> 20 ACHILLES: Your last service was sufferance. 'Twas not voluntary:
> no man is beaten voluntary. Ajax was here the voluntary,
> and you as under an impress.
> THERSITES: E'en so. A great deal of your wit, too, lies in your
> sinews, or else there be liars. Hector shall have a great catch an
> 25 a [if he] knock out either of your brains. A [he] were as good
> crack a fusty nut with no kernel.
> ACHILLES: What, with me too, Thersites?
> THERSITES: There's Ulysses and old Nestor, whose wit was
> mouldy ere your grandsires had nails on their toes, yoke
> 30 you like draught oxen and make you plough up the war.
> ACHILLES: What? What?

THERSITES: Yes, good sooth. To Achilles! To, Ajax, to –
AJAX: I shall cut out your tongue.
THERSITES: 'Tis no matter. I shall speak as much wit as thou
35   afterwards.

Under normal circumstances these four characters in the Greek camp
would address each other with *you* (like Achilles to Ajax in 4 and 11),
even though Thersites is a conscripted soldier (*impress* in 22 means
'compulsory military service'). Patroclus, even in irritation, says *you*
to Thersites in V.i.16: ' "Male varlet", you rogue? What's that?'; but
when he speaks in violent anger or extreme contempt, he switches to
thou, as in V.i.22–3: 'Why, thou damnable box of envy thou, what
mean'st thou to curse thus?' So do the other Greek leaders, like Ajax
in line 10 above and Achilles in V.i.5: 'Thou crusty botch of nature,
what's the news?' Thersites, in his vitriolic mockery, normally uses
thou even to the leaders, for whom he has little respect. It is important
to note that he wishes to show particular contempt for Ajax in this
scene. His scorn becomes clear, not only in his *thou* to him, but also
because this contrasts with his *you* to Achilles (9, 12) who is thus,
here, accorded relative respect, to the humiliation of Ajax. Achilles,
as already noted, uses *thou* whenever he wishes Thersites to feel his
contempt, but he does not do so in 20–2 above. This shows that his
explanatory remark about Thersites' service is coolly dignified, not
passionately angry nor especially contemptuous. It is noteworthy that
Ajax says *your* to Thersites in line 33: in spite of his words, he has
now cooled down. It is therefore particularly galling and humiliating
for him to receive a *thou* from Thersites in return.

The next extract is from *The Merchant of Venice* I.i.114ff. Antonio,
the merchant, and his friend Bassanio are having a conversation just
after their carefree friend Graziano has left them. Bassanio is in both
debt and love and tells Antonio of his plight:

BASSANIO: Graziano speaks an infinite deal of nothing, more than
    any man in all Venice. His reasons are as two grains of wheat
    hid in two bushels of chaff: you shall seek all day ere you find
    them, and when you have them they are not worth the search.
5 ANTONIO: Well, tell me now what lady is the same
    To whom you swore a secret pilgrimage,
    That you today promised to tell me of.
    BASSANIO: 'Tis not unknown to you, Antonio,
    How much I have disabled mine estate
10   By something showing a more swelling port
    Than my faint means would grant continuance,
    Nor do I now make moan to be abridged
    From such a noble rate; but my chief care
    Is to come fairly off from the great debts
15   Wherein my time, something too prodigal,

Hath left me gaged. To you, Antonio,
I owe the most in money and in love,
And from your love I have a warranty
To unburden all my plots and purposes
20   How to get clear of all the debts I owe.
ANTONIO: I pray you, good Bassanio, let me know it,
And if it stand as you yourself still do,
Within the eye of honour, be assured
My purse, my person, my extremest means
25   Lie all unlocked to your occasions.
BASSANIO: In my schooldays, when I had lost one shaft,
I shot his fellow of the selfsame flight
The selfsame way, with more advised watch,
To find the other forth; and by adventuring both,
30   I oft found both. I urge this childhood proof
Because what follows is pure innocence.
I owe you much, and, like a wilful youth,
That which I owe is lost; but if you please
To shoot another arrow that self way
35   Which you did shoot the first, I do not doubt,
As I will watch the aim, or [either] to find both
Or bring your latter hazard back again,
And thankfully rest debtor for the first.
ANTONIO: You know me well, and herein spend but time
40   To wind about my love with circumstance;
And out of doubt you do me now more wrong
In making question of my uttermost
Than if you had made waste of all I have.
Then do but say to me what I should do
45   That in your knowledge may by me be done,
And I am pressed unto it. Therefore speak.
BASSANIO: In Belmont is a lady richly left,
And she is fair, and, fairer than that word,
Of wondrous virtues. Sometimes from her eyes
50   I did receive fair speechless messages.
Her name is Portia, nothing undervalued
To Cato's daughter, Brutus' Portia;
Nor is the wide world ignorant of her worth,
For the four winds blow in from every coast
55   Renowned suitors, and her sunny locks
Hang on her temples like a golden fleece,
Which makes her seat of Belmont Colchis' strand,
And many Jasons come in quest of her.
O my Antonio, had I but the means
60   To hold a rival place with one of them,
I have a mind presages me such thrift
That I should questionless be fortunate.
ANTONIO: Thou know'st that all my fortunes are at sea,
Neither have I money nor commodity

65   To raise a present sum. Therefore go forth –
        Try what my credit can in Venice do;
        That shall be racked even to the uttermost
        To furnish thee to Belmont, to fair Portia.
        Go presently enquire, and so will I,
70   Where money is; and I no question make
        To have it of my trust or for my sake.

In the conversation immediately preceding this Graziano uses *you* to Antonio to begin with (I.i.73–4, 76), but he then switches to *thou* in a speech of carefree playfulness (79ff). As soon as he has gone, *you* is reverted to, at the beginning of our extract, between Antonio and Bassanio, i.e. the neutral, unmarked form among non-working class people. Bassanio then proceeds to tell his friend of his financial difficulties. In spite of his reference to Antonio's love (16–18) he still employs the 'proper' *you*. Antonio does the same even while urging Bassanio to tell him everything (21–5), and *you* remains Bassanio's pronoun as he asks Antonio for a loan: his request is somewhat indirect, couched as it is in an extended metaphor of arrow-shooting and retrieval, and thus cautious but well-mannered and respectful (32–8). Antonio's answer is very favourable, assuring Bassanio of his support in very positive terms and referring to his love for him – but he still uses *you*: Bassanio's problem is still vague, and Antonio still does not know the whys and wherefores of the matter. But then Bassanio opens his heart and speaks of Portia (47–58). He speaks about her so eloquently and with such beauty (his speech is among the most admired in Shakespeare) that his love for her is obvious. His final heartfelt pleading *O my Antonio . . .* (59–62) is both touching and genuinely desperate. And now for the first time in the scene Antonio's heart goes out to his friend in sympathy. He is deeply moved by Bassanio's love for Portia and his desperate situation. We see this, above all, in his change to *thou*, which goes with his details of the exceptionally generous assistance he eagerly urges him to accept.

The next passage, from *Much Ado About Nothing*, is a conversation between Beatrice and Benedick which ends Act IV.i. and starts at line 258. These two, in spite of being attracted to each other, are forever engaged in wordy warfare, and in this scene Beatrice tries to persuade Benedick to challenge Claudio for slandering her cousin Hero:

    BENEDICK: Lady Beatrice, have you wept all this while?
    BEATRICE: Yea, and I will weep a while longer.
    BENEDICK: I will not desire that.
    BEATRICE: You have no reason, I do it freely.
5   BENEDICK: Surely I do believe your fair cousin is wronged.
    BEATRICE: Ah, how much might the man deserve of me that
       would right her!

BENEDICK: Is there any way to show such friendship?

BEATRICE: A very even way, but no such friend.

10 BENEDICK: May a man do it?

BEATRICE: It is a man's office, but not yours.

BENEDICK: I do love nothing in the world so well as you. Is not that strange?

BEATRICE: As strange as the thing I know not. It were as possible

15 for me to say I loved nothing so well as you, but believe me not, and yet I lie not. I confess nothing nor I deny nothing. I am sorry for my cousin.

BENEDICK: By my word, Beatrice, thou lovest me.

BEATRICE: Do not swear and eat it.

20 BENEDICK: I will swear by it that you love me, and I will make him eat it that says I love not you.

BEATRICE: Will you not eat your word?

BENEDICK: With no sauce that can be devised to it. I protest I love thee.

25 BEATRICE: Why then, God forgive me.

BENEDICK: What offence, sweet Beatrice?

BEATRICE: You have stayed me in a happy hour. I was about to protest I loved you.

BENEDICK: And do it with all thy heart.

30 BEATRICE: I love you with so much of my heart that none is left to protest.

BENEDICK: Come, bid me do anything for thee.

BEATRICE: Kill Claudio.

BENEDICK: Ha! Not for the wide world.

35 BEATRICE: You kill me to deny it. Farewell.

BENEDICK: Tarry, sweet Beatrice.

BEATRICE: I am gone though I am here. There is no love in you.
– Nay, I pray you, let me go.

BENEDICK: Beatrice.

40 BEATRICE: In faith, I will go.

BENEDICK: We'll be friends first.

BEATRICE: You dare easier be friends with me than fight with mine enemy.

BENEDICK: Is Claudio thine enemy?

45 BEATRICE: Is he not approved in the height a villain, that hath slandered, scorned, dishonoured my kinswoman? O that I were a man! What, bear her in hand until they come to take hands, and then with public accusation, uncovered slander, unmitigated rancour – O God that I were a man! I would eat

50 his heart in the market place.

BENEDICK: Hear me, Beatrice.

BEATRICE: Talk with a man out at a window – a proper saying!

BENEDICK: Nay, but Beatrice.

BEATRICE: Sweet Hero, she is wronged, she is slandered, she is

55 undone.

BENEDICK: Beat –

BEATRICE: Princes and counties! Surely a princely testimony, a
goodly count, Count Comfit, a sweet gallant, surely. O that
I were a man for his sake! Or that I had any friend would be
60 a man for his sake! But manhood is melted into courtesies,
valour into compliment, and men are only turned into tongue,
and trim ones, too. He is now as valiant as Hercules that only
tells a lie and swears it. I cannot be a man with wishing,
therefore I will die a woman with grieving.
65 BENEDICK: Tarry, good Beatrice. By this hand, I love thee.
BEATRICE: Use it for my love some other way than swearing by
it.
BENEDICK: Think you in your soul the Count Claudio hath
wronged Hero?
BEATRICE: Yea, as sure as I have a thought or a soul.
70 BENEDICK: Enough, I am engaged, I will challenge him. I will
kiss your hand, and so I leave you. By this hand, Claudio
shall render me a dear account. As you hear of me, so think
of me. Go comfort your cousin. I must say she is dead. And
so, farewell.

Although Beatrice has made it clear earlier in the play that she loves
Benedick, she employs *you* throughout this passage: she keeps her
distance so as not to be thought of in any way as 'fast'. She wishes to
retain her dignity and give an impression of independence (*You have
no reason, I do it freely* (4)) and does not wish to be seen as somebody
who can be easily conquered. The distancing is also partly achieved
by her mockery (e.g. *It is a man's office, but not yours* (11)). Benedick,
on the other hand, employs both *thou* and *you*, starting off with the
latter in gently respectful, solicitous enquiry (1). He politely concurs
with her opinion that Hero has been wronged (*Surely I do believe your
fair cousin is wronged* (5)). His declaration of love in line 12 is still
with *you*, which should tell the actor that Benedick is as yet not too
forward, but his use of *thou* in 18 is a firm indication of the intensity
of his outburst. The reference to his manly dignity in 20–1 makes
him revert briefly to *you*, but after that he becomes very involved
emotionally: as Beatrice gets more and more worked up and upset,
Benedick becomes more and more impetuous and uses *thou* again and
again (24, 29, 32, 44, 65). The pronoun is particularly marked in line
65 after her long outburst about 'manhood': *Tarry, good Beatrice. By
this hand, I love thee.* Then, towards the end of the scene, Benedick
switches back to *you*. He does this to indicate to Beatrice that he is
genuine in his offer of help. His *you* in line 67 shows that not until
now does he really believe that there is something in what Beatrice
claims Claudio has done to Hero: *Think you in your soul the Count
Claudio hath wronged Hero?*. The change to *you* is here equivalent to
our 'do you honestly think that. . . ?'. Convinced, Benedick now

means business and reveals his seriousness of purpose by addressing Beatrice with *you* in the last three lines.

The last passage, from *3Henry VI* III.ii.36, is a conversation between King Edward the Fourth and Lady Elizabeth Gray, later to become his queen. Lady Gray is desperately trying to regain land lost after her husband's murder. The conversation is overheard by King Edward's brothers Richard and George:

KING EDWARD: Now tell me, madam, do you love your children?
LADY GRAY: Ay, full as dearly as I love myself.
KING EDWARD: And would you not do much to do them good?
LADY GRAY: To do them good I would sustain some harm.
5 KING EDWARD: Then get your husband's lands, to do them good.
LADY GRAY: Therefore I came unto your majesty.
KING EDWARD: I'll tell you how these lands are to be got.
LADY GRAY: So shall you bind me to your highness' service.
KING EDWARD: What service wilt thou do me, if I give them?
10 LADY GRAY: What you command, that rests in me to do.
KING EDWARD: But you will take exceptions to my boon.
LADY GRAY: No, gracious lord, except I cannot do it.
KING EDWARD: Ay, but thou canst do what I mean to ask.
LADY GRAY: Why, then, I will do what your grace commands.
15 RICHARD OF GLOUCESTER: (*to George*) He plies her hard, and much
   rain wears the marble.
GEORGE OF CLARENCE: As red as fire! Nay, then her wax must
   melt.
LADY GRAY: (*to King Edward*) Why stops my lord? Shall I not
   hear my task?
KING EDWARD: An easy task – 'tis but to love a king.
LADY GRAY: That's soon performed, because I am a subject.
20 KING EDWARD: Why, then, thy husband's lands I freely give thee.
LADY GRAY: (*curtsies*) I take my leave, with many thousand
   thanks.
RICHARD OF GLOUCESTER: (*to George*) The match is made – she
   seals it with a curtsy.
KING EDWARD: (*to Lady Gray*) But stay thee – 'tis the fruits of
   love I mean.
LADY GRAY: The fruits of love *I* mean, my loving liege.
25 KING EDWARD: Ay, but I fear me in another sense.
   What love think'st thou I sue so much to get?
LADY GRAY: My love till death, my humble thanks, my prayers –
   That love which virtue begs and virtue grants.
KING EDWARD: No, by my troth, I did not mean such love.
30 LADY GRAY: Why, then, you mean not as I thought you did.
KING EDWARD: But now you partly may perceive my mind.
LADY GRAY: My mind will never grant what I perceive
   Your highness aims at, if I aim aright.
KING EDWARD: To tell thee plain, I aim to lie with thee.

35 LADY GRAY: To tell *you* plain, I had rather lie in prison.
KING EDWARD: Why, then, thou shalt not have thy husband's
      lands.
LADY GRAY: Why, then, mine honesty shall be my dower;
      For by that loss I will not purchase them.
KING EDWARD: Therein thou wrong'st thy children mightily.
40 LADY GRAY: Herein your highness wrongs both them and me.
      But, mighty lord, this merry inclination
      Accords not with the sadness of my suit.
      Please you dismiss me either with ay or no.
KING EDWARD: Ay, if thou wilt say 'ay' to my request;
45   No, if thou dost say 'no' to my demand.
LADY GRAY: Then, no, my lord – my suit is at an end.
RICHARD OF GLOUCESTER: (*to George*) The widow likes him not –
      she knits her brows.
GEORGE OF CLARENCE: He is the bluntest wooer in Christendom.
KING EDWARD: (*aside*) Her looks doth argue her replete with
      modesty;
50   Her words doth show her wit incomparable;
      All her perfections challenge sovereignty.
      One way or other, she is for a king;
      And she shall be my love or else my queen.
      (*to Lady Gray*) Say that King Edward take thee for his queen?
55 LADY GRAY: 'Tis better said than done, my gracious lord.
      I am a subject fit to jest withal,
      But far unfit to be a sovereign.
KING EDWARD: Sweet widow, by my state I swear to thee
      I speak no more than what my soul intends,
60   And that is to enjoy thee for my love.
LADY GRAY: And that is more than I will yield unto.
      I know I am too mean to be your queen,
      And yet too good to be your concubine.
KING EDWARD: You cavil, widow – I did mean my queen.
65 LADY GRAY: 'Twill grieve your grace my sons should call you
      father.
KING EDWARD: No more than when my daughters call thee
      mother.
      Thou art a widow and thou hast some children;
      And, by God's mother, I, being but a bachelor,
      Have other some. Why, 'tis a happy thing
70   To be the father unto many sons.
      Answer no more, for thou shalt be my queen.

Lady Gray uses *you* throughout. Even when she finds the King's
request for sexual favours outrageous, she does not venture a *thou*:
his position is too exalted. The King first employs *you* (1–7), the
unmarked pronoun between people like himself and Lady Gray. The
switch to *thou* in the question *What service wilt thou do me . . . ?* (9)

tells us at once that the question is deliberately ambiguous, that the King is hinting at the more intimate, sexual sense of 'service'. Part of the tension of the conversation lies in Lady Gray's not catching on for quite some time. She probably takes the King's *thou* as a sign either of non-sexually based affection or possibly of the King's superior attitude. His innuendo over, Edward briefly reverts to *you* (11); but since Lady Gray is still totally unaware of where the conversation is leading, he resumes his intimate attitude (13, 20, 23, 26). Thinking she has now understood him, he goes back to a more businesslike *you* in 31. Exasperated, he finally throws caution to the winds and becomes blunt in his intimacy, switching back to *thou* (34). When she refuses to accept the bargain, the King, sulkingly or teasingly vindictive, sticks to *thou* (36, 39, 44, 45). However, his employment of *thou* after deciding to marry her, is quite different. It now signals affectionate, and not sexual, intimacy (58, 60, 66–7, 71), with one important exception, viz *you* in line 64, which shows how momentary irritation interferes with his affection.

It should be clear from these four examples how important the two pronouns are as signals of attitudes, emotions and relationships. These can change subtly, and often rapidly, within a scene, either completely or in a continually alternating manner. The subtleties are sometimes hard to appreciate, and some people may not agree with all my 'explanations' above; but we do ourselves a great disservice to the Renaissance writer if we remain immune to how different attitudes are hinted at by the interplay of *you* and *thou*.

10 The Third Person Personal Pronoun. *He* sometimes appears as *a* in unstressed position, especially, but not exclusively (see examples), in the speech of people from the lower classes:

> BEATRICE: . . . such a man would win any woman in the world, if a could get her good will.
> (*Much Ado About Nothing* II.i.14–15)

> POLONIUS: 'I know the gentleman
> . . .
> There was a gaming, there o'ertook in 's rouse'
> (*Hamlet* II.i.55, 58)

and *them* as *'em*: 'BRUTUS: Let 'em enter' (*Julius Caesar* II.i.76). This *'em* is a weakened form of the Middle English *hem* rather than *them* and is still current in colloquial spoken English, and in modern literature depicting it. The full form *hem* occasionally appears (together with *them*) in the early part of our period in writers like Caxton and Malory: 'And whan we se that ye have foughtyn with hem longe . . .' (*Morte Darthur*).

A rather, to us, peculiar use of *it* meaning 'he/she' may appear in sentences that define or describe, as in:

PANDARUS: I'll fetch her. It is the prettiest villain!
(*Troilus and Cressida* III.ii.31)

QUARLOUS: A notable hypocritical vermin it is; I know him.
(*Bartholomew Fair* I.iii.119)

Note that the descriptions in those two examples are of specific persons. Nowadays we could only use a defining *it* in general statements such as *it is a wise father that knows his own son*.

As in Middle English, *them* was often used as a demonstrative pronoun, i.e. 'those', before a relative pronoun. It is important that we do not regard this automatically as substandard or colloquial usage, which it would be in today's English:

I might be justly reckoned among the tardiest and the unwillingest of them that praise ye.

(*Aeropagitica* 152)

Occasionally a subject pronoun may be omitted:

. . . but he againe
Shooke him so hard, that forced him to speake.
(*The Faerie Queene* I.i.42)

i.e. 'that it (or he) forced . . .'

For the pleonastic (redundant) use of pronouns, see the next chapter on sentence structure, p. 101.

11 The Reflexive Pronoun. For the problem of personal pronoun *vs* reflexive pronoun *vs* zero after verbs, see section 5 above (Reflexive Verbs). Note also that a reflexive pronoun would sometimes be preferred to a personal one in cases where it would not happen today:

CALLAPINE: And never will we sunder camps and arms
Before himself or his be conquered.
(*2Tamburlaine* V.ii.52-3)

In Present-day English a reflexive pronoun on its own can only replace a personal one after *as, like, than,* and as in *he is not as old as myself / like yourself I have got problems / he said it was for you and myself*).

12 The Possessive Pronoun or Adjective. *Her* for *their* (as in Chaucer) occasionally appears early in our period (e.g. in Caxton) but it is rare after the Middle English period: 'These water-galls [rainbows] in her dim element / Foretell new storms to those already spent' (*The Rape of Lucrece* 1588).

His could sometimes appear instead of a possessive *-s*, especially after a noun ending in a sibilant, in which case the possessive *-s* would constitute a syllable, as in *George's house*. Since unstressed *his* would normally, as today, lose its *h-*, the pronunciation of *his* after a sibilant would be identical to possessive *-s*. This is the reason for its occasional appearance, as in the title of Thomas Nashe's *Pierce Penniless his Supplication to the Devil*. Other examples:

> . . . hee was quickly in *George* his pocket
>> (*The Pinder of Wakefield* 41)

> (*She catcheth out* Face *his sword*)
>> (stage direction in *The Alchemist* after I.i.115)

His was also originally the possesive for the neuter *its*. The latter is a late sixteenth-century development. Spenser and the 1611 Authorized Version of the Bible did not have *its* at all (Sugden 1936, 25); Milton used it only three times in his poetry (Emma 1964, 51); and according to Franz (1986, 287) *its* appears only ten times in the Shakespeare First Folio of 1623. Jonson uses *its* more frequently (Franz 1986, 287; Emma 1964, 51). Sometimes possessive *it* (i.e. without the *-s*), a form going back to the fourteenth century, was used during the Renaissance:

> ANTONY: It is just so high as it is, and moves with it own organs.
>> (*Antony and Cleopatra* II.vii.42–3)

and often *thereof*, as in *the tree and the leaves thereof*, would be preferred, and is very frequent in the 1611 Bible. Today *thereof* carries a solemnly archaic tone, but not in early Modern English:

> RICHARD GLOUCESTER: . . . he would make his son
> 'Heir to the Crown' – meaning indeed his house,
> Which by the sign thereof was termed so.
>> (*Richard III* III.v.75–7)

Since *his* was normal for inanimates, we must not automatically assume that it implies personification in Renaissance literature:

> . . . the life of that government drawes neere his necessarye periode
>> (*Arcadia* 145)

> . . . you are . . . as blind as a Flie in October, that will stand still while a man cuts of his head
>> (*The Gentle Craft* 75)

> PORTIA: How far that little candle throws his beams
>> (*The Merchant of Venice* v.i.90)

Regarding these three examples as instances of personification would be contrived overinterpretation.

Note the frequent construction 'demonstrative pronoun + possessive adjective + noun' (*this my friend*) where we would now use an *of*-phrase (*this friend of mine*), which was also current in early Modern English):

> Yet ye must grant at the least
> This my poor and small request
>
> (Wyatt, Song no. 106, 18–19)

> *Atheists* will ever be talking of that their opinion . . .
>
> (Bacon, *Of Atheisme* 52)

In certain cases the possessive adjective was so closely bound to its noun that another adjective would precede it rather than, as today, follow it. This was especially common with the noun *lord* (*good my lord*). Compare French *monsieur* (literally 'my sire' or 'my lord'):

> ARMADO: Name more – and, sweet my child, let them be men of good
> repute and carriage.
>
> (*Love's Labour's Lost* I.ii.66–7)

The so-called objective genitive was much more frequent in Renaissance English than it is now. We call *his* in *she talked about his murder* an objective genitive because in the corresponding construction with an active verb *his* would become the object *him* (*somebody murdered him*). Nowadays a phrase like *his love* would be understood as having either a possessive *his* (*his loved one*) or a *subjective* genitive *his*, which in the corresponding verb construction would become the subject *he* (*his deep love* → *he loves (someone) deeply*). In Renaissance English such a phrase could easily be an objective genitive. When Antonio, in *Twelfth Night*, says:

> For his sake
> Did I expose myself, pure for his love
>
> (V.i.78–9)

he means 'out of love for him'. Similarly in:

> CORBACCIO: . . . my heart
> Abhors his knowledge: I disclaim in him.
>
> (*Volpone* IV.v.106–7)

i.e. 'abhors any knowledge of him'. And in the following lines Gloucester puns rhetorically on the objective and possessive genitives:

> RICHARD GLOUCESTER: Speak it again, and even with the word
> This hand – which for thy love did kill thy love –
> Shall, for thy love, kill a far truer love.
>
> (*Richard III* I.ii.176–8)

The first and third instances of *thy love* are objective, i.e. 'love for thee', but the second is possessive (possibly subjective) i.e. 'the man thou lovedst'. This objective genitive is also found with nouns, sometimes in the equivalent *of*-phrase:

> RICHARD GLOUCESTER: What? Threat you me with telling of the King?
> Tell him, and spare not.
>
> *(Richard III* I.iii.113–4)

Telling of the King = 'the King's telling' = 'telling the King'.

13 The Relative Pronoun. The use of the relative pronouns in Renaissance English often differed from ours. Some constructions may appear odd or even obscure to a modern reader; some look distinctly archaic to us but were stylistically unmarked then; and often a relative pronoun appearing in the same kind of construction as today would have implications of meaning different from what it has today.

Of the three relative pronouns *who, which, that* the last has since early Middle English always remained the most common. *Who* as a relative was unusual in most Middle English texts except in the object form *whom* and the possessive *whose*. *That* was both then and during the Renaissance employed for both animates and inanimates. We still use *that* for persons (*the woman that rescued him got a medal*), but tend to prefer *who* in written language except perhaps after a superlative or superlative-like word such as *only*, for example in *he is the only man that can help us*. In other words our choice is normally governed by stylistic propriety, and this has been the case since the prescriptive pronouncements of eighteenth-century grammarians. But when we are confronted with Renaissance literature, we must not think that *that* referring to persons is in any way a sign of colloquial language; it occurs in high as well as middle and plain styles. Sidney's *Arcadia* is an example of the high one:

> *Zelmane* that had long long before doubted her selfe to be discovered by her, and now plainely finding it, was as the proverbe saith, like them that hold the wolfe by the eares . . .
>
> *(Arcadia* 12)

And it was still perfectly normal in Milton:

> Yet some there be that by due steps aspire
> To lay their just hands on that golden key
>
> *(Comus* 12–13)

It was common even in non-defining relative clauses. In a defining relative clause the relative pronoun is so closely linked to the preceding word it refers to (commonly called the 'antecedent') as to be essential to the meaning of the sentence. In a non-defining one, the link with the antecedent is looser, and a non-defining relative clause is rather similar to a parenthesis. Take the sentence *he ran up to the woman who grabbed her bag*. We indicate by not putting a comma after *woman* that the relative clause is to be understood as a defining one: he ran up to the woman who grabbed her bag as opposed to the woman (or women) who did not. But if we put a comma after *woman*, the relative clause becomes non-defining: he ran up to the woman (who then grabbed her bag). In Present-day English *that* is almost universally confined to defining relative clauses. Not so in Renaissance literature:

CRESSIDA: Blind fear, that seeing reason leads, finds safer footing
   than blind reason, stumbling without fear.
                     (*Troilus and Cressida* III.ii.68–9)

A modern editor has to put a comma before *that* (which in today's English would have to be a *which*) because here it introduces a non-defining explanatory clause. Cressida is not referring to the particular kind of blind fear that seeing reason leads, but to blind fear in general, which seeing reason leads.

   In spite of the frequency of *that* referring to persons, *who* and *which* began to gain ground during the Renaissance. The reason for this was the admiration for things classical, including the Latin language, whose relative pronouns (e.g. *qui, quod*) were more similar to *who, which* than to *that* (*qu-* corresponding to *wh-*; compare also the possessive *cuius* with *whose*).

   Which for persons was more common than *who* in the early part of the sixteenth century and is found throughout the period:

CALIBAN: For I am all the subjects that you have,
   Which first was mine own king
                     (*The Tempest* I.ii.343–4)

WARWICK: Then Warwick disannuls great John of Gaunt,
   Which did subdue the greatest part of Spain
                  (*3Henry VI* III.iii.81–2)

This survives today only in archaic biblical language (*Our father, which art in heaven*). We also sometimes find *the which* (for both animates and inanimates, and modelled on the French *lequel*), especially early in our period, but also occasionally later on, e.g. in Shakespeare and Milton: 'he wente and furnysshed and garnysshed two stronge castels of his, of the whiche the one hyght [was called] Tyntagil and the other castel hyght Terrabyl' (*Morte Darthur* 7); 'Queen Margaret saw / Thy murd'rous falchion [curved sword] smoking in his blood, / The which thou once didst bend against her breast' (*Richard III* I.ii.93–5).

When *who* is used for inanimates, there is often personification of some kind:

> SUBTLE: It turns to sulphur, or to quick-silver:
> Who are the parents of all other metals.
>
> > (*The Alchemist* II.iii.153–4)

Sometimes the personification is not unmistakably indicated by a word in the context the way it is by *parents* in the previous example; but in view of the scarcity of *who* for inanimates, it seems to be significant when it does occur. In the next example Ulysses is speaking of a man's merits or virtues being measured by their appreciative recognition by others:

> ULYSSES: Nor doth he of himself know them for aught
> Till he behold them formed in th'applause
> Where they're extended – who, like an arch, reverb'rate
> The voice again; or, like a gate of steel
> Fronting the sun, receives and renders back
> His figure and his heat.
>
> > (*Troilus and Cressida* III.iii.113ff)

(*Reverb'rate = reverb'rates*). The image is very powerful and *applause* seems to assume such force and influence that personification is very likely here, perhaps strengthened by the use of the verbs *receives* and *renders back*.

Who as an indefinite relative (i.e. a relative pronoun without an antecedent = 'he who' or 'whoever') was more frequent in Renaissance literature than it is today. We now regard this *who* as having an archaic or solemnly rhetorical ring to it. It was particularly frequent in *as who should say*, i.e. 'as if he would say', perhaps influenced by French *comme qui dirait*:

> TIBERIUS: Princes have still their grounds reared with themselves,
> Above the poor low flats of common men,
> And, who will search the reasons of their acts,
> Must stand on equal bases.
>
> > (*Sejanus* I.37ff)

> PORTIA: He doth nothing but frown, as who should say 'An you will
> not have me, choose'.
>
> > (*The Merchant Of Venice* I.ii.45–6)

The indefinite relative for inanimates is now *what* = 'that which', as in *what baffles me is that she came*. This was also current in Renaissance English, as was *that which*; but often *that that* or simply *that* (normal in Middle English) was used. Especially *that* as an indefinite relative meaning 'that which' could easily be confused at first reading with the conjunction *that*, as in the second example:

FORD: 'Love like a shadow flies when substance love pursues,
  Pursuing that that flies when substance love pursues'.
                         (The Merry Wives Of Windsor II.ii.201–2)

The blind master whom I have served so long,
  Grudging to hear that he did hear her say . . .
                              (Wyatt, Epigram no. 41)

QUARLOUS: That you are to undertake, is this
                          (Bartholomew Fair III.v.230)

It (. . .) *that* could also have this sense, giving *it* an emphasis that we have lost (except in different instances like *that's it!*):

LADY GRAY: This is it that makes me bridle passion
And bear with mildness my misfortune's cross.
                          (3Henry VI IV.v.19–20)

DOWNRIGHT: . . . it will never out o' the flesh that's bred i' the bone!
              (Every Man In His Humour II.i.68)

Omission of the relative as subject is today confined to colloquial language after *there is* (*was* etc), as in *there was a man came to see you*. Such an omission was perfectly respectable in early Modern English and not confined to *there is* sentences. It can sometimes obscure the syntax for a modern reader:

Like to an Eagle in his kingly pride,
  Soring through his wide Empire of the aire,
  To weather his brode sailes, by chaunce hath spide
  A Goshauke . . .
                         (The Faerie Queene V.iv.42)

According to modern syntax a *which* is missing before *by chaunce*. Another instance, from *Volpone*:

MOSCA: You still are, what you were, sir. Only you,
  Of all the rest, are he commands his love

                              (I.iii.1–2)

i.e. 'he who'.

14 The Interrogative Pronouns *What* and *Whether*. *What* was frequently used in three senses no longer current:

(a) 'who' in predicative questions (*what is he?*). This survival from Middle English lingered on until about 1700. But at the same time *what* could of course mean 'of what kind' just like today, as in:

> RICHARD GLOUCESTER: Let me put in your minds, if you forget,
>   What you have been ere this, and what you are;
>   Withal, what I have been, and what I am.
>   (*Richard III* I.iii.131–3)

It is important not to think that this qualitative sense ('what kind of . . .') is the only one. Predicative *what* is frequently used purely for identification, as in Macbeth's famous question, the answer to which is Macduff, who 'was from his mother's womb untimely ripped':

>   What's he
> That was not born of woman?
>   (*Macbeth* V.vii.2–3)

Similarly:

> ELDER BROTHER: That hallo I should know; what are you? speak.
>   (*Comus* 490)

When the qualitative 'what kind of' was intended, the construction *what . . . for* was often used (cp. e.g. German *was für* or Danish *hvad for*):

> DON JOHN: What is he for a fool that betroths himself to unquietness?
>   (*Much Ado About Nothing* I.iii.43)

Note also the use of *what* in:

> RICHARD GLOUCESTER: He that doth naught with her – excepting one –
>   Were best to do it secretly alone.
> BRACKENBURY: What one, my lord?
> RICHARD GLOUCESTER: Her husband, knave.
>   (*Richard III* I.i.100ff)

i.e. 'what man (is that)?' or 'who is that?'.

(b) Adverbially 'why':

> PANDARUS: What's all the doors open here?
>   (*Troilus and Cressida* IV.ii.21)

> What sit we then projecting peace and war?
>   (*Paradise Lost* II.329)

(c) Adverbially, when calling somebody impatiently:

PROSPERO: What, Ariel, my industrious servant, Ariel!

(The Tempest IV.i.33)

Whether was sometimes used in the sense 'which of the two':

MISTRESS PAGE: Whether had you rather, lead mine eyes, or eye
your master's heels?

(The Merry Wives Of Windsor III.ii.3–4)

15 The Pronoun *Other*. In the plural the *-s* had not become obligatory
even by the late seventeenth century:

these other wheel the north

(Paradise Lost IV.783)

If the preceding word is itself neutral as to number (unlike *these* which
obviously is plural), such as *the*, the *s*-less *other* could cause some
confusion:

GADSHILL: As we were sharing, some six or seven fresh men set
upon us.
SIR JOHN: And unbound the rest; and then come in the other.

(1Henry IV II.v.181–3)

Other would also sometimes dispense with the article we have in
another and *the other(s)*:

SURLY: What else are all your terms,
Whereon no one o' your writers grees with other?

(The Alchemist II.iii.182–3)

i.e. 'with another' or 'any other' or 'the others'. Note also *each* +
preposition + *other*, where today we have preposition + *each other*:

BUCKINGHAM: They . . .
Stared each on other . . .

(Richard III III.vii.24–6)

Adverbially = 'otherwise' or 'differently' *other* is used today only
before *than*, as in *it is difficult to tell her other than directly*; but in
Renaissance English this adverbial use was not such confined:

MACBETH: Will it not be received,
When we have marked with blood those sleepy two
Of his own chamber and used their very daggers,
That they have done't?
LADY MACBETH: Who dares receive it other

(Macbeth I.vii.75ff)

Similarly, in a passage from *Paradise Lost*, describing the angels fallen with Lucifer:

> The fellows of his crime, the followers rather
> (Far other once beheld in bliss), condemned
> For ever now to have their lot in pain
>
> (*Paradise Lost* I.606–8)

4

The Renaissance Sentence

Sentence Structure

In this section we shall take a look at the English-Renaissance sentence: its changing structure under the influence of Latin syntax following hard upon the extensive and intensive study of classical literature, literary habits and ideas. These syntactic changes first contrasted with the syntax of Middle English in general; but there were also considerable variation and divergent developments during the Renaissance period itself.

In discussions of sentence structure we distinguish between coordination and subordination of clauses. The most frequent coordinating conjunctions are *and, but, or*. Thus the following sentence:

> He went to Australia in the hope of staying there for a couple of months with a friend, but after only two weeks he came back sad and disillusioned.

consists of two coordinate clauses joined by *but*. We call a sentence that consists of coordinate (main) clauses, such as the one above, a 'compound sentence'.

There are many subordinating conjunctions. Most of them introduce subordinate adverbial clauses, such as *when, while, because, unless, as, since, as soon as*. The conjunction *that* introduces a subordinate noun clause, as in *he said that he could come*. When *if* means 'whether', it also introduces a noun clause, as in *he asked me if it was true or not*; otherwise *if* begins an adverbial clause: *I want to go if you do*. A sentence that consists of a main clause and one or more clauses that are subordinate to it is called a 'complex sentence'.

Relative clauses are also subordinate but not to a main clause; they are subordinate to the headword in a noun phrase. They commonly start with a relative pronoun (*who, which, that*) which refer to an antecedent (the headword in the noun phrase), as in:

The snakes that/which were writhing in the grass

The relative clause is *that were writhing in the grass*, in which *that* refers to the headword *snakes*.

Even in late Middle English (fourteenth century) sentence structure was relatively simple. There was plenty of subordination, as indeed there has always been in English, but it was limited in kind. Subordination with conjunctions other than *when, while, as, if* was much less common in the fourteenth century than one or two hundred years later. The following extract from *Mandeville's Travels* (c.1400) is typical of late fourteenth-century sentence structure which, in its use of chiefly compound sentences, showed much more coordination than most later patterns:

> Ethiope is departed in two princypall parties; and that is in the Est partie, and in the Meridionall partie, the whiche partie meridionall is clept Moretane. And the folk of that contree ben blake ynow, and more blake than in the tother partie; and thei ben clept Mowres. In that partie is a well, that in the day it is so cold that no man may drynke thereoffe; and in the nyght it is so hoot that no man may suffre hys hond therein. And beyonde that partie, toward the South, to pass by the See Occean, is a gret lond and a gret contrey. But men may not duell there, for the feruent brennynge of the sonne, so is it passynge hoot in that contrey.
>
> (96; *th* substituted for Þ and *y* for ȝ)

This coordinate style survives in the famous *Morte Darthur* by Thomas Malory, who finished the work between 1469 and 1470. Even by Malory's time this kind of sentence structure, which often seems artlessly naive to us nowadays, was by no means confined to casual or chatty writing. Even in the absence of any significant subordination, Malory's tone still manages to be ceremonious or stately when the occasion requires. The following extract, neither colloquial nor particularly courtly, describes a battle:

> Than sir Launcelot made hym redy and put the red slyeve uppon hys helmette and fastened it faste. And so sir Launcelot and sir Lavayne departed oute of Wynchestir pryvayly and rode untyll a litill leved woode behynde the party that hylde ayenste [held against] kynge Arthur party. And there they hylde hem stylle tylle the partyes smote togydirs [clashed]. And than cam in the Kynge of Scottis and the kynge of Irelonde on kynge Arthurs party, and ayenste them cam in the kynge of Northumbirlonde and the Kynge with the Hondred Knyghtes.
>
> And there began a gret medlé, and there the kynge of Scottis smote downe the kynge of Northumbirlonde, and the Kynge with the Hondred Knyghtes smote downe kynge Angwysh of Irelonde. Than sir Palamydes, that was one Arthurs party, he encountird with sir Galahalte, and ayther of hem smote downe othir, and aythir party halpe their lordys on horseback agayne. So there began a stronge assayle on bothe partyes.
>
> (*Morte Darthur* 1069–70)

Note also the pleonastic use of *he* in the last sentence but one, immediately after the subordination of the relative clause *that was one* [of] *Arthurs party*. We often use pronouns redundantly like this in spoken English, which is not unlike Malory's written variety, allowing for subsequent changes in vocabulary. Neither favours much subordination and when it occurs we, and here Malory, sometimes make up for the complexity by repeating the subject in the form of a pronoun. The difference is that today such a repetition would be considered bad grammar in written English. During most of the Renaissance period this was not so. Pleonastic *they* repeating the subject *thoughts* occurs in Shakespeare's *Richard II* in a speech by Richard which is anything but colloquial:

> Thoughts tending to ambition, they do plot
> Unlikely wonders
>
> (V.v.18–19)

A pleonastic *it*, equally 'respectable', was particularly common during the Renaissance:

> OTHELLO: That I have ta'en away this old man's daughter,
>   It is most true, true I have married her.
>
> (*Othello* I.iii.78–9)

Here the subject is the *that*-clause, so *it* is strictly speaking superfluous. Equally so in:

> OBERON: The next thing then she waking looks upon –
>   Be it on lion, bear, or wolf, or bull,
>   On meddling monkey, or on busy ape –
>   She shall pursue it with the soul of love.
>
> (*A Midsummer Night's Dream* II.i.179ff)

where *it* in the last line pleonastically repeats *the next thing* of the first line.

With the influence of Latin syntax on English during the sixteenth century, subordination, often called 'hypotaxis', became much more pervasive and the earlier typical pattern was increasingly relegated or confined to what came to be regarded as unsophisticated literature, such as popular stories or diaries. Here is a short extract describing a burial from *The Diary of Henry Machyn*, who was a citizen and merchant-taylor of London between 1550 and 1563:

> The xxiij day of July was bered my good lade [lady], the wyff of ser
> Wylliam Chester knyght and draper and altherman and marchand of the

stapull, and the howse and the cherche and the strette hangyd with blake
and armes, and she gayff to xx pore women good rossett gownes and
cottes [petticoats] to the nombur of a C. and to women gownes . . . and
ther was ij harold(s) of armes; and then cam the corse and iiij morners
beyryng of iiij pennon of armes abowtt, and cam morners a-for and
after, and the clarkes syngyng; and master Beycon dyd pryche over
nyght; and the morow after to the howse to dener . . .

(240)

It was not long before complex sentences, i.e. a subordinate sentence structure, became more frequent even in the least embellished
or least rhetorical prose literature, as in the following story called 'The
Tale of the Cobler and the Ape' which appears in *The Pinder of
Wakefield* (anon., 1632). There is still plenty of coordination, but relative clauses have become more frequent and note the use of the subordinate participial clauses *spoyling . . . neere* (7); *spying . . . him /
cutting his leather / whetting . . . whetstone* (10–12); *which Iacke perceiuing* (15), now taken for granted but much less common before the
Renaissance.

> There dwelt in *London* a rich Merchant that kept a great Ape,
> which when he had broke loose, would doe much mischiefe, and he
> could not see any thing done before him, but hee would be a doing
> the like. There dwelt a Cobler ouer-against this Gentlemans, which
> 5 the Ape would view how he cut out his Leather, and when the
> Cobler was gone abroad, Iacke would come ouer & play such reakes
> [pranks], spoyling all the shoes & leather he could come neere;
> which was much hinderance to the poore man, and he knew not
> how to be reuenged, because he had all his worke from thence; yet
> 10 at last a crotchet came into his head, and spying the Ape looking
> vpon him: to work hee went cutting his leather, and then whetting
> his knife of his whetstone, and then would he with the backe of the
> knife seeme to cut his throat: this did hee oftentimes; and out of
> the shop he goes, and leaues his knife and whetstone as sharp as a
> 15 razer; which Iacke perceiuing, vp he comes to the shop of the
> Cobler, and tooke the knife and whetstone, and as the Cobler had
> done, so did he, till at the last he cut his own throat.

(24–5)

We note in lines 4–5, in *which . . . Leather*, how relative constructions
had not yet quite settled down into the pattern we have nowadays.
Vacillation, or perhaps we should say considerable flexibility, was tol-
erated in the structure of relative clauses; not only in works like *The
Pinder of Wakefield* but also in, say, Sidney and Spenser. Here is a
typical example from the latter's *Faerie Queene*:

> There this old Palmer shewed himselfe that day,
> And to that mighty Princesse did complaine

Of grieuous mischiefes, which a wicked Fay
Had wrought, and many whelmd in deadly paine,
Whereof he crau'd redresse. My Soureraine,
Whose glory is in gracious deeds, and joyes
Throughout the world her mercy to maintaine,
Eftsoones deuisd redresse for such annoyes;
Me all vnfit for so great purpose she employes.

(II.ii.43)

To us it looks as if *glory* is the subject of the verb *joyes* in line 6. We would add an obligatory *who* before *joyes*. It is also very probable that *a wicked Fay* is not the subject of *whelmd* 'crushed' in 4, as our grammar would have her be, but that *which* in 3, although an object, is understood as the subject in 4; i.e. the *mischiefes* whelmed many in deadly pain. In the following example from Shakespeare:

RICHARD GLOUCESTER: And this is Edward's wife, that monstrous witch,
  Consorted with that harlot, strumpet Shore,
  That by their witchcraft thus have marked me.
        (*Richard III* III.iv.70–2)

That in the third line is a relative pronoun referring to both *Edward's wife* and *strumpet Shore*. According to our syntax this would be odd since those two are not in a coordinate structure like *and these are Edward's wife and strumpet Shore*. With the structure as it is, *that* in Present-day syntax could only have *strumpet Shore* as the antecedent. Note also the following, and very common Renaissance English, structure:

BUCKINGHAM: They spake not a word,
  But, like dumb statuas or breathing stones,
  Stared each on other and looked deadly pale –
  Which, when I saw, I reprehended them.
        (*Richard III* III.vii.24ff)

Today's syntax would demand coordination here: *and when I saw that, I reprehended them.*

Here are another few lines from *The Faerie Queene* to show how, in the best of writers, the rules about subordination and coordination were much less rigid than they are today:

As when the firie-mouthed steeds, which drew
The Sunnes bright wayne to *Phaetons* decay,
Soone as they did the monstrous Scorpion vew,
With vgly craples crawling in their way,
The dreadfull sight did them so sore affray,
That their well knowen courses they forwent

(V.viii.40)

The verb of the subordinate-clause subject *steeds* in the first line never appears. Instead we get, after the relative clause *which . . . decay*, another temporal clause *Soone as* [= as soon as] . . . *vew* with a subordinate prepositional phrase containing a participial clause *With vgly craples* [claws] . . . *way*, and *then* the main clause appears: *The dreadfull . . . affray*. The incompleteness of the *when*-clause does not interfere with the meaning, which is perfectly clear; but it could take aback people used to only one standard of grammatical structure.

Such vacillation or tolerance in syntax is also seen in Renaissance texts in the status of the conjunctions themselves. Before the system as we know it had become the norm, the increasing use of subordination was often given an extra marker in the shape of *that*: instead of only *when* or *though*, for instance, *when that* or *though that* was often preferred. This was a survival from Middle English; cp. the first line from Chaucer's *Canterbury Tales: Whan that Aprill with his shoures soote*. It is another construction that to us appears distinctly unorthodox but was perfectly acceptable in the sixteenth and most of the seventeenth century. It must not be considered substandard or part of a 'low' register or bad grammar; there is no need to find excuses such as the exigences of metre when Shakespeare has Mark Antony say in his famous speech in *Julius Caesar*:

> When that the poor have cried, Caesar hath wept
>
> (III.ii.92)

Sidney does the same with *though that* in prose:

> And therein did see, that though that people did not belong unto him, yet . . .
>
> (*Arcadia* 155)

and so does Deloney with *after that*:

> After that *Jack* had long led this pleasant life, beeing (though he were but poore) in good estimation: it was his Masters chance to dye, and his Dame to be a widow . . .
>
> (*Jack of Newberie* 3)

i.e. the *after that* clause is subordinate, the main clause starting after the colon. Similarly, we must take care not to be led astray by *after that* in the next quotation from *The Faerie Queene*, thinking it is a prepositional phrase. It is not; it is, as in the Deloney example, a composite conjunction:

> Or like the hell-borne *Hydra*, which they faine
> That great *Alcides* whilome ouerthrew,
> After that he had labourd long in vaine,
> To crop his thousand heads . . .
>
> (VI.xii.32)

We might even sometimes come across *that* (which is a subordinating conjunction) being used with the coordinating conjunction *or*, as on p 42 of *The Pinder of Wakefield*: 'he knew hee had it, or that he knew that some of his fellowes had it'.

Thus the whole system of clause ligatures was in a flux during the Renaissance period. In order to express new subtleties, or express subtleties differently in imitation of Latin hypotactic syntax, the inventory of conjunctions and prepositions was increased, mainly from the participles of verbs. Thus the earliest entry in the *Oxford English Dictionary* for *provided* as a conjunction = 'if' is 1460, and that of *providing* in the same sense was in 1632. Present-participle prepositions like *considering, during* and *notwithstanding* were first used by Chaucer and Wycliffe in the 1380s but did not become common until the Renaissance. One particularly important addition to the conjunctions was *because*. This comes from *by (the) cause that*. As a conjunction *because* was exceedingly rare in Middle English, the first *OED* entry being 1386 (Chaucer again). Middle English normally had *for* or *for that*. Malory uses *because* as a conjunction but at a time when it was by no means normal; and it had still not become regular by the late sixteenth century:

EDMOND: Wherefore should I
   Stand in the plague of custom and permit
   The curiosity of nations to deprive me
   For that I am some twelve or fourteen moonshines
   Lag of a brother?

                              (*King Lear* I.ii.2ff)

In the following speech from Shakespeare's *Othello*, the Quarto text has *for* (the Folio *when*). It is important to realize that this *for* does not start a main clause but a subordinate one and means 'just because':

OTHELLO: And heaven defend your good souls that you think
   I will your serious and great business scant
   For she is with me.
      (I.iii.263 in the Penguin edition by Kenneth Muir (1968))

Similarly, in the speech from *Richard II* from which we quoted above:

Thoughts tending to ambition, they do plot
Unlikely wonders: how these vain weak nails
May tear a passage through the flinty ribs
Of this hard world, my ragged prison walls;
And for they cannot, die in their own pride

                              (V.v.18–22)

and earlier in the same speech Richard uses *for* and *because* as a kind of compound conjunction, indicating the transitional phase:

I have been studying how I may compare
This prison where I live unto the world;
And for because the world is populous,
And here is not a creature but myself,
I cannot do it.

(1–5)

Sidney does the same in sonnet 29 of *Astrophel and Stella*:

But for because my chiefest prospect lyes
Upon the coast, I am given up for a slave.

And, just to complete the (confusing) picture, here is an instance of *because that*:

YORK: Because that I am little like an ape,
    He thinks that you should bear me on your shoulders.
                                    (*Richard III* III.i.130–2)

We cannot use as an argument that the conjunctions as employed in these three examples have been chosen for metrical reasons. It is irrelevant that these instances are from verse rather than prose. Nowadays, and indeed from c.1700 onwards, such constructions would not be considered acceptable even in poetry, and in any case they appear frequently in Renaissance prose too.

When sentences were according to our standards grammatically acceptable, as they were in most cases, they were often much longer. In such cases conjunctions were normally important signposts in the development of the sentence. Consider the following passage from Thomas Browne's *Religio Medici*:

I could never perceive any rationall consequence from those many texts which prohibite the children of Israel to pollute themselves with the Temples of the Heathens; we being all Christians, and not divided by such detested impieties as might profane our prayers, or the place wherein we make them; *or that* a resolved conscience may not adore her Creator any where, especially in places devoted to his service; where if their devotions offend him, mine may please him, if theirs profane it, mine may hallow it; . . .

(4)

The conjunctions *or that* (italicized in the passage by me) are far removed from the governing verb *perceive* of the main clause. Dividing *perceive* and *or that* is, among other things, a huge parenthetical participial clause *we being . . . make them* with two separate participles (*being* and *divided*), and itself containing a subordinate clause (*as . . . them*), which within itself contains a noun phrase with yet another subordinate clause, viz. the relative *wherein . . . them*. This heavily subordinate structure has resulted in a huge first object of *perceive*, viz *any rationall consequence . . . them* (lines 1–5), and we might by now have forgotten that it is an object; but *that*, which follows immediately after *or* in line 5, takes us back to *perceive* at once since this *that* introduces the second object of *perceive* (connected to the first by the *or* of line 5): *I could never perceive any rationall consequence . . . or* [perceive] *that a resolved conscience may not . . .*

Compared to much Renaissance literature Thomas Browne's example is relatively uncomplicated. Many writers, especially in the sixteenth century, were heavily influenced by Latin syntax, especially as it appeared in Cicero's works. The great Roman orator and rhetorician was greatly admired, and his long, perfectly controlled sentences came to be much imitated by writers like Sidney. Here are the first two sentences, the second starting in line 19, from Book 5 of his famous prose romance *Arcadia*:

> The daungerous division of mens mindes, the ruinous renting of all estates, had nowe brought *Arcadia* to feele the pangs of uttermost perill (such convulsions never comming, but that the life of that government drawes neere his [its] necessarye periode) when to the
> 5 honest and wise *Philanax*, equally distracted betwixt desire of his maisters revenge and care of the states establishment, there came (unlooked for) a *Macedonian* Gentleman, who in short, but pithye maner delivered unto him, that the renowmed *Euarchus*, king of *Macedon*, purposing to have visited his olde friend and confederate
> 10 the king *Basilius*, was nowe come within halfe a mile of the Lodges, where having understoode be [by, from] certayne Shepheards, the sodayne death of theyr Prince, had sent unto him, (of whose authoritye and faith he had good knowledge) desiring him to advertise [inform] him, in what securitie hee might rest there for that night,
> 15 where willinglye hee woulde (if safely hee might) helpe to celebrate the funeralls of his auncient companion and alye, adding hee neede not doubt [fear], since hee had brought but twentye in his companye, hee would be so unwise as to enter into any forcible attempte with so small force. *Philanax* having entertayned the Gentleman, aswell as
> 20 in the middest of so many tumultes hee coulde, pausing awhile with himselfe, considering howe it shoulde not onely be unjust, and against the lawe of Nations, not well to receyve a Prince whome good will had brought among them, but (in respecte of the greatnes of his might) very daungerous to geve him any cause of due offence;
> 25 remembring withall the excellent tryalls of his equitie, which made him more famous then his victoryes, hee thought hee might bee the fittest instrumente to redresse the ruynes they were in, since his goodness put hym without suspicion, and hys greatnesse beyonde envye.

(145)

Only two sentences and perfectly grammatical if we allow for an understood *he* before *had sent* in 12, and a pleonastic *hee* (26, first instance) repeating the subject *Philanax* in 19. What makes these sentences unusual from a modern viewpoint is the large number of participial clauses at different levels of subordination together with, to us, excessive use of other kinds of hypotaxis, both so typical of Latin syntax. Participial constructions became very widespread in Renaissance literature and would frequently play a parenthetical role. In the first sentence we find: *such convulsions never comming* (3), *equally distracted . . . establishment* (5–6), *unlooked for* (7), *purposing . . . Basilius* (9–10), *having understoode . . . Prince* (11–12), *desiring . . . him* (13), *adding . . . doubt* (16–17). The first of these (*such convulsions never comming*) is called an 'absolute' construction, i.e. a structure where the subject has no verb in the present or past tense at all, as in *this said and done, ...* These were particularly common in Latin and were often copied in English by many Renaissance writers.

The second sentence is perhaps even more marked in its complexity: it starts with the subject (*Philanax*) of a main clause which does not materialize until line 26, where the pleonastic *hee* is an almost necessary syntactic signpost. The heavy subordination between *Philanax* and *hee* is once again by means of participial clauses: *having entertayned . . . coulde* (19–20), *pausing . . . himselfe* (20–21), *considering . . . offence* (21–24), *remembring . . . victoryes* (25–26). And some of these contain clauses at lower levels of subordination, such as the comparative clause *aswell . . . coulde* (19–20) and the relative ones *whome . . . them* (22–23) and *which . . . victoryes* (25–26). Especially the second sentence, with extensive subordination coming immediately after the subject head-word, is typically Ciceronian.

It is important to bear in mind that a heavily hypotactic Latinate style was one of fashion rather than one belonging to a certain type of text or a certain register. We find similarly constructed sentences in otherwise widely different texts. The following example is from William Harrison's paraphrased English version (1587) of John Bellenden's Scots translation of Hector Boece's *Scotorum Historiae* (Bellenden's *Chroniklis of Scotland*). Harrison's version became Book 5 of Holinshed's *Chronicles*. This passage describes how Banquo's son Fleance, having escaped the murderers hired by Macbeth, felt it necessary to leave Scotland:

> It chanced yet by the benefit of the darke night, that though the father were slaine, the sonne yet by the helpe of almightie God reseruing him to better fortune, escaped that danger: and afterwards hauing some inkeling (by the admonition of some friends which he had in the court) how his life was sought no lesse than his fathers, who was slain not by

chance medlie (as by the handling of the matter Makbeth would haue had it to appeare) but euen vpon a prepensed deuise: wherevpon to auoid further perill he fled into Wales . . .

(Quoted from Görlach 1991, 335)

Note how the subject *sonne* (2) of the first main clause has been separated from its verb *escaped* in the next line by a long prepositional phrase incorporating a present-participial clause *reseruing*. . . . The second main clause, of which *he* in 8 is the subject, begins with *and afterwards* in 3. The subject has been suspended by so many subordinate structures that Harrison finds it necessary to add *wherevpon* (7) which to us may seem incorrect since the kernel structure is *and afterwards he fled into Wales*; but such cohesive links were perfectly acceptable before late seventeenth and eighteenth-century norms had been established, and actually clarify rather than impede the sense.

Hypotaxis to such a degree was by no means confined to the sixteenth century, but it became much more widespread and fashionable then than ever before or since. However, later writers such as Milton (and several in the eighteenth century) were by no means averse to extensive subordination as we can see from the next passage, taken from a page or two from the end of Milton's *Areopagitica* (1644), a magnificent discourse defending a free press:

> But if neither the check that Moses gave to young Joshua, nor the countermand which our Saviour gave to young John, who was so ready to prohibit those whom he thought unlicensed, be not enough to admonish our elders how unacceptable to God their testy mood
> 5 of prohibiting is; if neither their own remembrance what evil hath abounded in the church by this let of licensing, and what good they themselves have begun by transgressing it, be not enough, but that they will persuade and execute the most Dominican part of the Inquisition over us, and are already with one foot in the stirrup so active at
> 10 suppressing, it would be no unequal distribution in the first place to suppress the suppressors themselves, whom the change of their condition hath puffed up more than their late experience of harder times hath made wise.

(203–4)

Once again we do not get to the forceful main clause with its crowning conclusion (*it would be* . . . : 10) until rather late in the passage. Two long and parallel subordinate structures precede it: *if neither . . . be not enough . . . prohibiting is* (1–5) and *if neither . . . be not enough . . . at suppressing* (5–10); and their very parallelism with repetition of words, not only of structure, helps the reader to follow the argument. Note also the use of *that* in line 7 to signal subordination. Today we would have to leave it out because there is no 'logical' antecedent verb or other structure to justify it as far as our notions of grammatical cohesion go; but in long sentences like this its inclusion is justified on rhetorical rather than grammatico-logical grounds.

Today's students, who may find such syntax hard to cope with, should derive comfort in the knowledge that practice makes perfect. The more they expose themselves to earlier syntax of this kind without the prejudices of modern grammatical orthodoxy, the easier they will find the language and the more they will be able to appreciate and enjoy it.

The road taken by Sidney's and Milton's long sentences seems, like Cicero's, to be predetermined. They are carefully structured towards a goal: Sidney's first sentence moves towards a central climax in the Macedonian gentleman's message to Philanax concerning King Euarchus's visit, and is rounded up by the latter's experience on his arrival; his second sentence and that by Milton move towards a conclusion made emphatic because of the steps leading up to it.

By the early seventeenth century the formally composed, well-crafted Ciceronian sentence, not to mention the kind that displayed harmoniously rhetorical balancing of members in the Euphuistic manner, had come to be considered old-fashioned by some people (though evidently not by Milton), who preferred as a model another Roman, viz Seneca. His style now gained considerable prominence in prose with the result that early seventeenth-century sentences would often dispense with syntactic ligatures like conjunctions (i.e. they were *paratactic* rather than *hypotactic*) or use them much more sparingly than earlier, thereby giving the appearance of presenting the thoughts of the writer as they were coming to him. This style, sometimes called *stile coupé* or 'curt style', thus seems more spontaneous. As opposed to the Ciceronian sentence, the important point in a curt-style sentence is often stated first and then developed in a series of associative ideas, not necessarily logically linked. Such writing reflected a different way of thinking, a different attitude to literary expression. The following two sentences from Jonson's *Timber or Discoveries* illustrate the Senecan manner:

> If his [the poet's] wit will not arrive suddenly at the dignity of the ancients, let him not yet fall out with it, quarrel, or be over-hastily angry, offer to turn it away from study in a humour; but come to it again upon better cogitation, try another time with labour. If then it succeed not, cast not away the quills yet, nor scratch the wainscot, beat not the poor desk, but bring all to the forge, and file again, turn it anew.
>
> (585)

Although not denuded of conjunctions, this sentence is very unlike the deliberate symmetrical crafting of a Lyly or the carefully ligatured manner of a Sidney or Milton, and one cannot help irreverently recalling John Aubrey's comment on Seneca: 'Seneca writes as a Boare does pisse, by jirkes'. The curt-style sentence finds its own way as it goes along, hopping from one way of looking at things to another, one image giving birth to the next. The sense impressions are, as it were, set down as they occur and there is no attempt at formally well-balanced syntactic members. Jonas Barish gives a very interesting account of the new development by comparing Shakespeare's dramatic prose with that of Jonson, giving plenty of examples from their plays (Watson 1970, 114ff); and we could regard Donne's religious prose as illustrative of a stage midway between the older formal beauty and the new spontaneous expressiveness; see the discussion of an extract from one of Donne's sermons on pp. 178–82.

The *stile coupé* was of course not the only early seventeenth-century style. Another anti-Ciceronian alternative was a sentence less firmly controlled than the Ciceronian but frequently with just as much subordination in terms of e.g. participial clauses. This 'loose style', as it is sometimes called, would share with the curt one the impression of spontaneity, of lack of formal roundedness. Thomas Browne's prose in his *Religio Medici* is often couched in such loose-style sentences; and the effect it could have on drama can be seen in a fine speech by Antonio in Tourneur's *The Revenger's Tragedy* (1607), in which he gives vent to his rage after the rape of his wife by the Duchess's son and her subsequent suicide by poison:

    ANTONIO: You deal with truth my lord.
    Lend me but your attentions, and I'll cut
    Long grief into short words: last revelling night,
    When torchlight made an artificial noon
  5 About the court, some courtiers in the mask,
    Putting on better faces than their own,
    Being full of fraud and flattery: amongst whom
    The Duchess' youngest son – that moth to honour –
    Filled up a room; and with long lust to eat
 10 Into my wearing, amongst all the ladies
    Singled out that dear form, who ever lived
    As cold in lust as she is now in death,
    – Which that step-duchess' monster knew too well –
    And therefore in the height of all the revels,
 15 When music was heard loudest, courtiers busiest,
    And ladies great with laughter – O vicious minute!
    Unfit but for relation to be spoke of,
    Then with a face more impudent than his vizard
    He harried her amidst a throng of panders
 20 That live upon damnation of both kinds,
    And fed the ravenous vulture of his lust,
    – O death to think on't! – She, her honour forced,
    Deemed it a nobler dowry for her name
    To die with poison than to live with shame.

                              (I.iv.24ff)

Antonio proceeds sequentially as the events of the previous night unfolded, and this is how they come to his mind. Tourneur has Antonio use parenthesis and participial clauses (6–8, 13, 16–17, 22), not in order to build up a rounded sentence, but as a reflection of the thought processes of his agitated mind, of his comments on previous thoughts, of the associations that they bring about. *Anacoluthon* (i.e. grammatically unfinished structures) was a not infrequent ingredient of the loose style, and we note it here in the lack of a finite verb (i.e. a verb in the present or past tense) for the subject *some courtiers in the mask* (5), since *Filled up* (9) is parallel to *Singled out* (11) and has *The Duchess' youngest son* as subject. Note also how the conjunctive adverb *then* (18) helps the listener to connect *And therefore in the height of all the revels* (14) with *He harried her* (19).

When Shakespeare's characters are furious or desperate, they do not normally use complex sentences with participial and parenthetical constructions in a loose style. In such cases Shakespeare prefers syntax closer to the curt style, with phrases functioning as sentences and relatively little use made of conjunctions. When he used complex sentences with heavy employment of parenthesis, the effect was quite different. He would do so mainly in cases where the thinking itself was complex (which is not the case in Antonio's example above), and the result was much more in the Ciceronian vein, as in the following example from *Hamlet* I.iv.19ff:

> So, oft it chances in particular men
> That, for some vicious mole of nature in them –
> As in their birth, wherein they are not guilty,
> Since nature cannot choose his origin –
> 5   By the o'ergrowth of some complexion,
> Oft breaking down the pales and forts of reason,
> Or by some habit that too much o'erleavens
> The form of plausive manners – that these men,
> Carrying, I say, the stamp of one defect,
> 10   Being nature's livery or fortune's star,
> His virtues else be they as pure as grace,
> As infinite as man may undergo,
> Shall in the general censure take corruption
> From that particular fault.

This sentence is much more rhetorically formal than Antonio's, though what is common to both is that they are heavily hypotactic in their marked use of parenthesis and participial structures. The heavy parenthesis of lines 2–8 is essential to the argument Hamlet is presenting about the dangers of a certain kind of human flaw, and he gets us back to the main continuation by signposting it with a pleonastic *that* (8) repeating the conjunction of line 2. But as soon as we are on the main track, Hamlet highlights the circumstances of the flaw once again in a participial clause (*Carrying . . . defect*), to which is subordinated another (*Being . . . star*), which is followed by a subordinate concessive clause (*His virtues . . . undergo*, where *his* signals a sudden switch to the singular; we expect *their*). The concessive clause itself incorporates the comparative clause *as man may undergo*; and not until then do we get the long suspended predicate of *these men* in the last two lines: this is the important pronouncement and what precedes is a carefully structured argument in support of it.

The writer most influenced by Latin syntax was Milton. His linguistic structures in his epic poetry have often been criticized in modern times, most notably by F. R. Leavis (1936; the section on Milton's verse reprinted in Patrides 1967):

> reading *Paradise Lost* is a matter of resisting, of standing up against, the verse-movement, of subduing it into something tolerably like sensitive-ness, and in the end our resistance is worn down; we surrender at last to the inescapable monotony of the ritual.
>
> (Patrides 1967, 16)

> to admit the unusualness [of Milton's verse pattern] is to admit that commonly the pattern, the stylized gesture, and movement, has no par-ticular expressive work to do, but functions by rote, of its own momen-tum, in the manner of ritual . . . The sense that Milton's style is of that kind, the dissatisfied sense of a certain hollowness, would by most readers who share it be first of all referred to a characteristic not yet specified – that which evoked from Mr Eliot the damaging word 'magnil-oquence'. To say that Milton's verse is magniloquent is to say that it is not doing as much as its impressive pomp and volume seem to be asserting; that mere orotundity is a disproportionate part of the whole effect; and that it demands more deference than it merits.
>
> (*ibid*. 18)

Damaging criticism indeed, but Leavis's view is no more the current one; even T. S. Eliot changed his mind about the quality of Milton's verse. Nobody has done more in recent, or relatively recent, times to shift critical opinion than Christopher Ricks (1963). Especially in his chapter 'Syntax and Sense' he adduces convincing arguments for the expressive function, including the inherent sensitivity, of Milton's Latinate syntax. One feature of this is his frequent inversion of subject and object, as in

>   Him the Almighty Power
> Hurled headlong flaming from th' ethereal sky
> With hideous ruin and combustion down
> To bottomless perdition . . .
>
> (*Paradise Lost* I.44ff)

The power of these lines depends to no small extent on the position of *Him* (i.e. Satan), foregrounding both antagonists by the immediate juxtaposition and by forcing a stress on *Him* as strong as those on *Almighty Power*.

Another feature particularly typical of the Miltonic style is his imitation of the structure of the Latin periodic sentence. We saw an example of this in the prose passage from *Areopagitica* above. In his verse epics this imitation would frequently result in his famous suspensions *via* a long, complex sentence structure, frequently with *hyperbaton* (see p. 156). The effect this has on the opening of *Paradise Lost* is briefly discussed in the chapter on rhetoric (p. 156). Here is an example from his pastoral entertainment *Comus* (1634) 45ff:

> Bacchus, that first from out the purple grape
> Crushed the sweet poison of misused wine,
> After the Tuscan mariners transformed,
> Coasting the Tyrrhene shore, as the winds listed,
> On Circe's island fell.

The essential main clause is *Bacchus . . . / On Circe's island fell*. Separating so widely the subject head-word (*Bacchus*) and the verb (*fell*) is alien to English sentence structure but typical of Latin, as is indeed the absolute participle construction *After the Tuscan mariners transformed*, i.e. 'after the mariners had been transformed (by Bacchus into dolphins)' – Latin *post nautas mutatos*. Suspension of sentence completion like this was to become a feature typical of Milton's epic poetry, where it was often used with great mastery, as in the following short passage from *Paradise Lost*, shortly after Satan ('the superior Fiend') has been hurled from heaven. The first *He* of the passage refers to Beelzebub, who has just finished speaking:

>   He scarce had ceased when the superior Fiend
> Was moving toward the shore; his ponderous shield,
> Ethereal temper, massy, large, and round,
> Behind him cast; the broad circumference
> 5 Hung on his shoulders like the moon, whose orb
> Through optic glass the Tuscan artist views
> At ev'ning from the top of Fesole,
> Or in Valdarno, to descry new lands,
> Rivers or mountains in her spotty globe.
> 10 His spear, to equal which the tallest pine
> Hewn on Norwegian hills, to be the mast
> Of some great ammiral, were but a wand,
> He walked with to support uneasy steps
> Over the burning marl, not like those steps
> 15 On heaven's azure . . .

(I.283ff)

Amongst other things Milton is here describing Satan's enormous size. He first does this by comparing his shield to the moon, extending the simile evocatively as the cratered, heavenly object viewed from earth by Galileo ('the Tuscan artist') through his telescope. Next comes a description of Satan's spear. Note the syntax here: *His spear* (10) is the prepositional complement of *with* (13). To say *his spear he walked with* would already be a marked *hyperbaton* in its foregrounding of the spear; but to separate the complement from its preposition by a twenty-two-word simile is a daring suspension. The comparison is *the tallest pine* but the pine itself is aggrandized by two qualifications: *Hewn on Norwegian hills* and *to be the mast / Of some great ammiral* (meaning 'admiral's ship'). The effect is that the syntax mirrors the object: as the qualifications of the spear (including of course those of the pine) grow, so does the spear itself as we are reading about it. The main reason why we have a sense of this growth is that the sentence is leading 'upwards': we do not know the syntactic 'fate' of *His spear*. Is it going to be the subject, the object or what? Not until *He walked with* do we know, and the power behind such a spear now clashes almost pitifully with the *uneasy steps* (13) produced by the shock, mental as well as physical, that Satan has just experienced. Had Milton constructed his sentence differently and started with the normal *He walked with his spear*, the qualifications would have been in a loose, trailing sentence, and much of the mounting effect would have got lost.

It is not until around 1700 that we can say that a fixed standard for building up sentences had been reached, and with it a sharper distinction between coordination and subordination. The language that we write today, at least as far as the sentence structure of prose is concerned, is essentially a product of a late seventeenth-century formalism that had its origin in the rationalist philosophical thinking of Descartes. He and his followers regarded errors as springing from ill-assimilated sense impressions, which reason or intellect would have to sort out or categorize, and language did not escape categorization. This resulted in the establishment of new standards of acceptability or correctness, and from this followed:

> the study of the precise meaning of words; the reference to dictionaries as literary authorities; the study of the sentence as a logical unit alone; the careful circumscription of its limits and the gradual reduction of its length; . . . the attempt to reduce grammar to an exact science; the idea that forms of speech are always either correct or incorrect; the complete subjection of the laws of motion and expression in style to the laws of logic and standardization . . .
>
> (Croll, in Watson 1970, 109)

Such notions were not of the Renaissance and we must be careful not to judge writers of that period from our post-formalist and post-rationalist viewpoint.

Punctuation

Punctuation is closely related to the way we perceive a sentence and cannot be ignored. Indeed it is very important, in any discussion of sentence structure in written English, especially if that structure is different from our own. What today's punctuation practice and that of the Renaissance have in common is that the main punctuation signs form a hierarchy: the weakest is the comma, followed by the semi-colon; the second strongest is the colon, and the strongest the full stop (sometimes known as the period). The difference is that today's, based as it is mainly on eighteenth and nineteenth century precept, is essentially grammatical and logical; that of the Renaissance essentially rhythmical and elocutionary, although it began to be more closely related to clause and sentence structure in the early seventeenth century. The following example illustrates typical modern usage:

> Shakespeare's work falls into three main periods: an initial period domi-
> nated by comedy, both lighthearted and serious, and history plays; a
> middle period including the great tragedies, the Roman plays, and the
> so-called 'problem plays'; and a final period consisting of the late com-
> edies, sometimes called the 'romances'.

Although the separating force of the marks is to some extent pausal, their main function is grammatical and logical. The colon, for instance, is typically used to introduce an explanatory or particularizing statement, as in the first line. Post-qualifications that are felt to be essential are not separated by a comma: there isn't one before *dominated* in the first line, nor before *including* in the third; but *both lighthearted and serious* is surrounded by commas because this qualification is of a non-essential, non-defining nature. The semicolons separate the larger units of the list from the smaller ones within these.

Renaissance writers and printers were primarily concerned with separating by punctuation rhythmically balanced phrases, clauses and sentences to highlight, say, antithesis and parallelism, and with indicating, especially in dramatic texts, pauses for breath. The problem for a modern editor of Renaissance works is therefore obvious. Should he leave his editions unchanged in matters of punctuation and thus convey to the readers the early attitude to syntax and its expressiveness; or should he punctuate according to our views of sentence cohesion? Most editors opt for the latter since most modern students and readers in general are unfamiliar with Renaissance tradition in such matters and would consequently find texts subjected to highly unfamiliar punctuation practice confusing and difficult. Furthermore, printers (or proof-readers) would often alter their copy according to individual punctuation (and spelling) preferences or to the practice of the printing house; consequently, it is often dangerous to rely on the punctuation of a Renaissance edition as indicative of authorial usage. All the same, such an edition is likely to reflect general Renaissance habits; and ignoring these in a modern edition can sometimes distort the text. It is foolhardy of a modern editor to show the confidence of Samuel Johnson: 'In restoring the author's [Shakespeare's] works to their integrity, I have considered the punctuation as wholly in my power; for what could be their care of colons and commas, who corrupted words and sentences' (Johnson 1968, 107).

Since students are generally unfamiliar with Renaissance punctuation and because the editions they are likely to read are modern ones, most Renaissance text quotations in this book have been taken from editions with modern punctuation. Another reason is that early punctuation, as hinted above, could be somewhat idiosyncratic or even haphazard and downright incompetent. It has also been felt that when matters other than punctuation – even though these matters may be related to it – are being discussed, simultaneous 'interference' by features such as punctuation and spelling may prove counterproductive. All the same, as already said in the first chapter, some texts are available in editions only with original spelling and punctuation; and the serious student, once he has realized the importance of knowing about Renaissance punctuation, will (one hopes) seek occasional elucidation of an author's syntactic intent, from which may follow deeper interpretative insight. It therefore seems appropriate to say something about Renaissance pointing practice.

The earliest printed books (also called *incunabula*) only made use of the virgule (an oblique stroke), the colon and the full stop. In the early sixteenth century the virgule began to give way to the comma.

Below is a text extract from Caxton's translation (1481, from Dutch) of *The History of Reynard the Fox*, first with original spelling and punctuation, then in a modernized version of my own. Reynard has just been sentenced to death by the King and his council. Watching the sad exit from the court of Reynard's grief-stricken relatives (*nyghe of his kynne*), the King has second thoughts about the sentence; but Tybert (the cat) has not and tries to persuade Isegrim (the wolf) and Bruin (the bear) to get the hanging over and done with as swiftly as possible.

The only punctuation marks in the original text are the virgule and the full stop. The latter can appear in high, mid or low position, and the virgule may be long or short; but in this quotation I have put all full stops in the low position and made all virgules long. It should be clear from a comparison of the two versions that there is no simple modern correspondence to the use of the virgule. Sometimes we would use a comma, sometimes a full stop (or a semi-colon), in its place. And we should certainly not use a full stop after *vs* in line 7. The absence of one (or a virgule) after *thus* in 9 is probably unintentional. Capitalization is also different from ours, and note that direct speech is not signalled by quotation marks: *hier . . . lignage* lines 3–4; *sir bruyn . . . nyght* lines 5–10; *hier . . . galewis* line 11; *Isegrym . . . tarye* lines 12–15. We have to wait until the eighteenth century for those. Nor are there any question marks. These and exclamation marks were there in the sixteenth century but did not become fully established until the seventeenth:

> The kynge bithoughte hym and marked how many a yonglyng departed from thens al wepyng/ which were nyghe of his kynne/ and sayde to hym self/ hier behoueth other counseyl herto/ Though reynart be a shrewe/ ther be many good of his lignage/ tybert the
> 5   catte sayde/ sir bruyn and sir Isegrym/ how be ye thus slowe. it is almost euen/ hier ben many busshes and hedges. yf he escaped from vs. and were delyuerd out of this paryl he is so subtyl and so wyly and can so many deceytes that he should neuer be taken agayn/ shall we hange hym how stonde ye al thus er the galewis can be
> 10   made redy it shal be nyght/ Isegrym bethought hym tho and seyde/ hier by is a gybet or galewis/ And wyth that worde he sighed/ and the catte espyed that and sayde/ Isegrym ye be aferd/ ys it ayenst your wylle/ thynke ye not that he hym self wente and laboured that bothe your brethern were hanged/ were ye good and wyse ye sholde
> 15   thanke hym/and ye sholde not therwith so long tarye/
>
> (31)

> The King bethought him and marked how many a youngling departed from thence all weeping, which were nigh of his kin, and said to himself, 'Here behoveth other counsel hereto; though Reynard be a shrew, there be many good of his lineage.' Tybert the Cat said, 'Sir Bruin and Sir Isegrim, how be ye thus slow? It is almost even. Here are many bushes and hedges. If he escaped from us and were delivered out of his peril, he is so subtle and so wily and can so many deceits that he should never be taken again. Shall we hang him [i.e. if we are going to hang him], how stand ye all thus? Ere the gallows can be made ready it shall be night.' Isegrim bethought him then and said, 'Hereby is a gibbet or gallows.' And with that word he sighed, and the cat espied that and said, 'Isegrim, ye be afeard. Is it against your will? Think ye not that he himself went and laboured that both your brethren were hanged? Were ye good and wise, ye should thank him, and ye should not therwith so long tarry.'

It is worth noting what Renaissance writers themselves had to say about punctuation. Richard Mulcaster, in his *Elementarie* (1582) clearly thinks of the functions of the comma, colon and full stop (period) as pause marks:

> *Comma,* is a small crooked point, which in writing followeth som small branch of the sentence, & in reading warneth us to rest there, and to help our breth a litle, as *Who so shall spare the rod, shall spill the childe.* *Colon* is noted by two round points one above another, which in writing followeth som full branch, or half the sentence, as *Tho the daie be long: yet at the last commeth evensong. Period* is a small round point, which in writing followeth a perfit [perfect, complete] sentence, and in reading warneth us to rest there, and to help our breth at full, as *The fear of God is the beginning of wisdom.*
>
> (Mulcaster 1925, 166)

So does Puttenham:

> . . . the auncient reformers of language, inuented, three maner of pauses, one of lesse leasure then [than] another . . . The shortest pause or intermission they called *comma* as who would say a peece of a speach cut of [off]. The second they called *colon,* not a peece but as it were a member for his larger length, because it occupied twise as much time as the *comma.* The third they called *periodus,* for a complement or full pause, and as a resting place and perfection of so much former speach as had bene vttered . . .
>
> (74)

Simon Daines's later account in his *Orthoepia Anglicana* from 1640 (Daines 1967, 69–75) of the punctuation marks is even more revealing:

> The *Comma* . . . The use onely in long sentences, in the most convenient places to make a small pause for the necessity of breathing; or in Rhetoricall speeches (where many words are used to one effect) to make a kinde of Emphasis and deliberation for the greater majesty or state of Elocution.
>
> The *Colon* . . . is chiefly used in the division of sentences, and exacts halfe the pause of a *Period*; and halfe as much againe as a Comma-Colon [i.e. a semicolon].
>
> The *Period* . . . is altogether used at the end of every speech or sentence, . . . and signifies *conclusion.* The pause or distance of speaking hereto appropriate is sometime more, sometime lesse: for . . . when in the middle of a line it cuts off any integrall part of a complete Tractate, which goes not on with the same, but begins a new line, it requireth double the time of pause, that it doth when the treatise persists in the same line: being then foure times as long as a *Colon,* which in the same line is but twice.

Note in Daines the mention of the semicolon or comma-colon. This was introduced into England in 1569 (Treip 1970, 28), and is described further by Daines in the same section:

> The *Comma-colon* . . . to the Ancients was not knowne; but now in no lesse use than estimation, especially among Rhetoricians. Who in their long winded sentences, and reduplications, have it as a constant pack-horse, to make some short deliberation as it were of little sentences, as the *Comma* doth of words; the time of pause about double that of the *Comma* generally, which yet is very small.

The modern use of the colon to introduce a list or a particularization began in the eighteenth century. This restriction on the punctuation mark was alien to Renaissance writers and printers. Note the relative rhythmical or temporal force of colon and comma, and the parenthesis to indicate the clause of utterance (frequent in the sixteenth and seventeenth centuries), in the following snippet from Thomas Deloney's novel *Jacke of Newberie*, completed in 1596. The extract is from the printed edition of 1626:

> Alas, good Gossip (quoth the Widow) I perceiue no man hath drunke to thee yet.
> No truly (quoth the old woman): for Churchmen haue so much minde of yongue Rabbets, old men such ioy in young Chickens, and Batchelers in Pigs flesh take such delight, that an old Sow, a tough Henne, or a gray Cony are not accepted: and so it is seen by mee, else I should haue beene better remembred.
>
> (13)

A similar use of the colon and the comma as oratorically rhythmical marks in adducing an argument can be seen in the following longer sentence from Phillip Stubbes's *The Anatomie of Abuses* (1583). The passage condemns the popularity of bawdy books:

> And yet notwithstanding, whosoeuer will set pen to paper now a dayes, how vnhonest soeuer, or vnseemly of christian eares his argument be, is permitted to goe forward, and his work plausibly admitted and freendly licensed, and gladly imprinted without any prohibition or con-tradiction at all: wherby it is growen to this issue, that bookes & pam-phlets of scurrilitie and baudrie, are better esteemed and more vendible then [i.e. saleable than] the godlyest and sagest bookes that be: for if it be a godly treatise, reprooing vice, and teaching vertue, away with it, for no man (almost) though they make a floorish of vertue, and godlynes, will buy it, nor (which is lesse) so much as once touch it.
>
> (P.vii)

To illustrate more clearly the important rhetorical function of the colon in Renaissance literature, I have taken the first sentence of Thomas Nashe's *Pierce Penniless his Supplication to the Devil*, first as quoted from the original by Treip (1970, 24 – the misspelling 'eraely' for 'early' in line 5 is in the 1592 edition), then in the modern version by Wells (1964, 26):

> Having spent many yeeres in studying how to live, and liv'de a long time without mony: having tired my youth with follie, and surfetted my minde with vanitie, I began at length to looke backe to repentaunce, & addresse my endevors to prosperitie: But all in
> 5 vaine, I sate up late, and rose eraely, contended with the colde, and conversed with scarcitie: for all my labours turned to losse, my vulgar Muse was despised & neglected, my paines not regarded or slightly rewarded, and I my selfe (in prime of my best wit) laid open to povertie.

> Having spent many years in studying how to live, and lived a long time without money; having tired my youth with folly, and surfeited my mind with vanity, I began at length to look back to repentance and address my endeavours to prosperity. But all in vain. I sat up late and rose early, contended with the cold, and conversed with scarcity; for all my labours turned to loss, my vulgar muse was despised and neglected, my pains not regarded or slightly rewarded, and I myself, in prime of my best wit, laid open to poverty.

Note in the early version the relationship between comma (smaller rhetorical units) and colon (larger ones). Wells uses full stop or semicolon for the Renaissance colon in a grammatical way. The difference between the grammatico-logical way of seeing things and the rhetorical way of the original is particularly clear in lines 4–5, where the earlier version has a colon before *But* and only a comma after *vaine*, thus conveying no conception of a separate sentence *But all in vain* as in Wells's version. 'The prose unrolls in an ampler stream comparable to that of blank verse. Like blank verse, it moves with a larger ebb and flow than that of the sentence, and has its formal patternings overlying a simple groundbeat.' (Treip 24).

When we come to consider the punctuation of verse it was normal, in rhythmically regular lines of eight or more syllables, to put a comma in the middle of the line. Puttenham, comparing the poet to a highway traveller who stops regularly for refreshment (*baite*), equates the comma with a caesura:

> . . . our Poet when he hath made one verse, hath as it were finished one dayes iourney, & the while easeth him selfe with one baite at the least, which is a *Comma* or *Cesure* in the mid way, if the verse be euen and not odde, otherwise in some other place, and not iust in the middle.
>
> (74–5)

In the earliest printed books of verse the virgule had the same function, as can be seen in a stanza quoted from an edition that mirrors the original one of 1517 of Stephen Hawes's *The Passtyme of Pleasure*:

Your noble grace / and excellent hyenes
For to accepte / I beseche ryght humbly
This lytell boke / opprest with rudenes
Without rethorycke / or colour crafty
Nothynge I am / experte in poetry
As the monke of Bury / floure of eloquence
Whiche was in tyme / of grete excellence

(22–8)

In less regular verse, punctuation was normally a guide to the rhythmical flow of the verse, especially in longer poems or epics. Compare the following two versions of Milton's *Paradise Lost* V.64–73. The first is from Beeching's edition (1914), which follows that of 1667; the second from the modern edition (1966) by Douglas Bush. Eve is relating to Adam her dream of 'one shaped and winged like one of those from heav'n' plucking an apple from the Tree of Knowledge:

This said he paus'd not, but with ventrous Arme
He pluckt, he tasted; mee damp horror chil'd
At such bold words voucht with a deed so bold:
But he thus overjoy'd, O Fruit Divine,
Sweet of thy self, but much more sweet thus cropt,
Forbidd'n here, it seems, as onely fit
For Gods, yet able to make Gods of Men:
And why not Gods of Men, since good, the more
Communicated, more abundant growes,
The Author not impair'd, but honourd more?

This said he paused not, but with vent'rous arm
He plucked, he tasted; me damp horror chilled
At such bold words vouched with a deed so bold.
But he thus, overjoyed: 'O fruit divine,
Sweet of thyself, but much more sweet thus cropped,
Forbidden here, it seems, as only fit
For gods, yet able to make gods of men;
And why not gods of men, since good, the more
Communicated, more abundant grows,
The author not impaired, but honored more?

Comparing the 1667 edition of Book 1 of *Paradise Lost* with that of Milton's own manuscript (in which we only have Book 1) shows that the printers changed little in matters of punctuation; so we may feel justified that the punctuation in the remaining eleven books retains much of Milton's original punctuation (see Treip 1970, 97). The punctuation in both versions cited above points the changing rhythm, but there are differences. The comma in the fourth line in the 1667 edition suggests a very short pause before the address to the fruit (and note the absence of quotation marks which, as already mentioned, did not come into use until later), shorter than those signified by a semicolon or a colon. Douglas's colon has no such rhythmical implication. And because Douglas uses colon according to modern conventions, he cannot distinguish between the pausal differences between the seventeenth-century semicolon and colon. He uses the semicolon in both the second line and the seventh. In the latter, the earlier version highlights or foregrounds, with a rhetorical pause greater than that afforded by a semicolon, the dangerously insinuating and blasphemous question.

A few lines further on, Eve smells the fragrant fruit and

> Forthwith up to the Clouds
> With him I flew, and underneath beheld
> The Earth outstretcht immense, a prospect wide
> And various: wondring at my flight and change
> To this high exaltation; suddenly
> My Guide was gon, and I, me thought, sunk down,
> And fell asleep;
>
> (Beeching, 86ff)

> Forthwith up to the clouds
> With him I flew, and underneath beheld
> The earth outstretched immense, a prospect wide
> And various. Wond'ring at my flight and change
> To this high exaltation, suddenly
> My guide was gone, and I, methought, sunk down,
> And fell asleep;
>
> (Douglas, 86ff)

The punctuation differences in the fourth and fifth lines are significant. The 1667 version separates by colon and semicolon the participial clause *wondring . . . exaltation* from the surrounding text. Such pointing rhetorically and rhythmically suspends this brief moment of wonder. Douglas's full stop is too heavy, making it look as if it is the guide who does the wondering, especially since he uses only a comma before *suddenly*. This intriguing possibility, if that is what Douglas has in mind, is not warranted by the original text and the delicate suspension has gone.

Ambiguity, perhaps deliberate, may disappear in some cases because of modern punctuation:

> I never dranke of *Aganippe* well,
> Nor never did in shade of *Temple* sit:
> And Muses scorne with vulgar braines to dwell,
> Poore Lay-man I, for sacred rites unfit.
>   Some doe I heare of Poets fury tell,

But God wot, wot not what they meane by it:
And this I sweare by blackest brooke of hell,
I am no Pickepurse of an others wit.
    How fals it than, that with so smooth an ease
My thoughts I speake? And what I speake I showe
In verse; and that my verse best wittes doth please,
Gesse we the cause. What is it this? fie no.
    Or so? much lesse. How then? sure thus it is;
My lips are sure inspir'd with *Stellas* kisse.
                    (Sidney, *Astrophel and Stella*, sonnet 74)

The stanza is from Feuillerat's edition, which follows that of 1591.
Line 5 is ambiguous: according to modern pointing practice, it could
mean:

(a) Some do I hear of poets' fury tell
(b) Some, do I hear, of poets' fury tell
(c) Some do, I hear, of poets' fury tell

The tone of burlesque in the first eight lines is reinforced by this
ambiguity. When an editor like Kimbrough (1983), who uses modern
punctuation, chooses (a), he commits himself to that interpretation,
excluding the other two, because our punctuation method is syntactically logical. The Renaissance tradition allows for all three when the
line remains unpunctuated. Similarly, in line 12:

(a) What, is it this?
(b) What is it – this?

Kimbrough (who alters *this* to *thus* from the 1598 edition) opts for
'*What, is it thus?*', which is by no means certain. The trouble is that if
the editor elects to adopt modern pointing practice, he cannot leave
those four words unpunctuated unless he takes *what* in the old adverbial sense 'why', current at Sidney's time; but that is unlikely in view
of the next question *Or so*?

    In an epic like *Paradise Lost* the punctuation is relatively heavy so
as to create considerable variation in rhythm and pace. Things tend to
be different in shorter, more self-contained poems, such as Shakespeare's sonnets, in which the lines, unlike those in *Paradise Lost*, are
frequently end-stopped. In the 1609 edition of Shakespeare's sonnets,
a comma (less often a semicolon or colon) is thus often found at the
end of the first three lines of each quatrain but the caesural comma is
used rather sparingly, creating more flexibility. The exception is the
last couplet: since this tends to be in the nature of a summary conclusion, its pace is frequently made more deliberate by a caesural
punctuation mark, normally a comma. The rest of the punctuation
in these sonnets is mainly structural, highlighting the quatrains by
separating them, and thereby 'sectionalizing' the progressions of
thought development, either with full stops, with colons or with both,

depending on the degree of conceptual separation or on the individual punctuation preference, in this respect, of the two compositors involved in typesetting the sonnets (Salmon 1986, liv). The use of midline full stops is exceptional and therefore highly marked. The following two sonnets taken from the Wells/Taylor original-spelling edition (1986) are typical:

> That time of yeare thou maist in me behold,
> When yellow leaues, or none, or few doe hange
> Vpon those boughes which shake against the could,
> Bare ru'ind quiers, where late the sweet birds sang.
> In me thou seest the twi-light of such day,
> As after Sun-set fadeth in the West,
> Which by and by blacke night doth take away,
> Deaths second selfe that seals vp all in rest.
> In me thou seest the glowing of such fire,
> That on the ashes of his youth doth lye,
> As the death bed, whereon it must expire,
> Consum'd with that which it was nurrisht by.
>   This thou perceu'st, which makes thy loue more strong,
>   To loue that well, which thou must leaue ere long.

> (Sonnet 73)

> *Cupid* laid by his brand and fell a sleepe,
> A maide of *Dyans* this aduantage found,
> And his loue-kindling fire did quickly steepe
> In a could vallie-fountaine of that ground:
> Which borrowd from this holie fire of loue,
> A datelesse liuely heat still to indure,
> And grew a seething bath which yet men proue,
> Against strang malladies a soueraigne cure:
> But at my mistres eie loues brand new fired,
> The boy for triall needes would touch my brest,
> I sick withall the helpe of bath desired,
> And thether hied a sad distemperd guest.
>   But found no cure, the bath for my helpe lies,
>   Where *Cupid* got new fire; my mistres eyes.

> (Sonnet 153)

Sonnet 73 is discussed further on pp. 186–7.

In drama, punctuation can be particularly revealing. Renaissance practice, whether it reflected authorial intentions or not, naturally focussed on rhetorical pauses and oratorical delivery. The pointing was frequently used simply to indicate pauses of varying length, regardless of the grammatical logic. Many a punctuation mark which we find in modern editions is not there in the Renaissance ones. Conversely, many are there that have been omitted in modernized versions – many which mark the rhythm or are there to draw attention to an important word or words that follow, often for emotional reasons:

> The only rule for dealing with these supra-grammatical stops is to read the passage as punctuated, and then consider how it is affected by the pause at the point indicated. In the same way, if there is no stop where we expect one, or only a comma where we should expect a colon or even a full stop, we must try how the passage sounds with only light stops or none at all, and see what is the gain or loss to the dramatic impression.
>
> (Pollard 1917, 94)

Let us illustrate Pollard's point by quoting part of a speech by Lear followed by Gonerill's protestation of love for her father, first from the Penguin edition by G. K. Hunter (1972), then from the Folio text of 1623:

> LEAR: . . .   Tell me, my daughters,
> Since now we will divest us both of rule,
> Interest of territory, cares of state,
> Which of you shall we say doth love us most,
> That we our largest bounty may extend
> Where nature doth with merit challenge. Gonerill,
> Our eldest born, speak first.
>
> GONERILL: Sir, I love you more than word can wield the matter,
> Dearer than eyesight, space, and liberty,
> Beyond what can be valued rich or rare,
> No less than life, with grace, health, beauty, honour,
> As much as child e'er loved or father found;
> A love that makes breath poor and speech unable;
> Beyond all manner of 'so much' I love you.
>
> (*King Lear* I.i.48–61)

> LEAR: . . .   Tell me my daughters
> (Since now we will diuest vs both of Rule,
> Interest of Territory, Cares of State)
> Which of you shall we say doth loue vs most,
> That we, our largest bountie may extend
> Where Nature doth with merit challenge. *Gonerill,*
> Our eldest borne, speake first.
>
> GONERILL: Sir, I loue you more then words can weild ye matter,
> Deerer then eye-sight, space, and libertie,
> Beyond what can be valewed, rich or rare,
> No lesse then life, with grace, health, beauty, honor:
> As much as Childe ere lou'd, or Father found.
> A loue that makes breath poore, and speech vnable,
> Beyond all manner of so much I loue you.

The actor is guided more in the second version than in the first. In Lear's speech the bracket in the Folio indicates a lowering of intonation which sets *Which of you* into relief. But *Which of you* is also made to contrast with the majestic *we* of the next line because of the following pause that the rhetorical comma tells the actor to make. In Gonerill's speech *rich and rare* is made to stand out because of the comma preceding it; and it is by no means certain that this phrase is a complement of *what* as the Penguin edition would have it. In the Folio *rich or rare* may mean 'no matter how rich or rare', in which case the punctuation is grammatical as well as rhetorical. The actress (or actor, at Shakespeare's time) is given a choice. But the main point is that in either interpretation the Folio punctuation invites the actress to emphasize an alliteratively hypocritical hyperbole. Note also the colon after *honor*: its pausal force lends grandeur to the mounting *brachylogia* (a rhetorical figure denoting absence of conjunctions between words) that precedes it and foregrounds Gonerill's deceitful expression of filial emotion in the next line, in which the contrast between *Childe* and *Father* is emphasized by the comma. The last two lines of her speech, starting with her false *A loue*, are made particularly prominent because they are separated from the rest by a full stop (only a semicolon in the Penguin version).

5

The Art of the Matter

What is Rhetoric?

The great art historian Sir Ernst Gombrich said that 'in classical writings on rhetoric we have perhaps the most careful analysis of any expressive medium ever undertaken. Language, to these critics, is an organon, an instrument which offers its master a variety of different scales and "stops"' (1977, 317). It is certainly a subject with a very long tradition as a taught art form, stretching from the fifth century BC to the middle of the nineteenth century, although it began to decline with the advent of Romanticism, which preferred to set forth, with introspective force, the private responses and emotions of the author rather than using language to persuade the reader. The Romantics were concerned with the idiosyncratic creative faculty, i.e. more with themselves than with their readers.

The importance of rhetoric during the Renaissance cannot be over-estimated. Any writer of note would, then, have to be thoroughly familiar with its concepts and categories, and this familiarity would commence in childhood at school, where rhetoric figured prominently on the curriculum; and it can safely be said that without some knowledge of rhetoric the modern reader is at a grave disadvantage when confronted with Renaissance literature. He or she would not be attuned to the linguistic effects enjoyed as a matter of course by Renaissance readers and by audiences at plays. C. S. Lewis (1954, 61) reminds us that

> Nearly all our older poetry was written and read by men to whom the distinction between poetry and rhetoric, in its modern form, would have been meaningless. The 'beauties' which they chiefly regarded in every composition were those which we either dislike or simply do not notice. This change of taste makes an invisible wall between us and them . . . we must reconcile ourselves to the fact that of the praise and censure

which we allot to medieval and Elizabethan poets only the smallest part would have seemed relevant to those poets themselves.

The principle of rhetoric is not confined to oratory or literature. Gombrich (1977) and Vickers (1988, ch. 7) have shown its relevance to visual art, and every serious musician or opera singer knows about the importance of 'rhetorically' expressive effects such as *rubato, portamento* and *legato*. Recently there has been much discussion devoted to the tonal colours of the original instruments of, especially, the seventeenth and eighteenth centuries; and the realization of the ornamental and expressive value of the gracenote or *appoggiatura* in Mozart is making a significant comeback at the moment. The topicality of such issues is perhaps not unrelated to the increasing interest given to the importance of the rhetorical figures in literature. How recent this resurge of interest is follows from the Preface in Vickers (1970, 12), in which the author says that

> I have to part company with many distinguished historians of rhetoric. The accepted view of the tropes and figures of rhetoric is, to put it bluntly, that they are a nuisance, a quite sterile appendage to rhetoric to which (unaccountably) teachers, pupils and writers all over the world devoted much labour for over two thousand years. If this were true, their efforts would indeed have been absurdly wasted.

Not only the subject but also the word 'rhetoric' has suffered over the years. To most people it has a negative ring to it, which is reflected in a modern reference work like the *Collins Cobuild English Language Dictionary* (1987), which gives as its first definition: 'speech or writing that is presented in a forceful and dramatic way which appears to be clever and important; often used showing disapproval'. This is followed with the example *She simply ignored his bluster as empty rhetoric*. The pejoration of the word as a synonym of vacuous bombast is similar to that of 'theatrical', which often refers to unnatural or contrived behaviour for effect only. This does not mean that rhetoric, or certain forms of it, has been regarded pejoratively only in modern times: 'what looks like progress from the point of view of the mastery of a medium can also be viewed as decline into empty virtuosity. Polemics between the various schools of rhetoric make ample use of such moral arguments. Asiatic bombast is decried as a sign of moral decay, and the return to a pure Attic vocabulary is hailed as a moral victory' (Gombrich 1977, 8). For the terms 'Asiatic' and 'Attic' as applicable to ancient Greek schools of rhetoric, see below, p. 133.

The *Cobuild Dictionary*'s first and primary sense of 'rhetoric' is not going to be ours in this book. Its second (and last) definition comes closer to the, here, relevant meaning: 'a grand, poetic way of speaking which once used to be practised as an art'; but it is still a long way off. This definition does not seem to take account of writing as opposed to speaking and although, as we shall see, rhetoric has indeed its origins in the spoken medium, it is its relevance to literature that is of paramount importance during the Renaissance and beyond. The second definition also seems to imply that rhetoric is dead. It is not, as is clear in, for instance, Vickers (1988), whose eighth chapter is on rhetoric in the modern novel, and from Corbett (1990), which contains rhetorical analyses of texts by people like Dorothy L. Sayers, Somerset Maugham and Martin Luther King.

All the same, it is true that rhetoric was practised more consciously and more deliberately and certainly taught much more extensively and intensively in the past than now, no more so than during the Renaissance, when the works on the subject from classical Greece and Rome came to be widely known, admired and followed, and gave the impetus to the writing of a huge number of books on the subject.

A more useful definition, then, of rhetoric would be: the art of using language in such a way that it has a desired effect or impression on the listener and reader. Rhetoric and another branch of language, viz grammar, have sometimes been compared to a game. If we take the rules of soccer, for instance, it is obvious that without them soccer as we know it cannot be played. One rule is that we are not allowed to touch the ball with our hands, except for the goal keeper. Touching the ball with our hands during a soccer match corresponds in language to making a grammatical error such as *John are happy* or *John happy is*. These sentences are simply not English. Breaking such rules is 'breaking' the game or the language. In order to play soccer the rules must be observed; the same applies to language. But mere observation of the rules does not necessarily lead to winning the match. It does not even follow that the match will be played well. For this we need organization, strategies, tactics, manoeuverings. Similarly with language if we want it to be effective, convincing and persuasive; it is here that rhetoric comes in. It follows that good rhetoric, although stylized, does not come across as contrived or false. If it did, it would not be effective, convincing and persuasive. The emotional concern of rhetoric was imitation of the passions of real life and most of the rhetorical figures, as employed in the great literature of the Renaissance, simply constitute a conventional systematization and representation of word uses and word patterns that we give voice to when we are in some state of extreme or intense emotion. Even the grandest and most magniloquent of rhetorical language is therefore tied closely to sentiments and emotions of man's real nature, as recognized by the listener or reader; 'without nature, art can claim no being', as Ben Jonson says in *Timber or Discoveries* (586).

The systematization and codification of rhetoric began in ancient Greece and was continued and elaborated in the times of classical Rome. The works of the ancient rhetoricians became widely disseminated all over Europe during the Renaissance; and in order to understand the importance of rhetoric in that period, we must know something about the classical background.

The Origin and Development of Rhetoric: A Brief Survey

Rhetoric has its origins in natural eloquence, and in classical times it was concerned much more with speech (oratory) than with literature although both the Greeks and Romans showed considerable interest in the bearing of rhetoric on literary style. Eloquence was first carefully studied in ancient Greece where we start, or rather the Greek colonies in Sicily, for it was there, in the fifth century BC, that rhetoric, more specifically the rhetoric of the courtroom, was first systematically discussed and taught. The first to found a school of political and judicial rhetoric in mainland Greece was the Attic orator Isocrates 'that Old man eloquent' who the 'dishonest victory / At Chaeronea, fatal to liberty, / Killed with report' (in 338 BC) as Milton describes him in his sonnet *To the Lady Margaret Ley*. It is also of importance to note, in view of later developments, that Isocrates was not exclusively concerned with spoken rhetoric, but also with the style and rhythm of prose writing.

The most influential of the Greeks in the history of rhetoric was Aristotle (384–322 BC), whose *Rhetoric*, the first great work on the art of persuasion, became very influential, especially during the Renaissance although it had been translated in late medieval times, in the thirteenth century. As a philosopher Aristotle was naturally concerned with argument, with 'proving a case', and this is essentially what his rhetorical discussion is about. It is to Aristotle that we owe the famous three modes of persuasion: *ethos*, *logos* and *pathos*, which we can translate as, respectively, 'ethical, rational and emotional appeal'.

Ethos was concerned with gaining a receptive or willing audience by persuading it, during the course of his speech, of the speaker's righteous moral stance and integrity. The speaker had to appear to be trustworthy and inspire confidence. He might, for instance, do this by establishing a positive relationship with his listeners by flattering them in an intimately personal way, like Mark Antony at the beginning of his famous speech in Shakespeare's *Julius Caesar* (Act III.ii.): 'Friends, Romans, countrymen, lend me your ears'.

Logos, as the word implies, has much to do with logic and, as a purely philosophical concept, is discussed in detail by Aristotle in his *Organon* and *On Interpretation*. In rhetoric, which Aristotle regarded as an offshoot of logic, *logos* refers to persuasion through logical argument, either by induction or deduction. Inductive argument is based on generalizations from the observation of individual instances. The more instances, the more valid the generalization. In rhetoric where, unlike science, adducement of all the data on which the generalization is based would be intolerable and certainly ineffective, use is made of a typical example or two to illustrate the validity of the generalization, i.e. to support the argument. In deductive argument, in which inferences are made from statements, not from external phenomena, Aristotle's syllogisms play an important part, although in rhetoric the syllogism is implied rather than stated so that the appeal to reason is through probability rather than through the philosophical rigour of logical proof.

Pathos has to do with the way that a speech can sway us when the emphasis is on its emotional rather than its rational appeal. We are passionate creatures and the successful orator will bear that in mind. Thus there must be a place in the theory of rhetoric for a discussion of how to arouse, or sometimes allay, the emotions of an audience, and it is duly considered by Aristotle in Book 2 of his *Rhetoric*. This mode of persuasion was to be given particular emphasis in Renaissance writings on rhetoric; but, as we might expect, Aristotle found it inferior to *logos*. He rather seems to have accepted it as a necessity because of human nature being what it is. *Pathos* was certainly practised extensively in ancient Greek oratory, notably by Gorgias of Leontini who belonged to the fifth-century Greco-Sicilian group but, as ambassador, came to Athens where his appeal to the passions in his speeches was greatly admired. Gorgias was later immortalized by Plato in the famous dialogue that bears his name. This dialogue, together with *Phaedrus*, reveals Plato's distaste for, and suspicion of, rhetoric as a means of 'practical' persuasion but, ironically, in language that displays an extraordinary mastery of the art. All the same, Plato prefigures the medieval tendency to see rhetoric as a branch of logic in the sense that in *Phaedrus* he advocates the use of rhetoric for abstract philosophical distinction making.

We should be careful not to separate the three notions of *ethos*, *logos* and *pathos* too much. They would often work together. Giving the audience confidence in the speaker's moral integrity and competence (*ethos*) could often come from a clear exposition of rational argument (*logos*), and both would help to influence their emotions or frame of mind (*pathos*) in the listening process.

The rhetorical tradition established by the Greeks continued in ancient Rome, where the giants were Cicero (106–43 BC) and Quintilian (c.40–96 AD). Before we take a closer look at them, mention should be made of the anonymous *Rhetorica Ad Caius Herennium* (often referred to simply as *Ad Herennium* 'For Herennius') which until the end of the 15th century had been attributed to Cicero. This work, which was among the most influential in the Middle Ages, stems from the 80s BC, so its author must have been a contemporary of Cicero whose *De Inventione* was written about the same time. These two works were the first Latin books on rhetoric, and both are concerned essentially with the oratory of the courtroom (judicial rhetoric). *Ad Herennium* has the distinction of being the first work to have come down to us that includes a formal study of rhetorical figures of speech. In spite of the focus of these two books on specifically Roman law doctrine, they became two of the most widely read books on rhetoric during the Renaissance.

Besides *De Inventione*, Cicero wrote a number of books of rhetoric of which the most important are *De Oratore*, *Brutus* and *Orator*, the first two of these being dialogues, and the third in the form of a letter addressed to Brutus. During the time of Cicero there were two particularly prominent views on rhetoric, represented by the Atticists and the Asiatics. Whereas the former were in favour of a pure and plain style in the ancient Greek (Attic) manner, the latter advocated a much more flowery and ornate mode of expression, a style employed by orators from the Greek settlements in Asia. Cicero entered into the controversy between these two rhetorical parties in both *Brutus* and *Orator*, in which he tried to mediate between them. It is particularly clear from these works that he did not favour the Atticists who, for Cicero, were too cold; they lacked the emotional appeal of Aristotle's *pathos*. The difference between those two styles was similar to the differences between the styles of Seneca and Cicero in Rome, the former corresponding to the Attic, the latter to the Asiatic. During the Renaissance references were often made to, and arguments conducted about, the respective merits of the Senecan and the Ciceronian styles.

Aristotle's *Rhetoric* was translated into Latin during Cicero's lifetime, and his important threefold division of rhetorical appeal into *ethos*, *logos* and *pathos* reappeared in Cicero's works as *delectare* 'to delight' (with slight change of emphasis from the more moral notion of *ethos*), *docere* 'to instruct' and *(per)movere* 'to move', respectively. Amongst Cicero's contribution to rhetoric is his repeated emphasis on *movere*, on the importance in oratory of arousing the emotions of the audience. This element of the appeal triad now came to much greater prominence than in Aristotle, and was to be of paramount concern to the rhetoricians of the Renaissance.

But perhaps the extraordinary popularity of Cicero during the Renaissance should be attributed to the way he stressed the importance of rhetoric for an active life in politics, with a view to creating a better world with firm emphasis on the common good. This Humanist ideal demanded of the orator considerable wisdom, insight and knowledge:

> Unlike Aristotle, who held that rhetoric had no proper subject matter, Cicero felt that the perfect orator must have command of a wide range of knowledge. Accordingly, under the Ciceronian system the study of

rhetoric really became a liberal-arts course. This broadening of the scope of rhetoric helps to explain Cicero's appeal for the English and Continental Humanists when the study of rhetoric was revived during the Renaissance.

(Corbett 1990, 546).

Cicero had considerable influence, especially in his moral and humanist attitudes, on Quintilian, the other great Roman rhetorician, whose monumental work *Institutio Oratoria*, comprising twelve books, was to occupy a prominent position in the teaching of rhetoric during the Renaissance, not least because of Quintilian's accounts of the significance of literary criticism. It is to Quintilian that we owe the first systematic classification of the elements of rhetorical style into *tropes* and *schemes* (see below).

Mention should also be made of Longinus (1st century BC), whose *On the Sublime* is second to none in its praise of true rhetoric, i.e. the kind of rhetoric which, through art that conceals art, stays in tune with emotions we recognize and can empathize with:

> . . . in much the same way as dim lights vanish in the radiance of the sun, so does the all-pervading effluence of grandeur utterly obscure the artifices of rhetoric.
> Something of the same kind occurs in painting. For although light and shade as represented by colours may lie side by side on the same surface, it is the light that first catches the eye and seems to stand out, but also to be much nearer. So also is it with literature: by some natural affinity and by their brilliance, things that appeal to our feelings and sublime conceptions lie nearer to our hearts, and always catch our attention before the figures, overshadowing their artistry, and keeping it out of sight, so to speak.

(Longinus, in Dorsch 1965, 127–8)

Classical rhetoric was divided into five stages. The Latin names for these, and they are the ones that are generally used today, were *inventio, dispositio, elocutio, memoria* and *pronuntiatio*.

Inventio (the Greeks called it *heuresis*) denoted the search for, or discovery of, modes of persuasion (or arguments), for instance by reference to categories or *topics*, as they were called, such as cause and effect, similarity or difference, the possible *versus* the impossible, and the authority of precedents. (The inductive examples would come under this last *topic*.)

Under *dispositio* (Aristotle's *taxis*) would come the methods of organizing one's material, typically into an introduction (*exordium*), then a clear stating of the subject or case (*narratio*), followed by an effective organization of the points selected from the *inventio topics* (*confirmatio*), which would lead on to sections dealing with the proof and refutation of contrary arguments (*refutatio*), and then a conclusion (*conclusio*).

Elocutio (the Greek term was *lexis*) dealt with style, and three main styles were commonly distinguished: the high, the middle and the low. According to Quintilian, the high style was particularly suited to *delectare*, the middle to *movere*, and the low (or plain) to *docere*. It was also in his discussion of *elocutio* that Quintilian classified the rhetorical figures into *tropes* and *schemes* (in Book 9 of *Institutio Oratoria*).

A *trope* involves altering the meaning of a word or phrase to another, unusual or abnormal, meaning; i.e. a word or phrase is used in a sense that is outside its normal scope of meaning. *Irony*, in its classical definition of saying the opposite of what we mean, is a particularly clear example of a trope. So is the *metaphor*, which also implies a transfer of meaning, as when *haystack* refers to a certain kind of hairdo or headdress in *the haystack on her head*. Thus tropes are essentially semantically deviant.

Schemes, on the other hand, imply a change from the normal order or pattern of words to an abnormal one. They are morphologically, syntactically or phonologically deviant. For instance, selecting three words all starting with *b*-, as in Marlowe's *2Tamburlaine: Black is the beauty of the brightest day* (II.iv.1), is phonologically deviant and is an instance of the wellknown scheme *alliteration*. (The line is also a clear illustration of the trope *paradox* 'a contradictory statement'.) Choosing to give a number of words in a passage the same ending, as in *coming . . . going . . . running . . . falling* is employing the scheme *homoioteleuton*, which is an example of morphological deviance. And deliberately constructing a series of phrases or clauses in the same way, a scheme called *parison*, is doing something syntactically deviant. Shakespeare's *Julius Caesar* has an instance of this in I.i.58–9: *Run to your houses, fall upon your knees, / Pray to the gods . . .'*

Memoria, which had no counterpart in Aristotle's *Rhetoric*, is the part dealing with how to memorize speeches, mainly through word association or association with ideas or physical objects.

Finally, *pronuntiatio* (i.e. Aristotle's *hypocrisis*, a word that, revealingly, also meant 'acting') was concerned with delivery, i.e. how a speech was orally presented through voice modulation and rhythm, accompanied by suitable gestures. It is obviously irrelevant for literature except, of course, for the actors in drama. The word 'actor', incidentally, has always been closely tied up with the concept of rhetoric. During the Renaissance it was often used to refer to 'a pleader; he who conducts an action at law . . . an advocate in civil cases . . . a public prosecutor' (*Oxford English Dictionary*), meanings that stem from Roman Law.

During the Middle Ages rhetoric was one of the three university subjects in the undergraduate *trivium* course, the other two being logic and grammar. (The graduate course, the *quadrivium*, comprised geometry, arithmetic, astronomy and music.) But rhetoric in the

Middle Ages was not what it had been in previous centuries. A principal reason for this was, in an age when printing had not yet been invented, the relative unavailability of books on the subject. Thus Cicero's important works *Brutus* and *Orator* were unknown then although his *De Inventione* survived in a large number of manuscripts; but this work, referred to by Cicero himself in *De Oratore* (not widely known in the Middle Ages) as 'unfinished' and 'crude', only dealt with *inventio*. The important subject of *elocutio* or style could not even be studied in Quintilian's *Institutio Oratoria*, because the imperfect copies available had the relevant sections missing; but *Ad Herennium* was at least extant in a huge number of copies and contained, in Book 4, discussions of style. This and Cicero's *De Inventione* 'were the two most popular rhetoric-books of antiquity, and perhaps the two most disseminated works of any kind' (Vickers 1988, 28).

Another important reason for the diminished scope of rhetoric as a subject in medieval times was changing political circumstances. In the Middle Ages there were relatively few forums for free speech, and personal liberty and democratic ideals were severely curtailed. The result was some decline in the role of rhetoric before the advent of the Renaissance.

What happened to rhetoric in the Middle Ages is a complex question (see, for instance, McKeon 1942), but in general it can be said that it was subsumed under either logic or theology, or degenerated into the 'art' of writing business letters or petitions.

When it became subordinate to logic, rhetoric inevitably became more abstract and aridly intellectual, divorcing itself to a considerable extent from *pathos* or *movere*. But *movere* often came to the fore, though with scant reference to the specific effects of the rhetorical figures to that end, when rhetoric was assimilated to theology, a tendency that began with St Augustine (353–430 AD), and was put into the service of composing sermons, a branch of writing known as homiletics. This art of preaching was known in the Middle Ages as *ars praedicandi*. The great early thirteenth century prose work *Ancrene Wisse* 'guide for nuns', for example, belongs to this tradition; and in his rhetorical eloquence the anonymous author's concern is 'not to prove but to move. Even in his use of the forms of logical proof, his aim is to persuade, not to demonstrate a truth' (Shepherd 1959, lx).

The writing of letters and petitions came under what was called *ars dictaminis*. The scope of rhetoric in this sphere was narrow and closely tied up with grammar:

> Typically the form-letter shows the correct way to address someone superior or inferior (a lore that survives in modern protocol and etiquette books) . . . Whether begging-letters from students asking their parents for more money, or attempts to secure secular or ecclesiastical office, the model letters in these collections are supplicatory, or utilitarian.

They are not concerned with wider cultural issues, nor do they even encourage personal communication. The typical letter produced by this training has a single goal in mind, an item of business which will be mutually advantageous, or a request which, if granted, will benefit the writer, not the reader. The *dictamen* manual is written by one person to help another to write to a third to get what he or she wants.

(Vickers 1988, 234–5).

Guides to letter writing survived into the Renaissance, as is shown by the publication in 1522 of *Modus Conscribendi Epistolas* 'method for composing letters' by the great Dutch Humanist and rhetorician Erasmus, who worked for a time in England at the beginning of the sixteenth century, and in 1586 of *The English Secretorie* by Angel Day. These works are of considerable interest to the student of epistolary literature. Here is a short extract from one of Day's model letters, which he divided in typical rhetorical manner into appropriate discourse divisions, such as *exordium, propositio* (or *narratio*) and *conclusio* (or *epilogus*). The letter is 'an epistle monitorie to a father, touching the lewd and ill demeanor of his sonne', from which we shall quote the, to a modern reader, rather amusing *exordium*. This makes use of the *adagium*, i.e. 'adage' or 'proverb', which played an important part in rhetoric:

Exordium. Though it seeme an approued follye to caste pearles before swine, or to offer a golden saddle to an Asses backe; yet (not that I thinke either the Sowe worthy of the pearles, or the Asse fit for the saddle), I haue written vnto you, the one reason to manifest vnto you, the vile and bad parts of your sonne whereof you will take no notice, and of which this letter heerein closed shall beare sufficient testimony, the other for charities sake, to admonish you which are his father, to his benefit & timely looking to, to winde him from that, which by small sufferance may breed your woes and his irrecuperable destruction.

(Quoted in Görlach 1991, 357)

The perhaps rather negative view, indicated so far, of rhetorical teaching and writings in the Middle Ages does not mean, of course, that literary works did not make use of rhetoric. It means that rhetoric was not much studied as an element in literary criticism; but the literature of the Middle Ages is resplendent with rhetorical features, as any student of Chaucer and Gower will know; and see e.g. Salter (1962) on *Piers Plowman*.

One particularly notable feature of medieval literary rhetoric was the use of amplification, which manifested itself in various ways. The Anglo-Norman rhetorician Geoffrey de Vinsauf, who flourished at the beginning of the thirteenth century and taught for a while at Northampton, refers, in his *Nova Poetria*, to these various ways as *morae*, which means 'delays', 'as if the art of literature consisted in learning how to say much when you have little to say' (C. S. Lewis 1964, 192).

As opposed to the Renaissance emphasis on *amplificatio* as directed towards emotional arousal or bringing light to the subject in hand, i.e. towards the matter-content (*res* in Latin rhetoric books), medieval *amplificatio* was much more concerned with words for their own sake (*verba*).

One of the *amplificatio* delays was *ecphrasis* (Greek for 'speaking out', that is saying something in great detail), a separable decorative description, often introduced for a morally edifying purpose, of a character, object or situation, and therefore dear to medieval rhetoricians, who made frequent use of it in sermons. In medieval literature this figure would often result in elaborate descriptions of immense detail:

> one of the best examples in alliterative poetry is that of the Green Knight and his horse in *Gawain* [but] . . . the close and careful detail gives no impression of sensuous vividness, nor was this in general the medieval intention. Sensuous vividness, as seen, for example in Keats, depends upon the selection of significant detail: medieval descriptive convention depends upon the accumulation of all available detail . . . The description of the Green Knight is, in essence, a piece of conscious literary decoration.
>
> (Pearsall 1955, 130).

Ecphrasis or, as it is sometimes known, *hypotyposis* remained an important figure in Renaissance literary criticism. George Puttenham, the great sixteenth-century rhetorician, wrote eloquently of *ecphrasis* (or '*hypotiposis*', as he calls it):

> The matter and occasion leadeth vs many times to describe and set foorth many things, in such sort as it should appeare they were truly before our eyes though they were not present, which to do it requireth cunning [skill]: for nothing can be kindly [properly] counterfait or represented in his absence, but by great discretion in the doer. And if the things we couet to describe be not naturall or not veritable, than [then] yet the same axeth more cunning to do it, because to faine a thing that neuer was nor is like to be, proceedeth of a greater wit and sharper inuention than to describe things that be true.
>
> (238)

Since this book is on Renaissance language and literature, let us illustrate the effect of *ecphrasis* in a magnificent example from Spenser's *Fairie Queene*, Book I. In the ninth canto, stanzas 33–36, there is a detailed and powerful description of the Cave of Despair and of Despair himself. The effect this must have had on the Renaissance audience or reader must have been immense since they were familiar with similar pictures on woodcuts, emblems and paintings (Koller 1964, 135). The imagery is reminiscent of paintings like Hieronymus Bosch's (*c*.1450–1516) picture *St Jerome at Prayer* (in the Musée des Beaux-Arts, Ghent) in which, in a swampy grotto, rank with corruption and decay, we note the 'old stockes and stubs of trees' and 'the ghastly owl, sitting darkly on a branch whereon nor fruit, nor leaf was ever seene'; and Pieter Brueghel's *Triumph of Death* (in the Prado, Madrid, and painted during the 1560s), with its 'ragged rocky knees' and 'carcases . . . scattered on the greene, / And throwne about the cliffs':

> Ere long they come, where that same wicked wight
> His dwelling has, low in an hollow caue,
> Farre vnderneath a craggie clift ypight ['set'],
> Darke, dolefull, drearie, like a greedie graue,
> That still for carrion carcases doth craue:
> On top whereof aye dwelt the ghastly Owle,
> Shrieking his balefull note, which euer draue
> Farre from that haunt all other chearefull fowle;
> And all about it wandring ghostes did waile and howle.
>
> And all about old stockes and stubs of trees,
> Whereon nor fruit, nor leafe was euer seene,
> Did hang vpon the ragged rocky knees ['projections'];
> On which had many wretches hanged beene,
> Whose carcases were scattered on the greene,
> And throwne about the cliffs. Arriued there,
> That bare-head knight for dread and dolefull teene ['sorrow'],
> Would faine haue fled, ne durst approchen neare,
> But th'other forst him stay, and comforted in feare.
>
> That darkesome caue they enter, where they find
> That cursed man, low sitting on the ground,
> Musing full sadly in his sullein mind;
> His griesie lockes, long growen, and vnbound,
> Disordred hong about his shoulders round,
> And hid his face; through which his hollow eyne
> Lookt deadly dull, and stared as astound;
> His raw-bone cheekes through penurie and pine,
> Were shronke into his jawes, as he did neuer dine.
>
> His garment nought but many ragged clouts,
> With thornes together pind and patched was,
> The which his naked sides he wrapt abouts;
> And him beside there lay vpon the gras
> A drearie corse, whose life away did pas,
> All wallowd in his owne yet luke-warme blood,
> That from his wound yet welled fresh alas;
> In which a rustie knife fast fixed stood,
> And made an open passage for the gushing flood.

The power of this *ecphrasis* owes much to Spenser's emotive use of rhetorical figures, especially the schemes of repetition, such as *ploce* meaning repetition of the same word, here the repetition of the words *hollow, dolefull, carcases, drearie, gloomy* and *repulsive*; *polyptoton* i.e. repetition of the same word in a different form: *darke . . . darke-some*; *alliteration* (sometimes reinforcing a *polyptoton*), as in e.g. *darke, dolefull, drearie / greedie grave / carrion carcases / sadly . . . sullein* 'gravely . . . gloomily serious' / *penurie . . . pine*; *assonance*, which is using identical or similar vowels in close proximity: *carrion carcases / Musing full . . . sullein* (the last word pronounced with the vowel of *full* at the time); *consonance*, i.e. using the same or similar non-initial consonants in close proximity, such as [g] and [k] in *ragged rocky*, reinforced by the initial [k] in *knees*, still pronounced in Spenser's day.

The upsurge of interest in rhetoric during the Renaissance owes much to the Humanist movement. The Renaissance Humanists were opposed to the scepticism fostered by medieval philosophy of logic (scholasticism) and the suppression and devaluation of the individual. The medieval divinely determined hierarchy, celestial as well as terrestrial, in which everything and everybody had their fixed 'place' and 'degree' was now being undermined, partly through the rise of capitalism effecting greater social mobility. As the name implies, the Humanists put man in the centre and stressed his innate gifts, his potential for nobility and greatness. Hamlet expresses the essential Humanist sentiment eloquently:

> What piece of work is a man! How noble in reason, how infinite in faculty, in form and moving how express and admirable, in action how like an angel, in apprehension how like a god – the beauty of the world, the paragon of animals!
>
> (*Hamlet* II.ii.303–7)

Man was now recognized as having the power to question the mysteries of the universe outside the limits of theology. In this climate the dignity of eloquence seen as a power, gift or virtue in man for giving expression to his thoughts was elevated to new heights. The antiquities of ancient Greece and Rome were fuel to humanism, and the revival of learning that took place in the Renaissance ('rebirth', i.e. of the classical ideals) was based on them. Classical works on rhetoric now inspired a huge number of handbooks, some written in Latin, some in the various European vernacular languages. The discovery of texts lost in the Middle Ages:

> or the granting them true status . . . could only increase the autonomy of rhetoric, its recognition as an independent subject. The truly staggering number of editions, commentaries, and new works . . . testifies to the great eagerness with which rhetoric was cultivated. If there were perhaps two thousand rhetoric books published between 1400 and 1700, each in an edition of between two hundred and fifty and a thousand copies, and if each copy was read by anything from one reader to the dozens using a school text, then there must have been several million Europeans with a working knowledge of rhetoric. These included many of the kings, princes, and their counsellors; popes, bishops, ordinary clergymen . . . ,

all the professors, schoolteachers, lawyers, historians; all the poets and dramatists.

(Vickers 1988, 255–6).

This extraordinary dissemination of cultural ideas had been made possible by the invention of printing by the German Johannes Gutenberg in the mid-fifteenth century and introduced to Britain by William Caxton in 1476.

One of the most important developments in attitudes to rhetoric during the Renaissance was an increased emphasis on its relevance to literature, a fusion of classical rhetoric, which mainly had to do with oratory, and literary criticism (Clark 1922, 5ff). Ben Jonson in *Timber or Discoveries* (587):

> The *Poet* is the nearest borderer upon the orator, and expresseth all his virtues, though he be tied more to numbers; is his equal in ornament, and above him in his strengths . . . because in moving the minds of men and stirring of affections – in which oratory shows and especially approves her eminence – he chiefly excels.

Aristotle dealt with these two disciplines in separate works: rhetoric was discussed in his *Rhetoric*, literary criticism in his *Poetics*. But now the two subjects were amalgamated.

Several Continental rhetoricians were to exercise great influence on the development of rhetoric teaching in Britain. Amongst the most directly influential were Erasmus, Melanchthon and Susenbrotus.

The great Dutch Humanist Desiderius Erasmus (1466–1536) wrote a number of handbooks for schools on the instigation of John Colet, one of the principal Christian Humanists and reformers of his day in England, Dean of St Paul's and founder of St Paul's School, where later Milton was to learn the foundations of rhetoric. The most influential of these works by Erasmus was *De Copia Verborum ac Rerum* 'on the copiousness (of expression) of words and things', normally referred to simply as *De Copia*. It was common in the grammar schools of the time for rhetorical Latin composition, and many a Tudor pupil would learn from this work about how to use the *topics* of *inventio* and vary his style (*elocutio*) by paying close attention to the tropes and schemes.

Through his *Elementorum Rhetorices Libri Duo* 'two books on the elements of rhetoric' Philip Melanchthon (1497–1560) from Germany, like Erasmus highly anti-scholastic in his attitudes, became influential in his insistence on the *pathos* element of rhetoric and its methods to that end, which had suffered relative neglect in medieval times.

Joannes Susenbrotus's *Epitome Troporum ac Schematum*, published in 1541, paid particular attention to the tropes and schemes, which by some writers were considered less significant than the categories of *inventio* and *dispositio*. The *Epitome*, with its listing of 140 rhetorical

figures, became a highly popular textbook in sixteenth-century Britain.
Soon works in English followed, of which space allows only a few
to be mentioned.

Richard Sherry wrote *A Treatise of Schemes and Tropes* (1550),
which he revised with, significantly, greater emphasis on literature and
called it *A Treatise of the Figures of Grammer and Rhetorike* (1555).
Vickers, in drawing attention to the profound significance of rhetoric
in literature at the time, quotes Sherry: 'The common scholemasters
be wont in readynge, to saye unto their scholers: *Hic est figura* [here
is a figure]: and sometimes to ask them, *Per quam figuram?* [by what
figure?]' But, he says, 'what profit is herein if they go no further . . .
For thys darre I saye, no eloquente wryter maye be perceived as he
shulde be, wythout the knowledge of them' (1988, 259).

Thomas Wilson was enormously influential through his *Arte of
Rhetorique* (1553), with which Shakespeare might have been
acquainted (Craig 1931). Based on Aristotle and Quintilian and influenced by its Renaissance predecessors, its scope was comprehensive,
though the work is not particularly long: space was given to the five
categories *inventio, dispositio, elocutio, memoria* and *pronuntiatio*,
including discussion of eighty rhetorical figures; and Wilson does not
neglect the classical division of *dispositio* into *exordium, narratio, confirmatio, refutatio* and *conclusio*.

George Puttenham's *Arte of English Poesie* (1589) has added
immediate interest for the student of literature because of the author's
lively engagement with the new vernacular literature. His work contains numerous examples taken from great Renaissance poets such as
Sir Thomas Wyatt and Sir Philip Sidney. In the first brief chapter of
Book 3 (the last) of this work Puttenham, through exquisitely apposite
analogy that recalls Longinus (see above, p. 134), advises the poet to
exercise decorum and great discretion in his use of rhetorical devices:

> This ornament we speake of is giuen to it [poesie] by figures and figura-
> tive speaches, which be the flowers as it were and coulours that a Poet
> setteth vpon his language by arte, as the embroderer doth his stone and
> perle, or passements [lace] of gold vpon the stuffe of a Princely garment,
> or as th'excellent painter bestoweth the rich Orient coulours vpon his
> table of pourtraite: so neuertheless as if the same coulours in our arte
> of Poesie . . . be not well tempered, or not well layd, or be vsed in
> excesse, or neuer so litle disordered or misplaced, they not onely giue
> it no maner of grace at all, but rather do disfigure the stuffe and spill
> the whole workmanship taking away all bewtie and good liking from it,
> no lesse then [than] if the crimson tainte, which should be laid vpon a
> Ladies lips, or right in the center of her cheeks should by some ouersight
> or mishap be applied to her forhead or chinne, it would make (ye would
> say) but a very ridiculous bewtie, wherfore the chief prayse and cunning
> [skill] of our Poet is in the discreet vsing of his figures, as the skilfull
> painters is in the good conueyance of his coulours and shadowing traits

of his pensill, with a delectable varietie, by all measure and iust proportion, and in places most aptly to be bestowed . . .

(138)

Puttenham is also wellknown for his attempt to anglicize the Greek
names of the rhetorical figures. However vivid some of his English
terms are (*hyperbole* (exaggeration) he calls *the loud lier*), his attempt
has been in vain, partly perhaps because the English terms were often
no more informative than the Greek. *Anaphora*, for instance, which
means the repetition of words at the beginning of successive clauses,
he calls *the figure of report* where, of course, *report* directly translates
the Greek word, but only in the Latin sense (*reportare* 'carry back').
By Puttenham's time *report* had come to mean in everyday English
much the same as it means today, i.e. 'account' or 'reputation', but
since those meanings are irrelevant here, *report* is hardly more helpful
than *anaphora*.

Henry Peacham, in his *Garden of Eloquence* (1577, revised and
enlarged edition published in 1593), listed more figures (184) than any
other English writer and, more importantly, paid meticulous attention
to their expressive functions, especially in his second edition.

The scope of Abraham Fraunce's *Arcadian Rhetorike* (1588) was
confined to only two of the five rhetorical divisions, as he states laconi-
cally at the very start of his work: 'Rhetoric is an Art of speaking. It
hath two parts, Eloqution and Pronuntiation'. It is notable for his
consistent use of examples to illustrate the figures from, apart from
the classical authors, Sir Philip Sidney's works.

An excellent, though brief, work on rhetoric entitled *Directions
for Speech and Style* by John Hoskins appeared in 1600. He shows
considerable sensitivity to the expressive effect of a fair number of
figures, with illustrations taken mainly from Sidney's *Arcadia*.

Before we discuss *elocutio* (the tropes and schemes) in greater detail,
let us first take a closer look at *dispositio*, the division of rhetoric that
has to do with setting out the parts of a discourse, dividing it into
exordium, *narratio*, *confirmatio*, *refutatio* and *conclusio*. It is difficult
to find a better example of classical rhetorical discourse principles
applied to Renaissance literature than that afforded by Sidney's *Apolo-
gie for Poetrie*, also called *The Defence of Poesie*, published 1595, nine
years after Sidney's death, a great piece of literature in finely sculpted
prose, 'still the best analysis and the most persuasive justification of
this peculiar notion – that a sensible and comprehensive control over
human affairs can be learnt from splendid poems' (Shepherd, in his
edition (1965) 1). Sidney adds to the five two more parts, also recognized by many others, viz *propositio* and *divisio*. The latter was also
added to the famous five in *Ad Herennium* and defines the issues
between the statements of fact (*narratio*) and the proof (*confirmatio*).
We can regard *propositio* and *divisio* as extensions of the *narratio*.

In the short *exordium* (the introduction) Sidney immediately arouses our interest in a semi-anecdotal way by writing, in the first person, about the virtues of horsemanship as told to him by a certain John Pietro Pugliano:

> He said soldiers were the noblest estate of mankind, and horsemen the noblest of soldiers . . . no earthly thing bred such wonder to a prince as to be a good horseman. Skill of government was but a *pedanteria* in comparison . . . if I had not been a piece of a logician before I came to him, I think he would have persuaded me to have wished myself a horse.
>
> (95)

Such an introduction serves to amuse the reader and put him in a receptive frame of mind. It is an instance of what the Greeks meant by *ethos* and the Romans by *delectare*. *Ethos*, which also implied disposing the listeners or readers favourably towards their attitude to the character of the speaker or narrator, continues clearly a few lines later when Sidney with self-deprecating modesty asks for the reader's forbearance:

> . . . if Pugliano's strong affection and weak arguments will not satisfy you, I will give you a nearer example of myself, who (I know not by what mischance) in these my not old years and idlest times having slipped into the title of a poet, am provoked to say something unto you in the defence of that my unelected vocation, which if I handle with more good will than good reasons, bear with me, since the scholar is to be pardoned that followeth the steps of his master.
>
> (95)

Then follows the *narratio*, in which Sidney states as a matter of fact how fundamental poetry, which to Sidney includes prose fiction, has been to human mental endeavour since ancient Greek times:

> . . . that which, in the noblest nations and languages that are known, hath been the first light-giver to ignorance . . . let any history be brought that can say any writers were there before them [poets like Homer and Orpheus] . . . so among the Romans were Livius Andronicus, and Ennius. So in the Italian language the first that made it aspire to be a treasure-house of science [i.e. knowledge] were the poets Dante, Boccaccio, and Petrarch. So in our English were Gower and Chaucer . . .
>
> (96)

The *propositio*, a few lines only, defines poetry as:

> an art of imitation, for so Aristotle termeth it in his word *mimesis*, that is to say, a representing, counterfeiting, or figuring forth – to speak metaphorically, a speaking picture – with this end, to teach and delight.
>
> (101)

We recognize here immediately the reference to *docere* and *delectare*, which are taken up again in the *divisio* where we see, in the short extract below, that Sidney's reason for not specifying *movere* (*pathos*) lies in his including it under *delectare*, which to Sidney and other Renaissance writers, such as Francis Bacon, implied 'rhetoric's pleasurable seduction of the Imagination from the passions to good actions' (Harrison 1968, 258). The *divisio*, as the word implies, is Sidney's classification of poetry into religious, philosophical and imitative poetry, and into the different genres such as heroic, lyric, satiric and tragic. The 'imitative' poets, i.e. the poets of *mimesis*, are to Sidney the 'right' poets since they

> most properly do imitate to teach and delight . . . and delight to move men to take that goodness in hand, which without delight they would fly as from a stranger, and teach, to make them know that goodness whereunto they are moved
>
> (102–3)

The *confirmatio* then proceeds to discuss why poetry can claim to be greater than other disciplines, such as history and philosophy. We note here the force of rhetorical argumentation, based on the classical *topics* of difference and similarity (see above p. 134). In the following extract, from this relatively long section, Sidney tells us not only what the essential difference is between a philosopher and a historian, but also the similarity between them in both having great trouble in reaching the 'goal'. The difference between these two and the poet, in close relation to what has been said, is then examined:

> The philosopher . . . and the historian are they which would win the goal, the one by precept, the other by example. But both, not having both, do both halt. For the philosopher, setting down with thorny argument the bare rule, is so hard of utterance and so misty to be conceived, that one that hath no other guide but him shall wade in him [i.e. have to perform the tedious task of ploughing through the philosopher's works] till he be old before he shall find sufficient cause to be honest [i.e. good]. For his knowledge standeth so upon the abstract and general, that happy is the man who may understand him, and more happy that can apply what he doth understand. On the other side, the historian, wanting the precept, is so tied, not to what should be but to what is, to the particular truth of things and not to the general reason of things, that his example draweth no necessary consequence, and therefore a less fruitful doctrine.
>
> Now doth the peerless poet perform both: for whatsoever the philosopher saith should be done, he giveth a perfect picture of it in some one by whom he presupposeth it was done, so as he coupleth the general notion with the particular example. A perfect picture I say, for he yieldeth to the powers of the mind an image of that whereof the philosopher bestoweth but a wordish description, which doth neither strike, pierce, nor possess the sight of the soul so much as that other doth.
>
> (106–7)

We now come to the *refutatio*, in which Sidney anticipates the charges that the 'opposition' may adduce against poetry:

> . . . because we have ears as well as tongues, and that the lightest reasons that may be will seem to weigh greatly, if nothing be put in the counterbalance, let us hear, and, as well as we can, ponder, what objections may be made against this art, which may be worthy either of yielding or answering.
>
> (120–1)

He then, in the manner of good judicial rhetoric, proceeds to enumerate four distinct charges

> Now then go we to the most important imputations laid to the poor poets. For aught I can yet learn, they are these. First, that there being many other more fruitful knowledges, a man might better spend his time in them than this. Secondly, that it is the mother of lies. Thirdly, that it is the nurse of abuse, infecting us with many pestilent desires . . . And lastly, and chiefly, they cry out with an open mouth as if they outshot Robin Hood, that Plato banished them out of his commonwealth.
>
> (123)

– and then goes on to refute them one by one. Interestingly, the *refutatio* also contains an oration, itself divided into *narratio, propositio, confirmatio, refutatio* and *conclusio*, on how the poets of his time could profitably mend their ways.

The entire work ends with a short but impassioned *conclusio* or *peroratio* in which, as in the *exordium*, Sidney once more appeals to his reader for forbearance:

> . . . I conjure you all that have had the evil luck to read this ink-wasting toy of mine, even in the name of the Nine Muses, no more to scorn the sacred mysteries of Poesy, no more to laugh at the name of poets, as though they were next inheritors to fools . . . but to believe, with Aristotle, that they were the ancient treasurers of the Grecians' divinity; to believe, with Bembus [Pietro Bembo (1470–1547), Italian Humanist], that they were the first bringers-in of all civility . . . to believe, with me, that there are many mysteries contained in Poetry, which of purpose were written darkly, lest by profane wits it should be abused . . .
>
> (141–2)

Tropes and Schemes

It would probably be counterproductive or impractical, and certainly inappropriate in a book of this size, to give a full list of the tropes and schemes known to the Renaissance writers, so there will be no attempt to compete with Peacham's listing of 184 figures, let alone Sonnino (1968), who lists over 400. Only those that seem most important or common will be included, and the order will be alphabetical for ease of reference. There is often doubt as to the pronunciation of many of the terms, so the accent I have placed above the vowel-letter of the stressed syllable of less common words, should at least provide some help. The Greek, rather than the equivalent Latin, terms will be listed since they are now used much more extensively, except when a Latin term is the normal one (e.g. *alliteration, assonance, consonance, simile*). After the explanations and illustrations, we shall discuss the literary significance of figures in longer extracts.

(T) after a figure denotes a trope, (S) a scheme.

We recall that 'trope' is the rhetorical term for a figure that involves a deviation in meaning. Thomas Wilson, in *The Arte of Rhetorique*, defined it thus: '*A Trope* is an alteration of a worde or sentence, from the proper [i.e. natural] signification, to that which is not proper.' (1909, 172). Most of the tropes, although closely related to *pathos* in their effect, have their origin in the logical distinctions made in the *topics* of *inventio* (see p. 134). For instance, *antithesis, oxymoron, paradox* and the tropes of irony (*antiphrasis* and *paralipsis*) are tropes that have issued from the *topic* of contraries and contradictions; *metaphor, simile, onomatopoeia* and *auxesis* from the *topic* of comparison; *metonymy* and *synecdoche* from the *topics* of definition or division (genus vs species, whole vs part) or from the *topic* of essence and attributes. But some tropes are less related to *logos*, more to pure *pathos* only. These include *erotema* (rhetorical question), *apostrophe, ecphonesis* and *aposiopesis*.

A scheme involves a deviation from normal word form or word order. Marked repetition of a word, part of a word, or a sound would then normally be a scheme; but if the purpose of the repetition is to bring out a *basic* change of meaning, then we shall classify the figure as a trope. Compare *ploce* and *antanaclasis*: *ploce* means the repetition of a word with the same meaning, whereas *antanaclasis* means the repetition of a word in its different senses. Thus *ploce* is best seen as a scheme; *antanaclasis* as a trope.

However, 'meaning' is a complex concept. Deviation from the norm, 'foregrounding' as it is often called nowadays, brings out an emphasis which does affect the sense also in the case of schemes; but the change of meaning brought about by tropes is conceptually stronger, more a difference of kind than of degree. It should be added that even the rhetoricians, the Romans as well as those of the Renaissance, sometimes disagreed as to whether a certain figure was a scheme or a trope. For instance, Quintilian considered *prosopopoeia* a trope (rightly, in my view), but Puttenham called it a scheme.

1 Alliteration (S): The bestknown scheme, often abused, in which the same consonant is repeated at the beginning of words (or their stressed syllable) in close proximity, such as initial [p] and [f] in the following lines from Milton's *Comus* 7–8:

Confined and pestered in this pinfold here,
Strive to keep up a frail and feverish being

or [kl] in *eclipse* and *cloud* in Donne's *The Sun Rising* 13:

I could eclipse and cloud them with a wink

2 Anadiplósis (S): A word or words at the end of a clause being repeated in the next, as in Milton's *Lycidas* 37–8:

But O the heavy change, now thou art gone,
Now thou art gone, and never must return!

3 Anáphora (S): Beginning successive clauses or sentences with the same word(s). Hoskins, referring to its occurrence in oratory or drama, pertinently remarks that 'This figure beats upon one thing to cause the quicker feeling in the audience, and to awake a sleepy or dull person' (1935, 13). Here is an example from Spenser's *Amoretti*, sonnet 26, where the *anaphora* is reinforced by *antithesis*:

Sweet is the Rose, but growes vpon a brere;
    sweet is the Iunipere, but sharpe his bough;
    sweet is the Eglantine, but pricketh nere;
    sweet is the firbloome, but his braunches rough.
Sweet is the Cypresse, but his rynd is tough,
    sweet is the nut, but bitter is his pill;
    sweet is the broome-flowre, but yet sowre enough;
    and sweet is Moly, but his root is ill.

4 Antanaclasis (T): See **Puns**

5 Anthiméria (S): Nowadays often called *conversion*, this involves one word-class used for another. This became much easier after the loss of inflectional endings at the end of the Middle English period, so that a verb also function as a noun (see chapter 2, p. 23). Milton uses *pillow* as a verb in *On the Morning of Christ's Nativity* 229:

So when the sun in bed,
Curtained with cloudy red,
    Pillows his chin upon an orient wave

and *paradise* as a verb, together with *prosthesis* (see below), in *Paradise Lost* IV.506:

> Sight hateful, sight tormenting! thus these two
> Imparadised in one another's arms

Shakespeare frequently used *anthimeria* with great skill. Coriolanus gives us an instance when he says to his mother (II.i.173–4):

> Wouldst thou have laughed had I come coffined home,
> That weep'st to see me triumph?

and Lady Macbeth another with 'unsex me here' in *Macbeth* I.v.40.

6 Antimetábole (S): Repetition of the same phrases in successive clauses but in reverse order (*abba*), as in this example from *Paradise Lost* VII.24–6:

> More safe I sing with mortal voice, unchanged
> To hoarse and mute, though fall'n on evil days,
> On evil days though fall'n, and evil tongues

When the reversal does not involve the same words, we call it a **chiásmus**, as in the last line of Shakespeare's Sonnet 154, where the subject of the first clause is not identical with the object of the second (although *love* is repeated), and the verbs are different:

> Love's fire heats water, water cools not love

7 Antiphrasis (T): See **Irony**

8 Antíthesis (S and T): At once a figure of word-arrangement (scheme) and one of conceptual contrast (trope). In *antithesis* contrasting ideas are arranged in close proximity to each other, as in *Paradise Lost* V.897:

> Among the faithless, faithful only he

This *antithesis* also contains a *polyptoton* (see below).

9 Antonomasia (T): See **Periphrasis**

10 Aposiopésis (T): Breaking off an utterance, leaving the sense incomplete. This often signals intense emotion, as when Caius Martius, recently honoured with his 'addition', is greeted by his mother:

> My gentle Martius, worthy Caius,
> And, by deed-achieving honour newly named –
> What is it? – 'Coriolanus' must I call thee?
>
> (*Coriolanus* II.i.169–71)

or when King Lear rages against Gonerill and Regan:

> I will have such revenges on you both
> That all the world shall – I will do such things –
> What they are, yet I know not
>
>   (II.ii.453–5)

11 Apostrophe (T): A sudden moving away from addressing one person or topic to addressing another (often involving *prosopopoeia*, see below), frequently in an exclamation of intense emotion. Puttenham's English term is 'turntale' or 'turnaway': 'Many times when we haue runne a long race in our tale spoken to the hearers, we do sodainly flye out & either speake or exclaime at some other person or thing, and therefore the Greekes call such figure (as we do) the turnaway or turnetale' (237).

In Kyd's *The Spanish Tragedy* Isabella's outburst at discovering that her son has been murdered apostrophizes *tears* and *sighs*:

> Then is he gone? and is my son gone too?
> O, gush out, tears, fountains and floods of tears;
> Blow, sighs, and raise an everlasting storm
>
>   (II.v.42–4)

Nowadays, although the word *apostrophe* literally means 'turning away', it is often used to denote simply an address to an abstraction without necessarily moving away from a previous topic, as in the first line of George Herbert's poem *Death*:

> Death, thou wast once an uncouth hideous thing.

When the exclamation does not involve an address, the figure is known as **ecphonésis**. An example is 'O vicious minute' in a speech, which also illustrates *aposiopesis*, by Antonio in Tourneur's *The Revenger's Tragedy* I.iv.38–40:

> When music was heard loudest, courtiers busiest,
> And ladies great with laughter – O vicious minute!
> Unfit but for relation to be spoke of

Here 'O vicious minute!' is simply elliptical for 'O what a vicious minute!'

12 Assonance (S): The recurrence in close proximity of the same vowel or similar vowels, as in Gloucester's opening speech in *Richard III* where, after harping significantly on the word *I*, he echoes the vowel (or, to be precise, diphthong) in *I* once more and in *Why . . . piping time . . . delight . . . time*:

Why, I in this weak piping time of peace
Have no delight to pass away the time

(I.i.24–5)

13 Asýndeton (S): Absence of conjunctions between several successive phrases or clauses. '. . . the words come gushing out, as it were,
set down without connecting links, and almost outstripping the speaker
himself . . . The phrases, disconnected, but none the less rapid, give
the impression of an agitation which at the same time checks the
utterance and urges it on' (Longinus, in Dorsch 1965, 129), as in
Emilia's outrage at Othello's treatment of Desdemona. Here *asyndeton* is reinforced by *anaphora*:

I will be hanged if some eternal villain,
Some busy and insinuating rogue,
Some cogging, cozening slave, to get some office,
. . .
Why should he call her whore? Who keeps her company?
What place, what time, what form, what likelihood?
The Moor's abused by some most villainous knave,
Some base, notorious knave, some scurvy fellow

(*Othello* IV.ii.134ff)

But *asyndeton* is not confined to emotional outbursts; it is often
expressive for persuasive purposes in its foregrounding of 'logical divisions'. Hoskins quotes from Sidney's *Arcadia*:

Her skull with beauty, her head with wisdom, her eyes with majesty,
her countenance with gracefulness, her lips with lovingness

and goes on to say, with his usual insight: 'This is an excellent figure
in no place untimely if not too often. It fits well the even phrases and
interpretations of an eloquent tongue that seems to be rich and wise,
and to contain many parts (whereof each with a tedious man would
make a sentence) [which] stick in the hearer's senses. Thereof I called
it smooth and memorable. It hath been in request ever since the days
of Isocrates, whose orations are full of them.' (38)

When the conjunction is missing between single words, we call the
figure **brachylógia**, as in Donne's Elegy 19, *To his Mistress Going to
Bed*, 25–6:

Licence my roving hands, and let them goe
Behind, before, above, between, below.

and when the same word is repeated thus, the term is *epizeuxis*; see
ploce below.

14 Auxésis (T): moving from less to greater importance or emotional impact in successive words, phrases or clauses. Although Shakespeare uses it frequently for a serious purpose, as in *Othello* V.ii.274–5:

> Here is my journey's end, here is my butt
> And very sea-mark of my utmost sail

and in *Macbeth* II.iii.98–9:

> The spring, the head, the fountain of your blood
> Is stopped, the very source of it is stopped

he makes fun of it towards the end of *As You Like It* V.iv.86–94, when Jaques asks Touchstone

> Can you nominate in order now the degrees of the lie?

and Touchstone answers:

> I will name you the degrees . . . The Retort Courteous . . . the Quip Modest . . . the Reply Churlish . . . the Reproof Valiant . . . the Countercheck Quarrelsome . . . the Lie with Circumstance . . . the Lie Direct.

15 Brachylogia (S): See **Asyndeton**

16 Chiasmus (S): See **Antimetabole**

17 Climax (S): the Greek word for 'ladder'; the figure mirrors the progress up a ladder, step by step. In *climax* the last word or phrase of the first clause is repeated at the beginning of the second, the last word(s) of the second at the beginning of the third, etc. *Anadiplosis* is thus really the first step in this progression, but in *climax* three or more 'rungs' must be ascended. In Act II.i.119ff of Kyd's *The Spanish Tragedy* Balthazar says, with mounting intensity, of his 'destin'd plague' Horatio:

> First, in his hand he brandished a sword,
> And with that sword he fiercely waged war, .
> And in that war he gave me dangerous wounds,
> And by those wounds he forced me to yield,
> And by my yielding I became his slave.

Volpone, in his best mountebank manner, tries to impress Celia by using *climax*:

> Here is a powder, concealed in this paper, of which, if I should speak to the worth, nine thousand volumes were but as one page, that page as a line, that line as a word . . . Would I reflect on the price? Why, the

whole world were but as an empire, that empire as a province, that province as a bank, that bank as a private purse, to the purchase of it.

(*Volpone* II.ii.210ff)

18 Collatio (T): See **Simile**

19 Consonance (S): Repeating the same consonants or same type of consonants in words in close proximity. *Consonance* differs from *alliteration* in that the consonants do not necessarily begin the word. In the following example, where Lady Macbeth fiercely invokes the aid of the 'sightless substances', there is a marked use of the voiceless plosives, i.e. [p], [t] and [k], which, in spite of being articulated with greater energy than other consonants, have no sonority. Excessive use of such consonants hits the ear as harsh, explosive, spitting noise. Together with the abrupt caesura (a midline pause), they impede the harmonious flow of the verse and mirror Lady Macbeth's wish itself ('Stop up th' access and passage to remorse'). Note that *keen knife* probably alliterate since educated speech around 1600 still preserved *k*- in *kn*- (see chapter 1, pp. 9–10) though Shakespeare also has puns like *knight:night* (Kökeritz 1953, 305).

> Come, you spirits
> That tend on mortal thoughts, unsex me here,
> And fill me from the crown to the toe top-full
> Of direst cruelty. Make thick my blood,
> Stop up th'access and passage to remorse,
> That no compunctious visitings of nature
> Shake my fell purpose, nor keep peace between
> Th'effect and it. Come to my woman's breasts,
> And take my milk for gall, you murd'ring ministers,
> Wherever in your sightless substances
> You wait on nature's mischief. Come, thick night,
> and pall thee in the dunnest smoke of hell,
> that my keen knife see not the wound it makes,
> Nor heaven peep through the blanket of the dark
> To cry 'Hold, hold!

(III.v.39ff)

20 Ecphonesis (T): See **Apostrophe**

21 Epanalépsis (S): Repeating a word or words at the beginning and end of a clause, as in *Lycidas* 165:

Weep no more, woeful shepherds, weep no more

recalling a similar *epanalepsis* in the first line of the poem:

Yet once more, O ye laurels, and once more

22 Epanorthósis (S or T): In this figure the speaker, normally in an intensely emotional state, immediately corrects himself, like Tamburlaine:

> Ah, fair Zenocrate! divine Zenocrate!
> Fair is too foul an epithet for thee
>
> (1 Tamburlaine V.ii.72–3)

The vacillation I have shown in calling the figure 'S or T' is due to the relative emphasis one places on meaning *versus* parallelism of structure. In the example above the correction appears in an identical structure, as it often does in *epanorthosis*, and *fair* is repeated. This is scheme-like; so is the structural parallelism and repetition of the *epanorthosis* 'O eyes, no eyes' in the speech, from *The Spanish Tragedy*, analysed on pp. 182–3. But the self-correction is often expressed hyperbolically: 'O eyes, no eyes' is followed by 'but fountains fraught with tears', and a *hyperbole* (see below) is a trope. Cicero and Puttenham both classified *epanorthosis* as a scheme (Sonnino 1968, 65), whereas Hoskins (who calls it *correctio*) by listing it between *hyperbole* and *irony* evidently considers it a trope (29–30); and Miriam Joseph, by placing it under *topics* of *inventio*, also implies its trope-like character (1947, 153).

23 Epístrophe (S): Repeating the same word(s) at the end of successive clauses, as in Lyly's *Euphues: the Anatomy of Wit* 304:

> Who absolued *Mary Magdalene* from hir sinnes but Christ? Who forgaue the theefe his robbery and manslaughter but Christ? Who made *Mathew* the Publycane and tollgatherer, an Apostle and Preacher but Christ? Who is that good shepehearde that fetcheth home the straye sheepe so louingly vppon his shoulders but Christ?

24 Epizéúxis (S): See **Ploce**

25 Erótema (T): This is simply what is generally known as a rhetorical question, i.e. a question that is asked not in order to receive an answer but in order to assert something emotionally or persuasively, as in Lyly's example under *epistrophe* above or when Hieronimo exclaims:

> O heavens, why made you night to cover sin?
>
> (The Spanish Tragedy II.v.24).

Hendíadys (S): Expressing a single complex idea by two words connected by a conjunction or preposition; often two nouns thus connected instead of an adjective-noun construction, as when Giacomo says in *Cymbeline* V.ii.1:

> The heaviness and guilt within my bosom

for 'heavy guilt'.

or when Manoa, in *Samson Agonistes* 1733–5, expresses his wish to honour Samson's memory:

> there will I build him
> A monument, and plant it round with shade
> Of laurel . . .

for 'shady laurel': it is impossible literally to plant a shade. An example of the opposite process of this, i.e. a striking adjective + noun construction replacing what would normally be expressed by two nouns connected by a preposition or conjunction, appears later in the same work (574): *servile food* 'food for servants or slaves'. We shall call this *reverse hendiadys*. A *reverse hendiadys* comes close to the form of *hypallage* that is often called *transferred epithet*, but the latter is conceptually bolder in its looser semantic association of adjective with noun; see *hypallage* below.

26 Hirmus (S): See **Hyperbaton**

27 Homoeosis (T): See **Simile**

28 Homoioteléúton (S): Repeating the same ending on different words, as *nurture . . . Nature* and *pernicious . . . precious* in:

> an olde Gentleman in *Naples* . . . beganne to bewayle hys nurture: and to muse at hys Nature, beeinge incensed agaynste the one as moste pernicious, and enflamed wyth the other as moste precious
> (*Euphues: The Anatomy of Wit* 186)

Thus *homoioteleuton* is morphologically the opposite of *polyptoton* (see below).

29 Hypállage (S or T): Constructing clauses or phrases in such a way that the application of the words becomes absurd. Puttenham: 'A certain piteous louer, to moue his mistres to compassion, wrote among other amorous verses, this one *Madame, I set your eyes before mine woes*. For, mine woes before your eyes' (172). Bottom, in *A Midsummer Night's Dream*, gets hopelessly confused when he has to act in the play the mechanicals put on:

> I see a voice. Now will I to the chink
> To spy an I can hear my Thisbe's face

> (V.i.191–2)

The *transferred epithet*, which consists in using an adjective with a noun to which it does not literally apply, is also a *hypallage*, although the 'misapplication' does not result in absurdity but rather reinforces through compression, as in *turbulent liquor* in:

> I drank, from the clear milky juice allaying
> Thirst, and refreshed; nor envied them the grape
> Whose heads that turbulent liquor fills with fumes
>
> (*Samson Agonistes* 550–2)

The liquor itself is not turbulent; it causes turbulence (intoxication).

When *hypallage* simply refers to a disarrangement of the words, as in Bottom's case, it seems best to regard it as a scheme; but when it works as a *transferred epithet*, the deviance is more conceptual and the figure more of a trope than a scheme.

30 Hypérbaton (S): Marked deviance in word order, as in Spenser's:

> Dye would we dayly
>
> (*The Shepheardes Calender*, 'November' 186)

In the opening of *Paradise Lost*, Milton delays the verb *sing* and starts with a prepositional phrase which in non-deviant language would follow the verb. This *hyperbaton* foregrounds both what he wants the muse to sing about, i.e. the central topic of the epic, and *sing* itself:

> Of Man's first disobedience, and the fruit
> Of that forbidden tree, whose mortal taste
> Brought death into the world, and all our woe,
> With loss of Eden, till one greater Man
> Restore us, and regain the blissful seat,
> Sing, heav'nly Muse . . .

This particular form of *hyperbaton*, so characteristic of Milton in his periodic sentences, is sometimes called *hirmus* or *irmos*, which Puttenham defined as 'a maner of speach drawen out at length and going all after one tenure [tenor] and with an imperfit [imperfect] sense till you come to the last word or verse which concludes the whole premisses with a perfit sence' (176).

31 Hypérbole (T): Exaggeration for heightened effect. Hoskins, with his customary perspicuity, remarks of this figure: 'Sometimes it expresseth a thing in the highest degree of possibility, beyond the truth, that it descending thence may find the truth; sometimes in flat impossibility, that rather you may conceive the unspeakableness than the untruth of the relation' (29). Mistress Frankford, in Heywood's *A Woman Killed With Kindness*, exclaims:

In this one life I die ten thousand deaths

(IV.v.127)

and Isabella, in *The Spanish Tragedy*, II.v.43–4, gives vent to her grief after the loss of her son:

O, gush out, tears, fountains and floods of tears;
Blow, sighs, and raise an everlasting storm

The opposite of *hyperbole* is *meiosis* and *litotes*; see below.

32 Irmos = Hirmus (S): See **Hyperbaton**

33 Irony (T): The two central figures of irony in Renaissance rhetoric are *antiphrasis* and *paralipsis*.

Antiphrasis consists in using a word, clause or sentence in a sense opposite to what it would normally imply, as in Puttenham's example (1936, 191): 'when we deride by plaine and flat contradiction, as he that saw a dwarfe go in the streete said to his companion that walked with him: See yonder gyant'. When in drama a character's utterance has implications contrary to those understood by the speaker or listener, we call this *dramatic irony*, as when Lady Macbeth says to her husband:

A little water clears us of this deed

(*Macbeth* II.ii.65)

which contrasts cruelly with her later words in the Sleepwalking Scene: 'All the perfumes of Arabia will not sweeten this little hand' (V.i.48–9).

In **paralipsis** the speaker pretends to regard something significant as insignificant by passing lightly over it, thereby cleverly drawing attention to it. In *Othello* Iago uses *paralipsis* very effectively when he slowly rouses the Moor's suspicion:

IAGO: Ha! I like not that.
OTHELLO: What dost thou say?
IAGO: Nothing, my lord

(III.iii.33–5)

and a little later (96–100):

IAGO: Did Michael Cassio, when you wooed my lady,
    Know of your love?
OTHELLO: He did, from the first to last. Why dost thou ask?
IAGO: But for a satisfaction of my thought,
    No further harm

In *Julius Caesar* Mark Antony, in his great speech to his 'Friends, Romans, countrymen', shows his command of persuasive oratory by highly effective use of both *antiphrasis* and *paralipsis*:

> I come to bury Caesar, not to praise him.
> The evil that men do lives after them;
> The good is oft interred with their bones.
> So let it be with Caesar. The noble Brutus
> Hath told you Caesar was ambitious.
> If it were so, it was a grievous fault,
> And grievously hath Caesar answered it.
> Here, under leave of Brutus and the rest –
> For Brutus is an honourable man,
> So are they all, all honourable men –
> Come I to speak in Caesar's funeral.
> He was my friend, faithful and just to me.
> But Brutus says he was ambitious,
> And Brutus is an honourable man.
> He hath brought many captives home to Rome,
> Whose ransoms did the general coffers fill.
> Did this in Caesar seem ambitious?
> When that the poor have cried, Caesar hath wept.
> Ambition should be made of sterner stuff.
> Yet Brutus is an honourable man.
> . . .

(III.ii.75ff)

Mark Antony begins with a *paralipsis*: 'I come to bury Caesar, not to praise him . . . So let it be with Caesar', which anticipates another a little later when he refers to Caesar's generous will 'Which, pardon me, I do not mean to read' (132), developed further in 'Have patience, gentle friends, I must not read it. / It is not meet you know how Caesar loved you . . . 'Tis good to know not that you are his heirs' (141–2, 146).

The *antiphrasis* is in the repetition of 'Brutus is an honourable man', which the first time round appears so genuine, seemingly reinforcing 'noble Brutus' in the fifth line but *via* the later context turning out to be scathingly ironic.

34 Isocolon (S): See **Parison**

35 Litótes (T): One of two important tropes of understatement, the other being **meiósis**. *Litotes* tends to be emotionally positive, *meiosis* negative. *Meiosis* belittles; *litotes* heightens by understatement, as when we say colloquially 'this ain't half bad' for 'this is excellent'. Puttenham's example of *litotes* is 'I know you hate me not, nor wish me any ill,' on which he comments: 'Meaning in deede that he loued him very well and dearely, and yet the words doe not expresse so much, though they purport so much' (184). He continues: 'But if you diminish and abbase a thing by way of spight or mallice, as it were to depraue it, such speach is by the figure *Meiosis* or the *disabler*' and gives an example: 'A great mountain as bigge as a molehill' (185). Hamlet belittles himself in a famous *meiosis* in the nunnery speech:

> What should such fellows as I do crawling between heaven and earth?
> (III.i.129–31)

36 Meiosis (T): See **Litotes**

37 Metaphor (T): The bestknown trope of all. It expresses something in terms of something else that has something in common with it, as when Arden says in *Arden of Feversham* III.v.15–6:

> I climb'd the top bough of the tree
> And sought to build my nest among the clouds

The *metaphor* is different from the *simile* in that the former is an implicit comparison, the latter an explicit one with the grammatical word of comparison, such as *like* or *as*, expressed; see *simile* below.

38 Metónymy (T): Replacing a word with another closely associated with it, as when Prospero says to Ariel:

> Bravely, my diligence! Thou shalt be free
>
> (*The Tempest* V.v.244)

Because of the close association, *metonymy* is not generally as bold or imaginatively vivid as the *metaphor* although it can be very effective as we shall see later in a discussion of *Antony and Cleopatra* V.ii.76ff (pp. 184–6).

    Synécdoche is very similar, involving the replacing of the whole or the general with the part or the particular, or vice versa, as in *many hands make light work* (part for the whole) or when King John says in Shakespeare's play of the same name:

> So foul a sky clears not without a storm;
> Pour down thy weather
>
> (IV.ii.108–9)

where *weather* is the whole or general used for the particular *rain*.

39 Onomatopoeia: A wellknown sound-trope, using words whose sounds mirror natural sounds or suggest or reinforce the meaning, as in King Lear's oft-quoted outburst at the start of Act III.ii.:

Blow, winds, and crack your cheeks! Rage, blow,
You cataracts and hurricanoes, spout
. . .
                            all-shaking thunder,
Strike flat the thick rotundity o'th' world,
Crack nature's moulds, all germens spill at once
That makes ingrateful man

where the assonance of *crack* (twice) and *cataracts* and the harsh energy of the plosive consonants [k] and [t] in much of the passage are particularly echoic or suggestive.

40 Oxymóron (T): A contradictory expression, such as the last two words in Romeo's famous

Parting is such sweet sorrow
                            (*Romeo and Juliet* II.i.229)

and 'A heav'n on earth' (*Paradise Lost* IV.208). When the contradiction is in a statement rather than an expression, we call it a **paradox**:

Black is the beauty of the brightest day
                            (*2Tamburlaine* II.iv.1)

When my love swears that she is made of truth
I do believe her though I know she lies
                            (Shakespeare, Sonnet 138)

Oxymoron is a figure 'to stir admiration in the hearer and make them think it a strange harmony which must be expressed in such discords' (Hoskins, under the equivalent term *synoeciosis* (36)).

41 Paradox (T): See **Oxymoron**

42 Paralipsis (T): See **Irony**

43 Párison (S): Repeating the same grammatical construction in successive clauses or sentences. If these are of identical length, the figure is sometimes called **isocólon**. *Parison* and *isocolon* were not distinguished by the Renaissance rhetoricians, who normally referred to both by the Latin term *compar*; nor are they distinguished in modern times by e.g. Lausberg (1967, 110). In this book *parison* will be used to cover both terms. John Lyly was particularly fond of this scheme. Here are two examples from his *Euphues: The Anatomy of Wit*:

Alexander valiaunt in warre, yet gyuen to wine. *Tullie* eloquent in his gloses, yet vayneglorious: *Salomon wyse*, yet to[o] too wanton: *Dauid* holye but yet an homicide
                            (184)

Here the sentence-structures are the same: proper noun followed by two complements connected by *yet* and modifying the proper noun without a copula (*is*) intervening. In the first two sentences there is further parallelism in the prepositional phrase modifying the first complement (*in warre*/*in his gloses*).

The second example, which also illustrates *collatio* (see under *simile* below), has two clauses of exactly the same length, i.e. containing the same number of syllables (ignoring the clause-transitional *for*):

> for by howe much the more I am a straunger to you, by so much the more you are beholdinge to mee
>
> (187)

44 Paronomasia (T): See **Puns**

45 Períphrasis (T): Either (1) a way of describing something that would normally be said more briefly, or (2) using a proper noun for the typical quality or attribute associated with it. In sense (2) the figure is sometimes called **antonomásia**. Longinus appositely compares this figure, in the first sense, to its musical counterpart: 'No one, I think, would dispute that periphrasis contributes to the sublime. For as in music the sweetness of the dominant melody is enhanced by what are known as the decorative additions, so periphrasis often harmonizes with the direct expression of a thought and greatly embellishes it, especially if it is not too bombastic or inelegant, but pleasantly tempered' (Dorsch 1965, 137). A fine example of this sense of *periphrasis* occurs in *Macbeth* II.iii.66–7, when Macduff exclaims after the murder of King Duncan:

> Most sacrilegious murder hath broke ope
> The Lord's anointed temple

Temple means 'body' and recalls Paul's second letter to the Corinthians, 6:16, in the Bible: 'ye are the temple of the living God'. Macduff's *periphrasis* points eloquently to the horror of killing a man crowned king by divine right.

Two further famous instances of this figure (again in the first sense) are provided by *Doctor Faustus* V.i.97–8:

> Was this the face that launched a thousand ships, [i.e. Helen of Troy]
> And burnt the topless towers of Ilium? [i.e. Troy]

Shylock gives us an example of the second sense:

A Daniel come to judgement, yea, a Daniel!

(*Merchant of Venice* IV.i.220)

46 Personification: See **Prosopopoeia**

47 Ploce or **Ploche** (S): The occurrence of the same word(s) in a passage, mirroring the often dispairing or desperate mental focussing on an issue, notion or concept, as when Satan in *Paradise Lost* bewails his new-found state:

Me miserable! which way shall I fly
Infinite wrath, and infinite despair?
Which way I fly is hell; myself am hell;
And in the lowest deep a lower deep
Still threat'ning to devour me opens wide,
To which the hell I suffer seems a heav'n

(IV.73ff)

or Othello takes up the last word of Desdemona's preceding line ('Alas, what ignorant sin have I committed?') in IV.ii.73ff, where the first two instances of *committed* also form a urgent *anadiplosis*:

Was this fair paper, this most goodly book,
Made to write 'whore' upon? What committed?
Committed? O thou public commoner,
I should make very forges of my cheeks,
That would to cinders burn up modesty,
Did I but speak thy deeds. What committed?
Heaven stops the nose at it, and the moon winks;
The bawdy wind, that kisses all it meets,
Is hushed within the hollow mine of earth
And will not hear't. What committed?

When the word is repeated immediately, i.e. without any other word(s) intervening, the figure is called **epizéúxis**. This often signals extreme emotion, as when the blind Samson exclaims:

O dark, dark, dark, amid the blaze of noon

(*Samson Agonistes* 80)

48 Polýptoton or **Polyptóton** (S): Repeating the same word-base with different affixes, as in *human* / *inhuman* / *humanity* or when Mosbie in *Arden of Feversham* wistfully recalls the days before ambition ensnared him:

My golden time was when I had no gold

(III.v.11)

Another example, from *Paradise Lost* V.897:

Among the faithless, faithful only he

and one from *Othello* V.ii.368–9:

> I kissed thee ere I killed thee. No way but this:
> Killing myself, to die upon a kiss

49 Polysýndeton (S): Making use of an unusually large number of conjunctions; thus the opposite of *asyndeton* but can be just as striking in its cumulative effect:

> Thus with the year
> Seasons return; but not to me returns
> Day, or the sweet approach of ev'n or morn,
> Or sight of vernal bloom, or summer's rose,
> Or flocks, or herds, or human face divine
>
> > (*Paradise Lost* III.40ff)

50 Prosopopóéia or **Personification** (T): Investing the inanimate with human attributes, as in the case of *dew* in George Herbert's poem *Vertue*:

> Sweet day, so cool, so calm, so bright,
> The bridall of the earth and skie:
> The dew shall weep thy fall to night;
> > For thou must die.

51 Puns (T): In Classical and Renaissance rhetoric three important punning tropes were distinguished: *antanaclasis*, *paronomasia* and *syllepsis*.

In **antanáclasis** a word is repeated in two different senses. Peacham's example (also quoted in Sonnino 1968, 194) is 'in thy youth learne some crafte, that in thy age thou maiest get thy liuing without craft', where the first instance of *craft* means 'skill', the second 'cunning' or 'fraud'. Other examples are:

> Annihilating all that's made
> To a green Thought in a green Shade
>
> > (Marvell, *The Garden* 46–7)

and John of Gaunt in *Richard II* II.i.74 and 82:

> Old Gaunt indeed, and gaunt in being old / . . . / Gaunt am I for the grave, gaunt as a grave

eliciting from Richard: 'Can sick men play so nicely [subtly] with their names?' Well, nobody is better at that than Richard himself. In the great deposition scene, he uses a powerful *antanaclasis* on *care* (1) 'sorrow' or 'deep worry' and (2) 'responsibility, charge'. After Boling-broke curtly tells him that 'Part of your cares ['griefs, sorrows'] you give me with your crown', Richard replies ([1] = the first sense, [2] = the second):

> Your cares [2] set up do not pluck my cares [1] down.
> My care [1] is loss of care [2] by old care [2] done;
> Your care [1] is gain of care [1, 2] by new care won [2].
> The cares [1, 2] I give I have, though given away;
> They 'tend the crown, yet still with me they stay.
>
> (IV.i.185ff)

The paradox in the fourth line is effected by the two meanings inherent at the same time (*syllepsis*).

Paronomásia is a play on words that sound identical (homophones) or similar but have different meanings, as in this exchange between Prince Harry and Sir John Falstaff in *1Henry IV* II.v.439ff:

> SIR JOHN: . . . hang me up by the heels for a rabbit sucker, or a poulter's hare.
> PRINCE HARRY: Well, here I am set.
> SIR JOHN: And here I stand.

This *paronomasia* is not only in *hare* and *here* but also in *here* and *heir* in the Prince's line. He has just seated himself on the makeshift throne from which he has 'deposed' Falstaff during their pranks in the Boar's Head. Compare Falstaff saying to the Prince in I.ii.64–5: '. . . were it not here apparent that thou art heir apparent'.

Syllépsis denotes a pun similar to *antanaclasis*, but whereas the latter involves repetition of a word, *syllepsis* is more subtle since there the word occurs only once with both meanings at the same time, as in the flippant *her skirt was as tight as a flippin' money-lender*. When used seriously, it can have a profoundly evocative effect: Romeo, having just heard that Juliet lies dead in 'her kindred's vault', resolves to commit suicide and die next to her. His use of *lie* also recalls their former embraces:

> Well, Juliet, I will lie with thee tonight
>
> (*Romeo and Juliet* V.i.34)

Unfortunately the term *syllepsis* is also used for a scheme akin to *zeugma* (see below).

52 Rhetorical Question: see **Erotema**

53 Símile or **Homoeósis** (T): A figure of similitude, less bold than the metaphor because of the explicit word of comparison, typically *like* or *as*. Milton gives us a magnificent simile, one of many, in *Paradise Lost*

I.620, when he says of Satan who has just been hurled out of heaven:

> Tears such as angels weep burst forth

The Elizabethans, and in particular John Lyly, were fond of the simile that makes up balanced and often lengthy clauses in the shape *as X is/does, so Y is/does*. This kind of simile was known as **collatio**. Puttenham, although he does not use the term *collatio*, gives several examples, the first of which is 'But as the watrie showres delay the raging wind, / So doeth good hope cleane put away dispaire out of my mind' (241).

54 Syllepsis (T and S): See **Puns** and **Zeugma**

55 Synecdoche (T): See **Metonymy**

56 Transferred Epithet (T): See **Hypallage**

57 Zeugma (S or T): A verb-object construction in which a single verb is grammatically related to two or more objects across two clauses, as *lend* in *Romeo and Juliet* II. Prologue, 13:

> But passion lends them power, time means, to meet

Here the figure is a scheme; but the way the term is frequently employed today involves a change in sense as we move from the first to the second object, as in Pope's witty use of *take* incongruously governing both *counsel* and *tea*: 'Here thou, great Anna! whom three realms obey, / Dost sometimes counsel take – and sometimes tea' (*Rape of the Lock* III.7–8). There the figure is trope-like because of the clear conceptual leap.

Syllépsis is sometimes used for a scheme similar to *zeugma* but where the verb form is grammatically, though not semantically, incongruent with one of the objects, as in Brabantio's warning to Othello, in which the past tense does not go with *may*:

> She has deceived her father, and may thee

> (*Othello* I.iii.293)

To add to the confusion, some writers, e.g. Corbett (1990, 448), define *zeugma* the way we have just defined grammatical *syllepsis* and *vice versa*.

Rhetorical Analysis of Some Passages

This section does not pretend to be a chronological survey of how rhetoric developed during the years of the English Renaissance. But some references will be made to the development of certain patterns and different tastes in different periods.

For explanation of the rhetorical terms that will be employed extensively in the comments on the passages, the reader should refer to the preceding section.

The first clear sign of the new post-medieval poetry, incorporating the rhetorical teaching and example of the Humanists, is seen in the works of Sir Thomas Wyatt (1503?-1542) and Henry Howard, the Earl of Surrey (1517?-1547). Poems of theirs appeared posthumously in 1557 in a famous collection by Richard Tottel, entitled *Songes and Sonettes* and now normally referred to as *Tottel's Miscellany*. Puttenham's evaluation of these important pioneers is pertinent:

> In the latter end of the same kings [Henry VIII's] raigne sprong vp a new company of courtly makers, of whom Sir *Thomas Wyat* th'elder & *Henry* Earle of Surrey were the two chieftaines, who hauing trauailed into Italie, and there tasted the sweete and stately measures and stile of the Italian Poesie as nouices newly crept out of the schooles of *Dante* [,] *Arioste* [Ariosto] and *Petrarch*, they greatly pollished our rude [crude] & homely maner of vulgar [vernacular] Poesie, from that it had bene before, and for that cause may iustly be sayd the first reformers of our English meetre and stile . . . *Henry* Earle of Surrey and Sir *Thomas Wyat*, betweene whom I finde very little difference, I repute them (as before) for the two chief lanternes of light to all others that haue since employed their pennes vpon English Poesie, their conceits [concepts] were loftie, their stiles stately, their conueyance [forms of expression] cleanely, their termes proper, their meetre sweete and well proportioned, in all imitating very naturally and studiously their Maister *Francis Petrarcha*.
>
> (60, 62)

Besides the great Italian Francis Petrarch or Francesco Petrarca (1304–1374), the Classical Roman poet Virgil (70–19 BC) exercised considerable influence, for instance through his eclogues, i.e. pastoral poems in which the purpose is 'not . . . to counterfait or represent the rusticall manner of loues and communication: but vnder the vaile of homely persons . . . to insinuate and glaunce at greater matters' (Puttenham, 38). These influenced not only Petrarch and other Italian writers of the Renaissance, but also Spenser in his *Shepheardes Calender*. Appended to each eclogue of this work is a commentary by E.K. (see p. 21), which often contains elucidation and praise of rhetorical figures. Here are two stanzas (8 and 11) from the month of January:

> Thou feeble flocke, whose fleece is rough and rent,
> Whose knees are weake through fast and euill fare:
> Mayst witnesse well by thy ill gouernement,
> Thy maysters mind is ouercome with care.

5 Thou weake, I wanne: thou leane, I quite forlorne:
   With mourning pyne I, you with pyning mourne.

I loue thilke lasse, (alas why doe I loue?)
And am forlorne, (alas why am I lorne?)
Shee deignes not my good will, but doth reproue,
10 And of my rurall musick holdeth scorne.
Shepheards deuise she hateth as the snake,
And laughes the songes, that *Colin Clout* doth make.

We note extensive use of phonological schemes such as alliteration in lines 1–2, 4–8 and assonance in 1–2 in *feeble / fleece / knees* with [i:] and in line 5: *weake / leane with* [e:], foregrounding the semantic parallelism.

Spenser uses periphrasis in e.g. *feeble flocke* (1) and *rurall musick* (10), the kind that was later to become a mannerism in eighteenth-century poetic diction. Parison appears in e.g. lines 5, 7–8. Line 6 has a neat antimetabole. Lines 7–8 contain, besides alliteration and parison, a ploce that comes close to epanalepsis and highlights the lover's distress. E.K.'s comment on these two lines includes yet another two figures: 'a prety Epanorthosis in these two verses, and withall a Paronomasia or playing with the word', the paronomasia being of course *lasse / alas*, which eloquently stresses the lover's plight.

'The half-decade of *The Shepherd's Calendar* was decisive. It brought the writings of Sidney and a new generation of poets at Court' (Salingar 1955, 52). The model of Petrarch can be seen no more clearly than in Sidney's love-sonnet sequence *Astrophel and Stella*, written in the early 1580s but not published until after Sidney's death in 1586. The sonnets below are quoted from the first publication of 1591. This work may or may not be autobiographical: Stella may be Penelope Devereux, daughter of the first earl of Essex, but the evidence is inconclusive. The sonnet was a thirteenth-century Italian invention, refined by Petrarch, of whose sonnets *Astrophel and Stella* is a close imitation. Here are sonnets 6, 7 and 12:

Some Lovers speake, when they their Muses entertaine
Of hopes begott, by feare, of wot not what desires,
Of force of heavenly beames, infusing hellish paine;
Of lyving deathes deere woundes, faire storms and flashing fyres.
5   Some one his songes in *Jove* and *Joves* straunge tales attyres,
Bordered with Bulles and Swannes, poudered with golden raine:
An other humbler witte to shepheards pipe retyres,
Yet hiding royall blood, full oft in Rurall vaine.
     To some a sweetest plaint a sweetest stile affordes,
10   Whiles teares poure out his inke, and sighes breath out his wordes.
His paper pale despaire, and paine his penne doth move.
     I can speake what I feele, and feele as much as they,

But thinke that all the mappe of my state, I display.
When trembling voice bringes forth, that I do *Stella* love.

15 When nature made her chiefe worke, *Stellas* eyes,
In collour blacke, why wrapt she beames so bright?
Would she in beamy blacke like Painter wise,
Frame daintiest lustre mixte with shaddowes light?
    Or did she els that sober hewe devise,
20 In object best, to strength and knitt our sight:
Least if no vaile these brave beames did disguise,
They Sun-like would more dazell than delight.
    Or would she her miraculous power shewe,
That whereas blacke seemes Beauties contrarie,
25 Shee even in blacke doth make all Beauties flowe:
But so and thus, she minding Love should bee
    Plaste ever there, gave him this mourning weede:
    To honour all their deathes, who for her bleede.

Cupid because thou shin'st in *Stellas* eyes,
30 That from her lookes thy dimnesse nowe scapes free:
That those lips swelde so full of thee they be.
That sweet breath maketh oft the flames to rise,
That in her brest thy pap well sugred lyes,
    That grace even makes thy gracious wrongs; that she,
35   What word so ere shee speakes, perswades for thee:
That her cleere voice, lifteth the Sunne to Skyes.
    Thou countest *Stella* thine, like those whose powres
Having got up a breach, (by fighting well)
Cry victory, this happy day is ours:
40 Oh no, her heart is such a Cytadell.
    So fortified with wit, stor'd with disdaine:
    That to winne it, is all the skill and paine.

The punctuation is Elizabethan, but the only marks likely to confuse
a modern reader are four full stops where we would now use a comma:
in lines 10, 13, 31, 36 ('Thou countest Stella thine' is the main clause
on which 'because thou shin'st in Stellas eyes' (29) is dependent) and
40.

These sonnets are densely patterned with rhetoric. Anaphora in lines
2–4, 30–36 is conducive to the cumulative effect of the clauses in which
it occurs, and alliteration is used with considerable skill, reinforcing,
for instance, the two instances of oxymoron in 4 (*lyving deathes, deere
woundes*) and one in 17 (*beamy blacke*), anticipated by the antithesis
in 16. The syntactic scheme of parison in 10 develops into another
syntactic scheme in the next line, viz. zeugma, in which *His paper*
and *penne* are both objects of *doth move*. The ellipsis of the zeugma
concentrates powerfully the alliterative force of the line; but it also
serves an even more subtle purpose: *pale* may qualify *paper* or it may
qualify *despaire*, and the line is the richer for the ambiguity.

The trope syllepsis (a word used once but in at least two senses) was considered particularly elegant by the Elizabethans, and there are two fine instances here: *vaine* (8) in the literal sense of 'vein' first supports *blood* in the same line but is also to be understood figuratively in the sense of 'direction' or 'manner', supporting the general tenor of that sonnet, viz. various ways of writing poetry.

The other syllepsis is *light* in 18: the absence of an apostrophe (normal in the sixteenth century) makes *shaddowes* ambiguous; it can be *shadows* (plural), in which case *light* is its modifying adjective. This can mean either 'luminous' or 'delicate'. If it means 'luminous', it creates, together with its noun, a felicitous oxymoron lending express-ive weight to the contrast in *black* and *beauty* made more than once in that sonnet. If it means 'delicate', it is supported equally firmly by *daintiest* (*dainty* means 'delicate'). But *shaddowes* can also be a possessive (*shadow's* or *shadows'*), in which case it modifies *light*, now a noun. Both together would then, once again, constitute an appropriate oxymoron. It would be in the vein, and very much to the taste, of the Elizabethan poet to play, but to play significantly, with syntax and tropes in this manner. The ambiguity of *shaddowes* is destroyed as soon as an editor decides to use modern punctuation.

Allusions to classical mythology were frequent. Here they appear in periphrasis of Jove or Jupiter (Zeus to the Greeks) in line 6: Zeus abducted Europa in the shape of a white bull and mated with Leda after changing into a swan, and with Danae disguised as a shower of gold. The three periphrases are then metaphorically imagined as embroidery in 'straunge tales'.

The prosopopoeia of *nature* as *she* and that of *love* as *he*, common enough to be sure, are developed in the second and third sonnet. Almost the opposite or reverse figure of this appears with considerable elegance in the metonymy of *powres* for 'armed men' or 'soldiers' in 37, and the third sonnet culminates in an emotionally powerful epanorthosis (40–2) which, together with the rhetorical language else-where, mirrors the dazzled delight and emotional intensity of the lover.

The poetry of the 1590s slowly began, under the influence of the great dramas that had begun, or were shortly, to be written, to develop into language of terser expression: the kind of language that owed more to Seneca than Cicero. The more extravagant periphrases, often loosely structured metaphors and similes couched in long sentences in long poems (cp Marlowe in drama) began to give way to briefer stanzas or sinewy, more closely woven poetry, in which the language became more colloquial (cp Ben Jonson in drama). Sidney's sighing lover:

> I might, unhappy word, (woe me) I might,
> And then would not, nor could not see my blisse:
> Tyll now, wrapt in a most infernall Night,

I finde, how heavenly day (wretch) did I misse:
Hart rent thy selfe, thou doost thy self but right.
  No lovely *Paris* made thy *Helen* his,
  No force, no fraude, robd thee of thy delight,
No Fortune of thy fortune Author is;
But to my selfe, my selfe did give the blow . . .

                                        (*Astrophel and Stella*, sonnet 33)

gives way to Donne's:

For Godsake hold your tongue, and let me love,
  Or chide my palsie, or my gout,
My five gray haires, or ruin'd fortune flout,
  With wealth your state, your minde with Arts improve,
    Take you a course, get you a place,
    Observe his honour, or his grace,
Or the Kings reall, or his stamped face
Contemplate; what you will, approve
  So you will let me love.

                                        (*The Canonization*)

This development resulted in what we call 'metaphysical' poetry, first termed thus by Samuel Johnson in the eighteenth century. The deliberate and pervasive use of parallelism, of schemes, is much less prominent in metaphysical poetry; it is there, as it is in poetry of today, but it is no longer central to the creation of *pathos*. Tropes become more important, especially in the form of often intellectually demanding metaphors or similes, which we call 'conceits'. Donne's comparisons of two lovers' union to the mingling of sucked blood in a flea (in *The Flea*) and union in absence to a pair of compasses, (in *A Valediction: Forbidding Mourning*) are wellknown. The conceits were used less as decoration or ornament (however conducive to emotional arousal) in the manner of much Elizabethan poetry. They were more intrinsic to the meaning of the poem; were, indeed, sometimes the whole poem, as in Andrew Marvell's *The Coronet* or in the following poem *Discipline* by George Herbert, which is essentially one extended trope in which God is metaphorically seen as a strict teacher:

1 Throw away thy rod,
  Throw away thy wrath:
    O my God,
  Take the gentle path.

2 For my hearts desire
  Unto thine is bent:
    I aspire
  To a full consent.

5 Then let wrath remove,
  Love will do the deed:
    For with love
  Stonie hearts will bleed.

6 Love is swift of foot;
  Love's a man of warre,
    And can shoot,
  And can hit from farre.

3 Not a word or look
   I affect to own,
     But by book,
   And thy book alone.

4 Though I fail, I weep:
   Though I halt in pace,
     Yet I creep
   To the throne of grace.

7 Who can scape his bow?
   That which wrought on thee,
     Brought thee low,
   Needs must work on me.

8 Throw away thy rod;
   Though man frailties hath,
     Thou art God:
   Throw away thy wrath.

Schemes are, of course, still in evidence in this poem but they are matched more closely to the essence of the situation, as in the parison and anaphora of the fourth stanza, and in those of the first, lending emphasis to the desperate pleading repeated in the last stanza. The normally commonplace prosopopoeia of love is given paradoxical force in 'Love's a man of warre' (6), particularly effective after the preceding stanza in which 'Love will do the deed' after the removal of wrath.

The moving periphrasis 'That which wrought on thee' (7) for God's or Christ's love (for mankind) is here no decoration, but an essential ingredient in the 'argument'. It is followed by an equally moving syllepsis in *low*, first in the sense of the idiom 'bring low', secondly in the cosmic movement from heaven to earth. Another syllepsis in the third stanza draws attention, with condensed poetic expressiveness, to the pupil's frailty: *affect* in Renaissance English could mean both 'aspire' and, as now, 'pretend', and both senses are apt here. A third syllepsis, *consent* (2), is equally organic: in early Modern English it had, besides the general sense of 'agreement', the much more specific theological meaning of 'agreement in faith and doctrine', a meaning supported here by the third stanza. The second submissive sense of 'compliance' naturally fits in with the disciplinary situation and so does a third sense, viz 'sympathy, harmonius relationship', which we have now lost. Such density of meaning is typical of much metaphysical poetry.

As for prose, we will begin with two passages by John Lyly (1554?-1606), dramatist and author of a long prose work called *Euphues*. His plays, notable for being in prose, had no small reputation in late sixteenth-century Britain, coming immediately before Shakespeare. His *Euphues* is in two parts: *Euphues: The Anatomy of Wit* (1578) and *Euphues and his England* (1580), which are both concerned more with *docere* than *movere*. It is this work that has given the name to a certain kind of style called 'Euphuism' (discussed below) although by no means confined to *Euphues*; it appears in most of Lyly's work.

In spite of his popularity, Lyly received no solid patronage (although he was patronized for some time by Lord Burghley), and there exist two petitions of his to Queen Elizabeth in which he complains of hopes unfulfilled. Our first extract is from the second petition of 1593, as quoted in Minto (1881, 225):

Some land, some good fines, or forfeitures that should fall by the just fall of these most false traitors, that seeing nothing will come by the Revels, I may prey upon the Rebels. Thirteen years your Highness' servant, but yet nothing. Twenty friends that though they say they will be sure I find them sure to be slow. A thousand hopes but all nothing; a hundred promises but yet nothing. Thus casting up the inventory of my friends, hopes, promises, and times, the *summa totalis* amounteth to just nothing. My last will is shorter than mine invention: but three legacies, patience to my creditors, melancholy without measure to my friends, and beggary without shame to my family.

Lyly is doing well here in trying to persuade the monarch through the kind of rhetoric towards which she was favourably disposed, especially the use of the schemes of syntax. Some elements typical of his style can be seen in this short passage, particularly his use of parison or isocolon, forming an emotional auxesis: *patience . . . creditors / melancholy . . . friends / beggary . . . family*. If we adhere to the strict definition of parison as equality of grammatical construction and isocolon as identical length of phrases, clauses or sentences, we note that part of the culminating effect of the auxesis has been achieved through a perfect isocolon in *melancholy . . . friends* and *beggary . . . family* with eleven syllables in each.

Other rhetorical features include marked alliteration in *fines / forfeitures / fall / fall / false*, further foregrounded by the disadvantageous connotations of those words, by assonance in the last three and by the antanaclasis of *fall*, mirrored in the antanaclasis of *sure* in the third sentence; but the most striking feature of the passage lies in the *pathos* of the epistrophe of the word *nothing*.

The next passage is from Lyly's play *Endimion*. Endimion is in love with Cynthia, and his friend Eumenides with Semele. In Act III.iv.90ff Eumenides gives vent to his highly charged emotions after having seen at the bottom of a fountain 'in white marble engrauen these words, *''Aske one for all, and but one thing at all''* (80–2):

> Eum. Aske? so I will: and what shall I doo but aske? and whome
> should I aske but *Semele*? the possessing of whose person is a pleasure that cannot come within the compasse of comparison; whose golden lockes seeme most curious, when they seeme most carelesse;
> 5 whose sweete lookes seeme most alluring, when they are most chaste; and whose wordes the more vertuous they are, the more amorous they bee accounted. I pray thee, fortune, when I shall first meete with fayre *Semele*, dash my delight with some light disgrace, least imbracing sweetnesse beyond measure, I take a surfit without
> 10 recure: let her practise her accustomed coynesse, that I may dyet my selfe vpon my desires: otherwise the fulnesse of my ioyes will diminish the sweetnesse, and I shall perrish by them before I possesse them.

Why doe I trifle the time in words? The least minute, beeing
15   spent in the getting of *Semele*, is more worth then [than] the whole
worlde: therefore let mee aske. What nowe *Eumenides*? Whether
[whither] art thou drawn? Hast thou drawn? Hast thou forgotten
both friendship and duetie? Care of *Endimion*, and the commaundement of *Cynthia*? Shall hee dye in a leaden sleepe, because thou
20   sleepest in a golden dreame? I [Aye], let him sleepe euer, so I
slumber but one minute with *Semele*. Loue knoweth neither friend-
shippe nor kindred.

This speech by Eumenides exhibits many of the features of Euphuism. One of them is a penchant for erotema (rhetorical question), in this passage put to the service of reflecting emotional turmoil, in *Euphues* to further persuasive, moral argumentation. But its principal feature is parallelism, as seen in the extraordinarily frequent use of parison. We note this in the four relative clauses starting with *whose*. Not only are those parallel in being relative clauses, but parison occurs within them: *seeme most curious / seeme most carelesse / seeme most alluring / are most chaste* (4–6) and *the more vertuous they are / the more amorous they bee accounted* (6–7). Parison recurs in e.g. *imbracing sweetnesse beyond measure / take a surfit without recure* (9–10); *Care of Endimion / the commaundement of Cynthia* (even to the extent of proper noun, 18–19). Lyly's parallelism very often pinpoints antithesis, as in *curious* [elaborate] / *carelesse* (4), *alluring / chaste* (5–6), *vertuous / amorous* (6–7).

But Lyly does not leave his symmetrical patterning there. Within his parallel constructions of phrases and clauses, he makes use of morphological schemes, such as homoioteleuton (same ending on different words) in *vertuous / amorous* (6–7), highlighting the antithesis, and *measure / recure* (9–10), even if the pronunciation of the two *-ure* endings was not the same, though *measure* could still be stressed on the second syllable in verse rhyme. Polyptoton, another morphological scheme, repeating the same word in different forms, occurs in e.g. *delight / light* (8). We are here referring to word shape only: the *-light* of *delight* is of course not etymologically the same word as *light* although it received its spelling from association with it (see p. 14).

As for phonological schemes, Lyly is fond of alliteration, either the straight kind (a..a..a) or transverse (inter-linked) alliteration (a..b..a..b). Nowadays we normally regard two consonants as alliterating only if they occur initially in stressed syllables, but earlier also unstressed syllables would count, so that *compasse . . . comparison* (3) would have both [k] and [p] alliterating. The [k] alliteration is carried over into *curious / carelesse* in the next line. Transverse alliteration on [d] and [l] appears effectively in 8: *dash / delight / light /*

disgrace, the one on [d] being supported by the morphological scheme prosthesis (prefixing) of *delight* / *disgrace*.

A particularly good example of Lyly's complex patterning, conducive to *pathos*, can be seen in lines 18–20: parison in *Care of Endimion* / *the commaundement of Cynthia*, including alliteration on [k], and in *Shall hee dye . . . sleepe* / *thou sleepest . . . dreame*, with polyptoton in *sleepe* / *sleepest* and antithesis in *leaden* / *golden*. Transverse assonance creates a neat frame in *leaden* / *sleepe* / *sleepest* / *dreame*, -ea- and -ee- being pronounced differently, as we have seen, in the sixteenth century, as [e:] and [i:] respectively (*leaden* still had a long vowel). The alliteration of [sl] is carried over into the next line (*sleepe* / *slumber*) and culminates significantly as [s..l] with consonance in [m] from *slumber* in *Semele*, the object of Eumenides' affection.

Unfortunately the term 'Euphuism' has led many people to think that Lyly was the innovator of such a style. Although he polished it and employed it more than others, he had his models, themselves influenced by the language of fifteenth-century Italian Humanists. His chief models were probably Sir Thomas North's translation (1557) of Guevara's *The Diall of Princes* and George Pettie's *Pallace of Pleasure* (1576), although Euphuism can be detected in earlier English writing. Zandvoort (1970, 14) asks and answers the further pertinent question whether the style of *Euphues* might not derive from an older tradition:

> Since the publication of Feuillerat's *John Lyly* in 1910 we have known that the answer to this question is in the affirmative. In his chapter on the origins of Euphuism Feuillerat showed the untenability of Landmann's thesis of Guevara as its source and fountain-head, by quoting specimens of Euphuistic style from the English writings of Thomas More and other authors whose works antedate Thomas North's translation of Guevara's *Diall of Princes* in 1557. He went on to show how the rhetorical figures that are to be found in English prose throughout the sixteenth century are largely due to *classical* influence, going back, indeed, to the teachings of Gorgias and his fellow-sophists, and to the practice of Greek and Roman orators. Their influence was reinforced by the precepts of sixteenth-century handbooks of rhetoric, such as those by Wilson, Sherry and others, published long before Lyly's *Euphues* or even before North's Guevara.

All the same, we can say that Euphuism is 'if not the earliest, yet the first thorough and consistent attempt in English Literature to practise prose as an art . . . We shall be right in assigning to the Euphuist, as representing and including his special forerunners, North and Pettie, the praise of asserting, with an emphasis hitherto unknown, the absolute importance to prose-writing of the principle of Design' (Bond (1902) in his Lyly edition, vol. 1, 144–5).

Euphuism may seem artificial to us today but it was considered refined, elegant and beautiful in the sixteenth century. Although some writers, e.g. Sidney and Shakespeare, felt that Lyly went too far in not lending his sentences profundity of sense in due proportion to his patterning of language, his influence on Renaissance prose was considerable:

> The characterization of Euphuism as 'an equivalent of Pope's verse in *The Rape of the Lock*' was anticipated by René Pruvost in his . . . book on Robert Greene [1938], in which, after a reference to Pope, he wrote: 'or il nous semble que la structure de la phrase de Lyly représente, dans la prose anglaise du seizième siècle, un effort comparable à celui des versificateurs qui introduisirent le ''couplet'' dans la poésie anglaise au siècle suivant' (p. 92). So far from being regarded as a mere freak of fashion, the style which we continue to call Euphuism is recognized as a positive contribution to the development of literary expression in the sixteenth and seventeenth centuries.
>
> (Zandvoort 1970, 20)

Lyly understood that it is not only in poetry that the reader wants to experience the pleasure derived from harmonious phrasing. There is pleasure to be had in language other than the kind that provides fresh insight or knowledge, although Lyly's style is nearly always admirably clear. And a highly patterned style can sometimes be positively advantageous in the conducting of an argument. Francis Bacon's style is generally not densely rhetorical but every now and then he will adorn his thoughts or views with rhetorical syntax in the Euphuistic manner. In the following example from his essay *Of Truth*, the syntax actually mirrors the clarity of thought admirably, mainly because of the felicitous use of parison. Also note the rhetorical punctuation separating, and thereby emphasizing, the parisonic units by semicolons:

> But howsoever these things are thus, in mens depraved Judgements, and Affections, yet *Truth*, which onely doth judge it selfe, teacheth, that the Inquirie of *Truth*, which is the love-making, or Wooing of it; The knowledge of *Truth*, which is the Presence of it; and the Beleefe of *Truth*, which is the Enjoying of it; is the Soveraigne Good of humane Nature.
>
> (8)

One of those who must have admired the eloquence of Euphuism was the Queen herself. Bond (in his edition of Lyly (1902), vol. 1, 136) quotes a letter written by Elizabeth to Edward VI as early as 1552, i.e. before North's *Diall of Princes*. Edward had asked for her picture and Elizabeth wrote a reply which contains syntactic parallelism and antithesis much in the way of Lyly's:

> My picture I mean: in which if the inward good mind toward your grace might as well be declared as the outward face and countenance shall be seen, I would not have tarried the commandment, but prevented it [i.e. issued it earlier], nor have been the last to grant but the first to offer it . . . Of this also yet the proof could not be great, because the occasions

have been so small; notwithstanding, as a dog hath a day, so may I perchance have time to declare it in deeds, which now I do write them but in words.

This letter also illustrates a certain figure typical of Euphuism, that of the balanced simile also known as *collatio* and praised by Puttenham: 'As well to a good maker and Poet as to an excellent perswader in prose, the figure of *Similitude* is very necessary, by which we not onely bewtifie our tale, but also very much inforce & inlarge it' (240); see further under Simile, p. 165. It was in this spirit that Lyly and Elizabeth used collatio, such as the one in the letter quoted above: *as a dog . . . in deeds*. It is especially this feature, together with general wordiness and the balanced antithesis, that Shakespeare ridicules so magnificently – to the undoubted delight of many a courtly spectator – in *1Henry IV* when Falstaff, acting the King in the Boar's Head Tavern, upbraids Prince Harry and refers favourably to himself (Oldcastle = Falstaff) in what he considers to be the stilted language of the King:

> Harry, I do not only marvel where thou spendest thy time, but also how thou art accompanied. For though the camomile, the more it is trodden on, the faster it grows, yet youth, the more it is wasted, the sooner it wears . . . If then thou be son to me, here lies the
> 5 point. Why, being son to me, art thou so pointed at? Shall the blessed sun of heaven prove a micher, and eat blackberries? – A question not to be asked. Shall the son of England prove a thief, and take purses? – A question to be asked. There is a thing, Harry, which thou hast often heard of, and it is known to many in our land
> 10 by the name of pitch. This pitch, as ancient writers do report, doth defile. So doth the company thou keepest. For Harry, now I do not speak to thee in drink, but in tears; not in pleasure, but in passion; not in words only, but in woes also. And yet there is a virtuous man whom I have often noted in thy company, but I know not his name
> 15 . . . now I remember me, his name is Oldcastle. If that man should be lewdly given, he deceiveth me; for, Harry, I see virtue in his looks. If, then, the tree may be known by the fruit, as the fruit by the tree, then peremptorily I speak it – there is virtue in that Oldcastle.
>
> (II.v.402ff)

We recognize Lyly at once in *For though . . . wears* (2–4) with its parison, antithesis and alliteration. The humour, apart from the marked parallelism, lies in the mundane example of the camomile being trodden on, which can be compared to the bathos of *pitch* (10) in such supposedly elevated style.

In lines 5–8 there is further obvious sentence symmetry, and the antimetabole of lines 17–18 is downright silly because of its second half, made sillier by the solemn echoing of a 14th-century proverb (the first half) and a possible, and even more solemn, reference to the biblical 'by their fruits ye shall know them' (*Matthew* 7:20).

The word *sun* (6) also means 'son'; cp the opening of *Richard III*: 'Now is the winter of our discontent / Made glorious summer by this son of York.' In the sixteenth century both words were often spelt *son* or *sonne*. But whereas the syllepsis is quite brilliant in *Richard III*, it is deflated here by the almost irrelevant triviality of the sentence in which it occurs.

The height of the ridicule is perhaps in the would-be antitheses of lines 12–13; 'would-be', for they miss being antithetical in spite of the syntax, unless Shakespeare wants *passion* to be seen as a ludicrous syllepsis, i.e. not only in the sense of 'aroused emotion' but also in the sense of 'suffering', as in Christ's passion on the cross.

But this does not mean that Shakespeare was averse to using a Euphuistic style when required. The pointing of antithesis and balancing of syntactic members are essentially features belonging to oratory. Lyly tried to assimilate these features into a pervasive style in his novels and prose plays; Shakespeare employs the style seriously in the situation to which he thinks it belongs, viz in the Roman forum. Brutus's forum speech (in prose) in *Julius Caesar* is highly rhetorical in the Euphuistic manner, and it is so in order to persuade the crowd of the justice in killing Caesar:

BRUTUS: Be patient till the last.
Romans, countrymen, and lovers, hear me for my cause, and be silent that you may hear. Believe me for mine honour, and have respect to mine honour, that you may believe. Censure me in your
5 wisdom, and awake your senses, that you may the better judge. If there be any in this assembly, any dear friend of Caesar's, to him I say that Brutus' love to Caesar was no less than his. If then that friend demand why Brutus rose against Caesar, this is my answer: not that I loved Caesar less, but that I loved Rome more. Had you
10 rather Caesar were living, and die all slaves, than that Caesar were dead, to live all free men? As Caesar loved me, I weep for him. As he was fortunate, I rejoice at it. As he was valiant, I honour him. But as he was ambitious, I slew him. There is tears for his love, joy for his fortune, honour for his valour, and death for his ambition.
15 Who is here so base that would be a bondman? If any, speak, for him have I offended. Who is here so rude that would not be a Roman? If any, speak, for him have I offended. Who is here so vile that will not love his country? If any, speak, for him have I offended. I pause for a reply.

(III.ii.12ff)

This speech is as highly patterned as anything in Lyly, but here the rhetoric is put to the service of swaying a crowd that has just screamed *We will be satisfied! Let us be satisfied!*. Brutus starts off with balanced, pleading imperatives (2–5) which include persuasive epanalepsis in *hear . . . hear / Believe . . . believe* (2–4) round emotive *ethos* words like *cause, honour* and *respect*, followed by sound-parallelism in *Censure / senses* (4–5), *censure* being pronounced *censor*. The parallel hypothetical structures *If . . . If . . .* (5–9) incorporate the antithetically prominent parison *not that I loved Caesar less, but that I loved Rome more* (8). The Euphuistic structures continue in the erotema *Had you . . . free men?* with its chiastic *living . . . die / dead . . . live* (10–11), followed by three parisonic sentences each beginning with the reasoning *As* and setting forth Caesar's virtues, but ending most effectively in a fourth that highlights his essential vice: *But as he was ambitious, I slew him* (11–13). The unjustifiability of Caesar's ambition regardless of his virtues is pithily stressed by Brutus in the parallel noun phrases that follow *There is* (13–14), each mirroring its preceding sentence counterpart; and the speech culminates in three parisonic rhetorical questions, each followed generously by its own parallel invitation to object. All highly effective and sufficient to satisfy the crowd (*None, Brutus, none*) – at least until Mark Antony takes over.

Although we can call this style Euphuistic, it does not mean that Shakespeare necessarily borrowed it from Lyly. As shown above, Lyly had his precursors in the great rhetorical tradition, and it seems safer to assume that it was this, perhaps in his desire for a kind of verisimilitude, that Shakespeare exploited in Brutus's speech.

Fine examples of later Renaissance prose in which rhetoric is used with magnificently persuasive force are afforded by Donne's sermons. Euphuism has still not lost its grip: 'Donne's prose, Euphuistic in inspiration, spills over its boundaries and hurries the reader onward' (Webber 1963, 4); it is more apparently spontaneous. Here is an extract from his Second Prebend Sermon, preached at St Paul's on January 29, 1625. The sermon is based on the biblical quotation from *The Book of Psalms* 63:7: 'Because thou hast been my help, therefore in the shadow of thy wings will I rejoice.'

> Let me wither and weare out mine age in a discomfortable, in an unwholesome, in a penurious prison, and so pay my debts with my bones, and recompence the wastfulnesse of my youth, with the beggary of mine age; Let me wither in a spittle under sharpe, and
> 5 foule, and infamous diseases, and so recompence the wantonnesse of my youth, with that loathsomnesse in mine age; yet, if God with-draw not his spirituall blessings, his Grace, his Patience, If I can call my suffering his Doing, my passion his Action, All this that is temporall, is but a caterpiller got into one corner of my garden,

10   but a mill-dew fallen upon one acre of my Corne; The body of all,
the substance of all is safe, as long as the soule is safe. But when I
shall trust to that, which wee call a good spirit, and God shall deject,
and empoverish, and evacuate that spirit, when I shall rely upon a
morall constancy, and God shall shake, and enfeeble, and enervate,
15   destroy and demolish that constancy; when I shall think to refresh
my selfe in the serenity and sweet ayre of a good conscience, and
God shall call up the damps and vapours of hell it selfe, and spread
a cloud of diffidence, and an impenetrable crust of desperation upon
my conscience; when health shall flie from me, and I shall lay hold
20   upon riches to succour me, and comfort me in my sicknesse, and
riches shall flie from me, and I shall snatch after favour, and good
opinion, to comfort me in my poverty; when even this good opinion
shall leave me, and calumnies and misinformations shall prevaile
against me; when I shall need peace, because there is none but
25   thou, O Lord, that should stand for me, and then shall finde, that
all the wounds that I have, come from thy hand, all the arrows that
stick in me, from thy quiver; when I shall see, that because I have
given my selfe to my corrupt nature, thou hast changed thine; and
because I am all evill towards thee, therefore thou hast given over
30   being good towards me; When it comes to this height, that the fever
is not in the humors, but in the spirits, that mine enemy is not an
imaginary enemy, fortune, nor a transitory enemy, malice in great
persons, but a reall, and an irresistible, and an inexorable, and an
everlasting enemy, The Lord of Hosts himselfe, The Almighty God
35   himselfe, the Almighty God himselfe onely knowes the waight of
this affliction, and except hee put in that *pondus gloriæ*, that
exceeding waight of an eternall glory, with his owne hand, into the
other scale, we are waighed downe, we are swallowed up, irrepar-
ably, irrevocably, irrecoverably, irremediably.

(96–7)

Compared to our notions of grammatical cohesion as to what consti-
tutes a sentence or clause Donne's, and those of other Renaissance
writers, were different, as we saw in chapter 3. Donne's distinctions
between full stop, semicolon and comma are rhetorical or rhythmical
rather than grammatical. His units are what we call 'rhetorical periods',
which have more to do with the emphases and pace of delivery and
with thought completion and associative unity.

According to the modern convention of punctuation this longish
extract consists of only two sentences, separated by the full stop in
line 11. These are by no means ungrammatical, but they are unpredict-
able in their movement; they are explorative rather than expository:
our minds are continually being asked to focus on smaller units within
the sentence, units that are charged with considerable associative and
emotional energy.

The first sentence is full of schemes which serve to illustrate the powerful contrast between the hardship and misery envisaged in the first part (down to *yet* in 6) and its insignificance if suffered 'in the shadow of thy wings': The two anaphoric *Let me wither* clauses starting in 1 and 4 themselves contain many instances of parison, sometimes with a cumulative, sometimes with an antithetical effect: *in . . . / in . . . / in . . .* (1–2) cumulative; *the wastfulnesse of my youth / the beggary of mine age* (3–4) and *the wantonnesse of my youth / that loathsomnesse in mine age* (5–6) cumulative when taken together, antithetical when taken separately. The second part, starting in line 6, uses parallelism to highlight the contrast between God and his subject: *my suffering his Doing, my passion his Action; suffering* corresponds to *passion* (in its Latin sense, as in *Christ's passion*), and *Doing* to *Action*. The homoioteleuton foregrounds the 'victim – victimizer' contrast in both pairs by connecting the words in each even further: *suffering / Doing*; *passion / Action*. The repetition of *suffering / Doing* in equivalent Latinate words emphasizes, in its stylistic elevation, the more learnedly theological concept of the situation. Like Shakespeare, Donne was a master at gaining the attention of the learned and unlearned alike.

As in Shakespeare's sonnet 73, discussed below, the fusion of schemes and tropes, persuasively and imaginatively reinforcing each other, more than anything else makes this great prose. Continuing our analysis of the first sentence, take the metaphors *but a caterpiller got into one corner of my garden, but a mill-dew fallen upon one acre of my Corne*. Part of the effectiveness of them is their gentle simplicity. Donne is here aware of the important element of oratorical *ethos* gaining his hearers' confidence and sympathy by intimately drawing their attention to the familiar. Many of his congregation would be farmers, attending to their daily duties in the vicinity of St Paul's, where they would see cows grazing the fields, instead of today's highrises. The metaphors are in simple language with many monosyllables, and foregrounded through parison: a noun *caterpiller / mill-dew* modified by an elliptical relative clause which consists of a participle *got / fallen* + a prepositional phrase *into one corner / upon one acre*, itself modified by another prepositional phrase *of my garden / of my Corne*. There is even harmonious parallelism in the prepositions themselves: those in the first structure are disyllabic (*into / upon*), those in the second a monosyllabic repetition (*of / of*). It is this harmony of the syntactic units, together with the artless vocabulary, that makes these metaphors memorable.

We note a similar concord of metaphor and scheme in 26–7: *all the wounds that I have, come from thy hand, all the arrows that stick in me, from thy quiver*. This is strongly reinforced by further parison in 27–30 (*because . . . / because . . .*), the persuasiveness of which is strengthened by the fearful antithesis (*I . . . my / thou . . . thine*) and the chiasmus or antimetabole in the second half of the parison (*I . . . thee / thou . . . me*).

The huge second sentence, beginning in line 11, consists of a large number of subordinate clauses (many of them containing other subordinate clauses), all starting anaphorically with *when*, signposting the steps in a powerful auxesis which keeps the listener in excited suspense, maintained partly through the parallelism described in the previous paragraph, and through another in lines 31–33: negative *not / nor* + noun phrase (*an imaginary enemy / a transitory enemy*), each with its own apposition (*fortune / malice in great persons*). This parison is lit by the homoioteleuton in *imaginary / transitory* and by the ploce of *enemy*. The subordinate clauses culminate, highly appropriately, in the first instance of *The Almighty God himselfe* (34). Donne then dwells for a moment at the 'top' in the anadiplosis of this phrase before the long-suspended release in the relatively short main clause which warns us of dangers to the soul, moving through another parison (*we are waighed downe, we are swallowed up*) – not antithetical but cumulative in spite of the two strong, monosyllabic, antithetical adverbs in emphatic final position – to the finality of the last four adverbs, given enormous weight by brachylogia, prosthesis (the prefixing in *ir-* and *re-*) and homoioteleuton (*-ably*).

Powerful use of prosthesis also occurs in the first part of the second sentence, first in the three parallel verbs *deject . . . empoverish . . . evacuate* (12–13) which form a fearful auxesis, *evacuate* threatening finality in its sense of 'make totally void or worthless' (cp. *vacuum*). These violent verbs are then followed by another five (14–15), just as potent. The last four of these are once again made prominent by cumulative linking through prosthesis, this time involving repetition, as in the last line. Again the verbs create a mounting auxesis culminating in *demolish* 'reduce to ruin', written at a time before the word became too familiar with overuse. The two prosthetic groups (with *en-* and *de-*) are individually polysyndetic, their members being conjoined by *and*, but form as groups together an asyndetic construction. This shifting way of conjoining adds considerably to their prominence through rhythmical cadence. Part of the rhetorical pace of the passage is achieved by such variation of asyndeton and polysyndeton; cp. lines 1–2 and 7 (asyndeton), 12–22 (markedly polysyndetic) and the last two powerfully asyndetic lines.

The lines with the prosthetic verbs (12–15) are couched in what is sometimes called a verbal style, i.e. a style in which most of the meaning is in the verbs. Being instinctively aware of how overuse of this would be counterproductive since it could easily become unimaginatively repetitious or even clumsy, Donne then slows down to a nominal style, where nouns or noun phrases carry the semantic load, in a series of metaphors of increasing solidity, forming another auxesis – *serenity and sweet ayre / damps and vapours / cloud / impenetrable crust* (15–18) – before resuming a style in which the verbal is equally balanced with the nominal.

In this passage the schemes of syntax, word and sound frame the tropes, pointing to contrasts and similarities, fuelling auxesis and continually shifting the pace of the language, as in the interplay of asyndeton and polysyndeton; tropes reinforce schemes so that they are never purely ornamental; the simple words are balanced with the learned, and the energetic verbal style with the slower, but equally effective, heaviness of the nominal. All the stylistic categories work together in the beauty of great art towards one common end: to arouse, to move, and to persuade.

In the latter half of the sixteenth century there was a marked tendency to focus on rhetorical parallelism, i.e. on schemes in particular. Later on in our period tastes changed to some extent towards less obvious or rigid patterning, although the Donne passage above, written for persuasion through speech, still exhibits this to a large extent; but in Donne the stylistic momentum is quite different from Lyly's. The changing emphasis applies not only to prose works and poems but to verse drama as well. To illustrate earlier Renaissance dramatic verse, here is a famous speech from Kyd's *The Spanish Tragedy* III.ii.1ff, in which Hieronimo gives vent to his grief and outrage at his son's murder and resolves to take revenge:

> O eyes, no eyes, but fountains fraught with tears;
> O life, no life, but lively form of death;
> O world, no world, but mass of public wrongs,
> Confus'd and fill'd with murder and misdeeds!
> 5   O sacred heavens! if this unhallowed deed,
> If this inhuman and barbarous attempt,
> If this incomparable murder thus
> Of mine, but now no more my son,
> Shall unreveal'd and unrevenged pass,
> 10 How should we term your dealings to be just,
> If you unjustly deal with those that in your justice trust?
> The night, sad secretary to my moans,
> With direful visions wake my vexed soul,
> And with the wounds of my distressful son
> 15 Solicits me for notice of his death.
> The ugly fiends do sally forth of hell,
> And frame my steps to unfrequented paths,
> And fear my heart with fierce inflamed thoughts.
> The cloudy day my discontents records,
> 20 Early begins to register my dreams,
> And drive me forth to seek the murtherer.
> Eyes, life, world, heavens, hell, night, and day,

See, search, show, send some man, some mean, that may –
What's here? a letter? tush! it is not so! –
25   A letter written to Hieronimo!

In lines 1–3 there are three instances of the scheme epanorthosis, which mirror Hieronymo's inability to think clearly in his deeply distraught state. Their power of *pathos* lies not only in the the hyperbole of the first or in the oxymoron of the second, but also in being foregrounded in parallel clauses of parison with anaphora. Another syntactic scheme brachylogia (22–3) reflects the passion of the speaker, not only because of the absence of conjunctions but also through the repetition in line 22 of visions or imaginings from earlier in the speech but still at the forefront of his inflamed mind.

Phonological parallelism is obvious in the liberal use of alliteration throughout, particularly expressive when it brings into relief words that either reinforce each other through sense connotation, as in lines 18 and 23, or are in an antithetical relationship, like *heavens* and *unhallowed* in line 5.

Morphological parallelism is marked through prosthesis in *inhuman / incomparable* (6–7) and *unreveal'd / unrevenged* (9), all four words paralleling each other in their negative prefixes. Hieronimo's mental occupation with revenge and justice finds expression in the powerful polyptoton (10–11) of *just / unjustly /justice*, given extra force by the rhyme with *trust*.

Tropes are of course in evidence, as in the prosopopoeia of *night* (12–15) and, antithetically, that of *day* (19–21); but it is schematic parallelism, more than anything else, that is conducive to the *pathos* of this speech.

The later rhetorical development, with a taste for greater use of striking tropes, is particularly clearly reflected in Shakespeare's verse. His earlier plays exhibit relatively close attention to syntactic schemes in conjunction with relatively regular metre and a tendency to end-stopped lines, i.e. verse in which syntactic boundary and sense coincide with the end of the line. Such features were also typical of e.g. Spenser's *Faerie Queene* and, in drama, e.g. Kyd (witness the passage above) and Marlowe. Shakespeare's later plays show more imaginative use of tropes and imagery, less schematic parallelism in the syntax, less rigid metre and more run-on lines where the syntax is interrupted, or held in suspense, at the end of lines.

Let us take a look at two passages, admittedly rather extreme cases, the first from early Shakespeare and the second from a later play, to illustrate this difference. *The Two Gentlemen of Verona* belongs to Shakespeare's early period. It had certainly been written by 1598 and 'most scholars would place its composition from four to eight years earlier on the grounds of its style and its relationship to other plays' (Sanders 1968, 7). Here is one of Julia's speeches from Act IV:

> Alas, poor Proteus, thou hast entertained
> A fox to be the shepherd of thy lambs.
> Alas, poor fool, why do I pity him
> That with his very heart despiseth me?
> 5　Because he loves her, he despiseth me.
> Because I love him, I must pity him.
> This ring I gave him when he parted from me,
> To bind him to remember my good will.
> And now am I, unhappy messenger,
> 10　To plead for that which I would not obtain;
> To carry that which I would have refused;
> To praise his faith, which I would have dispraised.
> I am my master's true-confirmed love,
> But cannot be true servant to my master
> 15　Unless I prove false traitor to myself.
> Yet will I woo for him, but yet so coldly
> As, heaven it knows, I would not have him speed.
>
> (IV.iv.89ff)

The iambic metre shows a high degree of regularity. The syntactic sense is firmly matched to line boundaries in whole sentences (5–6) and main clause (13); the relative-clause modifier of *him* occupies line 4, full adverbial clauses lines 8, 15, 17, and three main-verb predicates lines 10–12. The passage makes extensive use of schemes, such as ploce, arranged antimetabolically or transversely in the second-half lines of 3–6: *pity / despiseth / despiseth / pity*. Parison occurs in lines 5–6 and 10–12 with anaphora in both cases and antithesis with chiasmus in the first (*he despiseth me / I love him*) and also in lines 14–15, again with antithesis: *true / false, master / myself (servant)*.

Compare that passage to Cleopatra's famous speech in Act V of *Antony and Cleopatra*, written between 1606 and 1608:

> CLEOPATRA: I dreamt there was an Emperor Antony.
> 　O, such another sleep, that I might see
> 　But such another man!
> DOLABELLA:　If it might please ye –
> CLEOPATRA: His face was as the heav'ns, and therein stuck
> 5　A sun and moon, which kept their course and lighted
> 　The little O o'th' earth.
> 　DOLABELLA:　Most sovereign creature –
> CLEOPATRA: His legs bestrid the ocean; his reared arm
> 　Crested the world. His voice was propertied
> 　As all the tuned spheres, and that to friends;
> 10　But when he meant to quail and shake the orb,
> 　He was as rattling thunder. For his bounty,

There was no winter in't; an autumn 'twas,
That grew the more by reaping. His delights
Were dolphin-like; they showed his back above
15   The element they lived in. In his livery
Walked crowns and crownets. Realms and islands were
As plates dropped from his pocket.

(V.ii.75ff)

This passage shows much greater use of run-on lines (enjambement) with their bolder syntactic breaks (2, 4, 5, 7, 11, 13–16) and often containing a heavy caesura (8, 11–16), interfering with metrical regularity which, at this stage of his career, Shakespeare had evidently come to regard as an impediment to *pathos*.

The speech produces this not so much through syntactic schemes as through tropes: hyperbole, meiosis, metaphor, metonymy, simile, anthimeria, paradox, and possibly apostrophe if we consider the elliptical *O, such another sleep* an instance of this; see Apostrophe above, p. 150. Sometimes a trope is helped by syntactic suspension foregrounding it, such as *stuck* (4), which is a highly effective instance of the trope meiosis, here belittling the sun and moon in one of the enormous hyperboles making up most of the passage. These are expressed in similes (4, 9, 11, 14 and 17), bold metaphors (12–13), or in metonymy: *crowns and crownets* for 'kings and dukes etc.' Masterly use of anthimeria in *crested* and *propertied* (nouns used for verbs, 8) heightens their respective hyperboles, and the metaphor *an autumn . . . reaping* is given further prominence through paradox.

The contrast between love and scorn in Julia's speech from *The Two Gentlemen of Verona* was foregrounded through the schemes of parison, anaphora, chiasmus and antithesis. But in Cleopatra's speech the contrast between Antony's anger and joy is couched in striking hyperbole and simile: *When he meant to quail and shake the orb, / He was as rattling thunder / . . . His delights / Were dolphin-like; they showed his back above / The element they lived in.* Contrasting so magnificently with the violence and elemental noise of the first image, the glimpse of frolicking dolphins jumping out of the sea in unbounded joy and playfulness is particularly felicitous: thus did Antony's delights make him appear, not in the element where his delights were found, but above it. The sexual implication, though probably secondary, of the image (*his back above*) is unmistakable: man delighting in woman.

The hyperboles expressed thus with references to the heavenly bodies, the seasonal cycle and the elements, tell us that to Cleopatra, in her dream, Antony is above perfection as we know or imagine it, by their pervasive pointing to the most perfect of shapes, the circle, which has no beginning and no end but, despite this perfection, is merely a part of him or 'below' him: *sun / moon / The little O o'th' earth / world / spheres / orb / crowns / crownets / plates* [i.e. coins].

This concentration on tropes can often be seen in Shakespeare's sonnets, most of which were probably written shortly before the turn of the century, after the sonnet vogue had begun with the publication in 1591 of Sidney's *Astrophel and Stella*. We shall not go into detail about the formal stanzaic differences between Sidney's Petrarchan variety and Shakespeare's sonnet form, but simply point out Shakespeare's greater imaginative use of the tropes, often similar to the extended conceits of the metaphysical poets. Two notable instances of this can be seen in sonnets 87 and 134, in the organic use of tropes taken from the world of finance. But Shakespeare was often at his most impressive when he used schemes to reinforce his metaphorical brilliance, as in sonnet 73:

> That time of year thou mayst in me behold
> When yellow leaves, or none, or few, do hang
> Upon those boughs which shake against the cold,
> Bare ruined choirs where late the sweet birds sang.
> 5   In me thou seest the twilight of such day
> As after sunset fadeth in the west,
> Which by and by black night doth take away,
> Death's second self, that seals up all in rest.
> In me thou seest the glowing of such fire
> 10   That on the ashes of his youth doth lie
> As the death-bed whereon it must expire,
> Consumed with that which it was nourished by.
> This thou perceiv'st, which makes thy love more strong,
> To love that well which thou must leave ere long.

The way in which Shakespeare employs the metaphor of fading light compared to fading life is masterly. It is structured firmly across the three quatrains, going from a broader perspective to a narrower one, from the darkening days of autumn in the first, to the end of the day in the second, to a barely flickering fire in the third, i.e. from the less immediate to the more immediate and imminent. The transitions of the progression are facilitated by the harmony of parison and anaphora in 5 and 9, the parison being in a chiastic relationship to the very first line, while the anaphora of *In me* focuses sharply on the dying man, balancing the focus on the darkening season in line 1.

Within each quatrain, complex tropes create the imaginative vision: in *shake against the cold* (3) the condensed force of the enemy winter (and death) is foregrounded by the metonymy of *cold* in its nakedness (for 'cold winds'), elevating the word from the status of attribute to that of essence. This metonymy permits a syllepsis in *shake*, meaning both 'move' (in the wind) and 'shiver' (in the cold), which momentarily lets us glimpse the boughs as animate (prosopopoeia). This is followed, in the description of these, by another metonymy of evocative compactness in *choirs* for the place of summer's bird chorus or choir, appealing simultaneously to our auditory as well as our visual sense. But the modifier *ruined* also turns the metonymy into a powerfully appropriate syllepsis pointing to physical decay: behind the primary image we are afforded the sad vision of ruined churches with their bare choirs (in the architectural sense), which may indeed be the place 'where late the sweet birds sang' in the poet's vision.

In line 2 the modifiers *none / few* follow *yellow leaves*. Normal word order would be 'no, or few, yellow leaves', but Shakespeare's hyperbaton manages to foreground both the head-phrase *yellow leaves* (*late* autumn) and the barrenness implied by the modifiers.

The metaphor of fading light peeps into the imminent future *via* the metaphor of night as *Death's second self* (8). The prosopopoeia of the fire in the last quatrain takes its greatness from the word *youth* (*his* meaning 'its'), which is in immediate antithesis to the simile of *death-bed* in the next line, continuing the prosopopoeia; and the quatrain culminates in a meaningful paradox of reflective melancholy: *Consumed with that which it was nourished by*. The 'summing up' in the final couplet is movingly enhanced by the fusion of the schemes polyptoton and anadiplosis: *love* as noun and as verb (polyptoton) with their respective, semantically corresponding adjective and adverb (*strong / well*) ending one line and beginning the next (anadiplosis).

This sonnet owes much of its beauty not only to the rich tapestry woven by the subtle interplay of schemes and tropes. This complexity is miraculously balanced by the simplicity of the mainly Anglo-Saxon vocabulary: of the 121 words (each instance counted), only nine are of French origin, viz. *ruined, choirs, fadeth, second, seals, expire, consumed, nourished, perceiv'st*. None of these is exceptionally learned, and several are as basic as the homely, native words, which are often simple monosyllables, quite a few of them repeated.

Our last example, written seventy-odd years after the Shakespeare sonnet above, is from Milton, 'the last . . . Renaissance humanist writing in English' (Partridge 1971, 261). It comes from the beginning of his tragedy *Samson Agonistes*, modelled on the ancient Greek tragedies. Apart from receiving a comprehensive rhetorical education in the Renaissance manner, Milton had a thorough knowledge of both Latin and Greek, and some of his linguistic habits have their syntactic origin in those languages. Examples of this occur in the following passage but need not concern us here unless they are relevant to our rhetorical analysis.

Milton's play is based on the biblical story of Samson and the Philistines, as told in *The Book of Judges*, chapter sixteen. The tragedy opens after Delilah's betrayal, through which Samson lost his superhuman strength and after which 'the Philistines took him, and put out

his eyes, and brought him down to Gaza, and bound him with fetters
of brass; and he did grind in the prison house' (*Judges* 16:21):

> SAMSON: A little onward lend thy guiding hand
> To these dark steps, a little further on,
> For yonder bank hath choice of sun or shade;
> There I am wont to sit, when any chance
> 5 Relieves me from my task of servile toil,
> Daily in the common prison else enjoined me,
> Where I, a prisoner chained, scarcely freely draw
> The air imprisoned also, close and damp,
> Unwholesome draught. But here I feel amends,
> 10 The breath of heav'n fresh-blowing, pure and sweet,
> With day-spring born; here leave me to respire.
> This day a solemn feast the people hold
> To Dagon their sea-idol, and forbid
> Laborious works; unwillingly this rest
> 15 Their superstition yields me; hence with leave
> Retiring from the popular noise, I seek
> This unfrequented place to find some ease,
> Ease to the body some, none to the mind
> From restless thoughts, that like a deadly swarm
> 20 Of hornets armed, no sooner found alone,
> But rush upon me thronging, and present
> Times past, what once I was, and what am now.
> O wherefore was my birth from Heaven foretold
> Twice by an angel, who at last in sight
> 25 Of both my parents all in flames ascended
> From off the altar, where an off'ring burned,
> As in a fiery column charioting
> His godlike presence, and from some great act
> Or benefit revealed to Abraham's race?
> 30 Why was my breeding ordered and prescribed
> As of a person separate to God,
> Designed for great exploits, if I must die
> Betrayed, captived, and both my eyes put out,
> Made of my enemies the scorn and gaze;
> 35 To grind in brazen fetters under task
> With this Heav'n-gifted strength? O glorious strength,
> Put to the labor of a beast, debased
> Lower than bondslave! Promise was that I
> Should Israel from Philistian yoke deliver;
> 40 Ask for this great deliverer now, and find him
> Eyeless in Gaza at the mill with slaves,
> Himself in bonds under Philistian yoke.

As in late Shakespeare, syntactic sense often straddles the lines,
which show enjambement (e.g. 4, 7, 13, 16, 21, 24, 28) and sometimes
have a heavy caesura (9, 11, 15, 36, 38), making the rhythm of the

verse closer to natural speech. The highly charged ecphonesis in line 36 (*O glorious strength*) is marked further by occurring immediately after such a mid-line pause, and by repeating the noun *strength* (ploce).

Samson's blindness is referred to at once and with pitiful economy in *these dark steps*, a hypallage (transferred epithet) of arresting compression: his steps are faltering because he cannot see. The phrase is made to stand out in solemn melancholy partly because of Milton's use of *these* rather than *my*, an idiom common in Greek, Latin and Italian poetry. Moreover *these* (here) contrasts with *yonder* (over there) in the next line, making the effort of free movement particularly painful.

Ecphrasis (graphic description) in the Homeric manner, so typical of Milton especially in his extended (epic) similes, appears in the first of two long rhetorical questions, which starts in line 23 (the second begins in 30). As so often in this work and in *Paradise Lost*, the similes refer to events or situations in the Bible, which is also gently evoked in the lovely periphrasis of *day-spring* for 'dawn' (11), recalling *Luke* 1:78: 'Through the tender mercy of our God; whereby the dayspring from on high hath visited us'. Milton's knowledge of Latin is often used for the purpose of meaningful syllepsis, as in *prescribed* (30) at the beginning of the second rhetorical question: it has the original Latin sense of 'laid down beforehand' but also the later modern sense of 'ordered', synonymous with the preceding verb of the line (see further chapter 2, pp. 20–21)

Another powerful simile appears in the comparison of *restless thoughts* to *a swarm / Of hornets armed* (19–20). The fierceness of the image is strengthened not only by the assonance of *swarm / armed* (the *w-* had not yet, by Milton's time, rounded a following *-a-*) but also by the pitiful sigh of the anadiplosis *ease / Ease* (17–18) and by the antithetical chiasmus (18), which focuses attention on Samson's mental torture rather than his physical suffering and develops the antithetical polyptoton of *rest / restless* (14, 19). The peace he seeks contrasts with the joyful celebrations around him, which have been foregrounded in the reverse hendiadys *popular noise* 'noise of the people', reminding us of the same figure in Coriolanus's *at once pluck out / The multitudinous tongue* 'tongues of the multitude' in *Coriolanus* III.i.158–9. Equally effective is the foregrounding of the noun *scorn* in a 'genuine' hendiadys: *scorn and gaze* (34) for 'scornful gaze'.

Phonological parallelism occurs again in the fine rhyme *servile toil* (5) – *toil* was pronounced *tile* – which reinforces the meaning of both words. A similar effect is achieved by the prosthetic *beast, debased* (37), which still rhymed at Milton's time, *debased* thus yoking *beast* and *Lower* in the next line. The polyptoton *prison / prisoner / imprisoned* (6–8) effects painfully Samson's thoughts on his captive state, with prosopopoeia in 8: in this dungeon even the air is a prisoner.

The passage ends with a truly great parison filling the last two lines. These consist solely of prepositional phrases, arranged in a sequence that focuses more and more narrowly on Samson's plight: *Eyeless in Gaza→at the mill→with slaves→Himself in bonds→under Philistian yoke*. The last phrase is first to be taken literally, but *yoke* is also a syllepsis implying 'dominance' and in this sense contrasts cruelly and ironically with lines 38–9.

Bibliography

1 Illustrative examples from literature have been taken from the following editions unless otherwise stated:

Arden of Feversham: MCILWRAITH, A. K. (ed.) 1971: *Five Elizabethan tragedies*. Oxford: Oxford University Press. (Originally published in World's Classics Series, 1938.)

Bacon, Sir Francis: KIERNAN, M. (ed.) 1985: *Sir Francis Bacon: the essayes or counsels, civill and morall*. Oxford: Clarendon Press. (*Of Atheisme; Of Ceremonies and Respects; Of Envy; Of Truth.*)

Browne, Sir Thomas: MARTIN, L. C. (ed.) 1964: *Sir Thomas Browne: Religio Medici and other works*. Oxford: Clarendon Press. (*Religio Medici.*)

Caxton, William: BLAKE, N. F. (ed.) 1970: *William Caxton: The history of Reynard the Fox*. Early English Text Society 263. London: Oxford University Press.

Chaucer, Geoffrey: ROBINSON, F. N. (ed.) 1957: *The works of Geoffrey Chaucer*. (2nd edition) London: Oxford University Press. (*The Miller's Prologue; The Pardoner's Tale.*)

Day, Angel: GÖRLACH, M. 1991: *Introduction to early Modern English*. Cambridge: Cambridge University Press. (First published in 1978 in German as *Einführung ins Frühneuenglische*. Heidelberg: Quelle & Meyer.) (*An Epistle Monitorie to a Father.*)

Deloney, Thomas: MANN, F. O. (ed.) 1912: *The works of Thomas Deloney*. Oxford: Clarendon Press. (*The Gentle Craft; Jacke of Newberie.*)

Donne, John: GARDNER, H. (ed.) 1972: *The metaphysical poets*. 2nd ed. London: Penguin. (*A Hymne to God the Father*; 'Batter my heart'; *The Canonization; The Flea; The Good-Morrow; Satyre: Of Religion; The Sun Rising; To his Mistress Going to Bed.*)

—MUELLER, J. M. (ed.) 1971: *Donne's Prebend sermons*. Cambridge, Mass.: Harvard University Press. (*Second Prebend Sermon*, January 29, 1625.)

Elizabeth I: in Bond 1902 (see Lyly) (Letter to Edward VI).

Harrison, William: in Görlach 1991 (see Day) (*The Chronicles of Scotland*).

Hawes, Stephen: MEAD, W. E. (ed.) 1928: *Stephen Hawes: The passtyme of pleasure*. Early English Text Society OS 173. London: Oxford University Press.

Herbert, George: in Gardner 1972 (see Donne). (*Death; Discipline; The Pulley; Vertue.*)

Heywood, Thomas: in McIlwraith 1971 (see *Arden of Feversham*). (*A Woman Killed With Kindness.*)

Jonson, Ben: WILKES, G. A. (ed.) 1988: *Ben Jonson: five plays*. Oxford: Oxford University Press. (*The Alchemist; Bartholomew Fair; Every Man In His Humour; Sejanus; Volpone.*)

—DONALDSON, I. (ed.) 1985: *Ben Jonson*. Oxford: Oxford University Press. (*Timber or Discoveries.*)

Kyd, Thomas: in McIlwraith 1971 (see *Arden of Feversham*). (*The Spanish Tragedy.*)

Lyly, John: BOND, R. W. (ed.) 1902: *The complete works of John Lyly*. (3 vols.) Oxford: Clarendon Press. (*Endimion; Euphues.*)

—MINTO 1881: *Manual of English prose literature*. Edinburgh and London: William Blackwood and Sons. (Second Letter of Petition, 1593.)

Machyn, Henry: NICHOLS, J. G. (ed.) 1848: *The diary of Henry Machyn*. Camden Society 42. London: Nichols and Son.

Malory, Sir Thomas: VINAVER, E. (ed.) 1967: *The works of Sir Thomas Malory*. (2nd ed., 3 vols.) Oxford: Clarendon Press. (*Morte Darthur.*)

Mandeville, Sir John: SISAM, K. (ed.) 1921: *Fourteenth century verse and prose*. Oxford: Clarendon Press. (*Mandeville's Travels.*)

Marlowe, Christopher: STEANE, J. B. (ed.) 1969: *Christopher Marlowe: The complete plays*. London: Penguin. (*Dido, Queen of Carthage; Doctor Faustus; Edward the Second; The Jew Of Malta; The Massacre At Paris; 1Tamburlaine, 2Tamburlaine.*)

Marvell, Andrew: in Gardner 1972 (see Donne). (*The Garden.*)

Milton, John: BUSH, D. (ed.) 1966: *Milton: poetical works*. Oxford: Oxford University Press. (*Comus; Lycidas; On the Morning of Christ's Nativity; Paradise Lost; Samson Agonistes.*)

—BUSH, D. (ed.) 1949: *The portable Milton*. New York: The Viking Press. (*Aeropagitica.*)

—BEECHING, H. C. (ed.) 1914: *The poetical works of John Milton*. London: Oxford University Press. (Original spelling and punctuation version of *Paradise Lost*.)

Nashe, Thomas: WELLS, S. (ed.) 1964: *Thomas Nashe*. London: Edward Arnold. (*Pierce Penniless his Supplication to the Devil.*)

Pinder of Wakefield, The: HORSMAN, E. A. (ed.) 1956: *The Pinder of Wakefield*. Liverpool: Liverpool University Press.

Shakespeare, William: WELLS, S. and TAYLOR, G. (general eds.) 1988: *William Shakespeare: The complete works*. Oxford: Clarendon Press. (*All's Well That Ends Well; Antony and Cleopatra; As You Like It; The Comedy Of Errors; Coriolanus; Cymbeline; Hamlet; 1Henry IV; 2Henry IV; 1Henry VI; 2Henry VI; 3Henry VI; Henry VIII; Julius Caesar; King John; King Lear; Love's Labour's Lost; Macbeth; Measure For Measure; The Merchant Of Venice; The Merry Wives Of Windsor; A Midsummer Night's Dream; Much Ado About Nothing; Othello; The Phoenix and Turtle; The Rape Of Lucrece; Richard II; Richard III; Romeo and Juliet; Sonnets; The Taming*

Of The Shrew; The Tempest; Timon of Athens; Troilus and Cressida; Twelfth Night; The Two Gentlemen Of Verona; Venus and Adonis; The Winter's Tale.)
—WELLS, S. and TAYLOR, G. (general eds.) 1986: *William Shakespeare: The complete works.* Oxford: Clarendon Press. (Original spelling and punctuation passages.)
Sidney, Sir Philip: FEUILLERAT, A. (ed.) 1922: *The complete works of Sir Philip Sidney*, vol. 2. Cambridge: Cambridge University Press. (*Arcadia; Astrophel and Stella.*)
—SHEPHERD, G. (ed.) 1965: *Sir Philip Sidney: An apology for poetry.* London: Nelson.
Spenser, Edmund: SMITH, J. C./DE SELINCOURT, E. (eds.) 1912: *Spenser: poetical works.* Oxford: Oxford University Press. (*Amoretti; The Faerie Queene; The Shepheardes Calender.*)
Stubbes, Phillip 1583: *The anatomie of abuses.* (Facsimile edition.) *The English Experience* 489. Amsterdam, 1972.
Tourneur, Cyril: SALGÃDO, G. (ed.) 1965: *Three Jacobean tragedies.* London: Penguin. (*The Revenger's Tragedy.*)
Wyatt, Sir Thomas: REBHOLZ, R. A. (ed.) 1978: *Sir Thomas Wyatt: the complete poems.* New Haven and London: Yale University Press. (*A Paraphrase of the Penitential Psalms*; Epigram no. 41; Songs nos. 106, 117; *Iopas's Song.*)

2 References

Ad Herennium, see *Rhetorica ad Herennium*.
Aristotle 1926: *Art of Rhetoric.* Transl. Freese, J. H., Loeb Classical Library. London: Heinemann.
Barber, C. 1976: *Early Modern English.* London: André Deutsch.
Barish, J. A. 1970: Jonson's dramatic prose. In Watson, 1970, 111–55. Originally in Barish, J. A. (ed.) 1960: *Ben Jonson and the language of prose comedy* Cambridge, Mass.: Harvard University Press, 41–89. Also reprinted in a slightly shorter extract as 'Prose as prose' in Fish, S. (ed.) 1971: *Seventeenth century prose* New York: Oxford University Press, 309–35.
Cicero 1939; rev. 1962: *Brutus* and *Orator.* Transl. Hendrickson, G. L. and Hubbell, H. M. Loeb Classical Library. London: Heinemann.
—1942: *De oratore.* Transl. Sutton, E. W. and Rackham, R. (2 vols.) Loeb Classical Library. London: Heinemann.
—1949: *De inventione* and *De optimo genere oratorum* and *Topica.* Transl. Hubbell, H. M. Loeb Classical Library. London: Heinemann.
Clark, D. L. 1922: *Rhetoric and poetry in the Renaissance: a study of rhetorical terms in English Renaissance literary criticism.* New York: Columbia University Press.
Corbett, E. P. J. 1990: *Classical rhetoric for the modern student.* (3rd edition.) New York, Oxford: Oxford University Press.

Craig, H. 1931: Shakespeare and Wilson's *Arte of Rhetorique. Studies in Philology* 28, 618–30.

Croll, M. 1970: The Baroque style in prose. In Watson 1970, 84–110. Originally in Malone, K. and Ruud, M. B. 1929: *Studies in English philology: A miscellany in honor of Frederick Klaeber*. Minneapolis: University of Minnesota Press, 427–56. Also reprinted in Fish, S. (ed.) 1971: *Seventeenth century prose*. New York: Oxford University Press, 26–52.

Daines, S. 1640: *Orthoepia Anglicana*. Facsimile edition. London: Menston 1967.

Danielsson, B. 1948: *Studies on the accentuation of polysyllabic Latin, Greek, and Romance loan-words in English*. Stockholm: Almqvist & Wiksell.

Day, A. 1586: *The English Secretorie* (Facsimile edition). London: Scolar Press, 1974.

Dobson, E. J. 1968: *English Pronunciation 1501–1700*. (2nd edition. 2 vols.) Oxford: Clarendon Press.

Dorsch, T. S. (ed. and transl.) 1965: *Classical literary criticism*. London: Penguin.

Ellegård, A. 1953: *The auxiliary do*. Stockholm: Almqvist & Wiksell.

Emma, R. D. 1964: *Milton's grammar*. The Hague: Mouton.

Erasmus, D. 1978: *De duplici copia verborum ac rerum*. Transl. Knott, B. I. In vol. 24 (*Literary and Educational Writings 2*) of *Collected Works of Erasmus*. Toronto.

Fraunce, A. 1588: *The Arcadian Rhetorique*. (Facsimile edition). London: Menston, 1969.

Franz, W. 1986: *Die Sprache Shakespeares in Vers und Prosa*. (4th edition.) Tübingen: Niemeyer. (Reprint from 1939 edition. Halle: Niemeyer).

Gombrich, E. H. 1977: *Art and illusion: a study in the psychology of pictorial representation*. (5th edition.) London: Phaidon.

Harrison, J. L. 1968: Bacon's view of rhetoric, poetry, and the imagination. In Vickers, B. (ed.), *Essential articles for the study of Francis Bacon* (Hamden, Connecticut: Shoestring Press), 253–71. Originally in *Huntingdon Library Quarterly* 20 (1957), 107–25.

Hoskins, J. 1935: *Directions for speech and style* (1600). Ed. Hudson, H. H. Princeton, New Jersey: Princeton University Press.

Hughes, G. 1988: *Words in time: a social history of the English vocabulary*. Oxford and New York: Blackwell.

Hulme, H. M. 1962: *Explorations in Shakespeare's language*. New York: Longman.

Isocrates 1928–45: *Isocrates*. (3 vols.) Transl. Norlin, G. and Van Hook, L. Loeb Classical Library. London: Heinemann.

Johnson, S. 1968: *Johnson on Shakespeare*. Ed. Sherbo, A. *The Yale Edition of the Works of Samuel Johnson 7*. New Haven: Yale University Press.

Joseph, Sister M. 1947: *Shakespeare's use of the arts of language*. New York: Hafner.

Kimbrough, R. (ed.) 1983: *Sir Philip Sidney: selected prose and poetry*. Madison: University of Wisconsin Press.

Kökeritz, H. 1953: *Shakespeare's pronunciation*. New Haven: Yale University Press.

Koller, K. 1964: Art, rhetorique and holy dying in *The Faerie Queene. Studies in Philology* 61, 128–39.

Lausberg, H. 1967: *Elemente der literarischen Rhetorik.* (3rd edition.) Munich: Max Hueber.

Lewis, C. S. 1954: *English literature in the sixteenth century.* Oxford: Clarendon Press.

—1964: *The discarded image.* Cambridge: Cambridge University Press.

Longinus 1965: *On the sublime.* In Dorsch, 1965, 97–158.

McKeon, R. P. 1942: Rhetoric in the Middle Ages. *Speculum* 17, 1–32.

Melanchthon, P. 1968: *Elementorum rhetorices libri duo* (Wittenberg 1531). Ed. and transl. Sister La Fontaine, J. M. PhD dissertation: University of Michigan.

Minto, W. 1881: *A manual of English prose literature.* Edinburgh and London: William Blackwood & Sons.

Mulcaster, R. 1925: *Mulcaster's Elementarie* (1582) Ed. Campagnac, E. T. Tudor and Stuart Library. Oxford: Clarendon Press.

Partridge, A. C. 1971: *The language of Renaissance poetry.* London: André Deutsch.

Partridge, E. 1968: *Shakespeare's bawdy.* London and New York: Routledge & Kegan Paul.

Patrides, A. (ed.) 1967: *Milton's epic poetry.* London: Penguin.

Peacham, H. 1577: *The Garden of Eloquence.* (1st edition) Facsimile edition. London: Menston, 1971.

— 1593: *The Garden of Eloquence.* (2nd edition.) Facsimile edition, by Crane, W. G. New York, 1977.

Pearsall, D. A. 1950: Rhetorical 'descriptio' in *Sir Gawain and the Green Knight. Modern Language Review* 50, 129–34.

Pennanen, E. 1951: *Chapters on the language in Ben Jonson's dramatic works.* Turku: Turun Yliopisto.

Plato 1952: *Phaedrus.* Transl. Hackford, R. Cambridge: Cambridge University Press.

— 1979: *Gorgias.* Transl. Irwin, T. Oxford: Clarendon Press.

Pollard, A. W. 1917: *Shakespeare's fight with the pirates and the problems of the transmission of his text.* London: Alexander Moring.

Puttenham, G. 1936: *The arte of English poesie* (1589). Ed. Willcock, G. and Walker, A. Cambridge: Cambridge University Press.

Quintilian 1921–2: *Institutio oratoria.* Transl. Butler H. E., (4 vols). Loeb Classical Library. London: Heinemann.

Rhetorica ad Herennium 1954. Transl. Caplan, H. Loeb Classical Library. London: Heinemann.

Ricks, C. 1963: *Milton's grand style.* Oxford: Clarendon Press.

Ridley, M. R. (ed.): *Shakespeare: Antony and Cleopatra.* Arden edition. London: Methuen.

Rubinstein, F. 1989: *A dictionary of Shakespeare's sexual puns and their significance.* (2nd edition.) London: Macmillan.

Salingar, L. G. 1955: The Elizabethan literary Renaissance. In Ford, B. (ed.), *The age of Shakespeare* in *Pelican Guide to English Literature 2.* London: Penguin, 51–116.

Salmon, V. 1986: The spelling and punctuation of Shakespeare's time. In

Wells, S. and Taylor, G. (general eds.), *William Shakespeare: The complete works* (Oxford: Clarendon Press), xlii-lvi.

Salter, E. 1962: '*Piers Plowman*': *an introduction*. Oxford: Blackwell.

Samuels, M. L. 1972: *Linguistic evolution*. Cambridge: Cambridge University Press.

Sanders, N. 1968: Introduction to his edition of Shakespeare's *Two Gentlemen of Verona*. London: Penguin.

Shepherd, G. (ed.) 1959: *Ancrene Wisse*. London: Nelson.

Sherry, R. 1550: *A treatise of schemes and tropes*. Facsimile edition by Hildebrandt, H. W. Gainesville, Florida: University of Florida Press 1961; repr. New York, 1977.

Sonnino, L. A. 1968: *A handbook to sixteenth-century rhetoric*. London: Routledge & Kegan Paul.

Sugden, H. W. 1936: *The grammar of Spenser's Faerie Queene*. Philadelphia: University of Pennsylvania Press.

Susenbrotus, J. 1541: *The 'Epitome troporum ac schematum' of Joannes Susenbrotus: text, translation and commentary*, by Brennan, J. X. Ph.D. dissertation: University of Illinois 1953.

Tarselius, R. 1968: 'All colours will agree in the dark': a note on a feature in the style of Francis Bacon. In Vickers, B. (ed.), *Essential articles for the study of Francis Bacon*. Hamden, Connecticut: Shoe String Press, 293–99. (Originally in *Studia Neophilologica* 25 (1958), 55–60).

Treip, M. 1970: *Milton's punctuation*. London: Methuen.

Vallins, G. H. 1965: *Spelling*. (2nd edition), revised by Scragg, D. G. London: André Deutsch.

Vickers, B. 1988: *In defence of rhetoric*. Oxford: Clarendon Press.

Watson, G. (ed.) 1970: *Literary English since Shakespeare*. London: Oxford University Press.

Webber, J. 1963: *Contrary music: the prose style of John Donne*. Madison: University of Wisconsin Press.

Wells, S. 1979: *Modernizing Shakespeare's spelling*. Oxford: Clarendon Press.

Wilson, T. 1909: *Arte of rhetorique* (1553). Ed. Mair, G. H. Oxford: Oxford University Press.

Wright, J. 1905: *The English dialect grammar*. Oxford: Clarendon Press.

Zandvoort, R. W. 1970: What is Euphuism? *Collected papers II* (Groningen Studies in English 10), 12–21. Originally in *Mélanges Fernand Mossé* (Paris 1959), 508–17.

3 Suggestions for further reading. (Books and articles already listed in section 2 above will be referred to by author and year only, and so will works if listed more than once (under different subheadings) in this section.)

For general surveys, especially on sounds, spellings, vocabulary and attitudes to language, there are several histories of English, for instance:

Baugh, A. C. and Cable, T. 1978: *A history of the English language*. (3rd edition). Englewood Cliffs, New Jersey: Prentice-Hall.

Leith, D. 1983: *A social history of English*. London: Routledge & Kegan Paul.

Pyles, T. and Algeo, J. 1982: *The origins and development of the English language*. (3rd edition). New York: Harcourt Brace Jovanovich.

Suitable works with more specific reference to the Renaissance period are:

Barber, 1976.

Görlach, 1991.

Partridge, A. C. 1969: *Tudor to Augustan English*. London: André Deutsch.

Useful because of their emphasis on language as a literary medium in particular are:

Lewis, 1954.

McKnight, G. H. 1968: *The evolution of the English language*. New York: Dover. (First published in 1928 with the title *Modern English in the making*. New York: Appleton.)

Partridge, 1971.

Sounds and spellings:

Cercignani, F. 1981: *Shakespeare's works and Elizabethan pronunciation*. Oxford: Clarendon Press.

Danielsson, 1948.

Dobson, 1968.

Kökeritz, 1953.

Partridge, A. C. 1964: *Orthography in Shakespeare and Elizabethan drama*. London: Edward Arnold.

Pollard, 1917.

Salmon, 1986.

Scragg, D. G. 1974: *A history of English spelling*. Manchester: Manchester University Press.

Vallins, 1965.

Wells, 1979.

Wyld, H. C. 1923: *Studies in English rhymes from Surrey to Pope*. London: John Murray.

Vocabulary and meaning:

Biese, Y. M. 1941: *Origin and development of conversions in English*. Annales Academiae Scientarum Fennicae B XLV.2. Helsinki.

Blake, N. F. 1983: *Shakespeare's language*. London: Macmillan.

Brook, G. L. 1976: *The language of Shakespeare*. London: André Deutsch.

Groom, B. 1937: The formation and use of compound epithets in English poetry from 1579. Society for Pure English, Tract 49, 293–322. Oxford: Clarendon Press.

Hughes, 1988.

Hulme, 1962.

Jespersen, O. 1954: *Growth and structure of the English language.* (9th edition). Oxford: Blackwell.
Lewis, C. S. 1967: *Studies in words.* (2nd edition). Cambridge: Cambridge University Press.
Partridge, 1968.
Pennanen, 1951.
Rubinstein, 1989.
Schäfer, J. 1973: *Shakespeares Stil: germanisches und romanisches Vokabular.* Frankfurt: Athenäum.
Serjeantson, M. S. 1935: *A history of foreign words in English.* London: Routledge & Kegan Paul.
Sheard, J. A. 1954: *The words we use.* London: André Deutsch.
Ullmann, S. 1959: *The principles of semantics.* (Rev. edition) Glasgow: Jackson.

Syntax and punctuation:

Abbott, E. A. 1872: *A Shakespearian Grammar.* (Rev. edition). London: Macmillan.
Ando, S. 1976: *A descriptive syntax of Christopher Marlowe's language.* Tokyo: University of Tokyo Press.
Banks, T. H. 1927: Miltonic rhythm: a study of the relation of the full stops to the rhythm of *Paradise Lost. Publications of the Modern Language Association of America* 42, 140–5.
Barish, 1970.
Blake, 1983.
Brook, 1976.
Charleston, B. M. 1941: *Studies on the syntax of the English verb.* Bern: Francke.
Croll, M. W. 1966: *Style, rhetoric and rhythm.* Princeton: Princeton University Press.
—1970.
Dahl, L. 1969: *Nominal style in the Shakespearean soliloquy.* Turku: Turun Yliopisto.
Ellegård, 1953.
Emma, 1964.
Franz, 1986.
Fridén, G. 1948: *Studies on the tenses of the English verb from Chaucer to Shakespeare.* Stockholm: Almqvist & Wiksell.
Fries, C. C. 1925: Shakespearian punctuation. *Studies in Shakespeare, Milton and Donne.* University of Michigan Publications in Language and Literature, vol. 1, New York: Macmillan, 65–86.
Jespersen, O. 1909–49: *A Modern English grammar on historical principles.* (7 vols). London: Allen and Unwin.
Kakietek, P. 1970: *May* and *might* in Shakespeare's English. *Linguistics* 64, 26–35.
—1972: *Modal verbs in Shakespeare's English.* Poznan: Universytet im Adama Mickiewicza.

Kisbye, T. 1971: *An historical outline of English syntax*. (2 vols.) Aarhus: Akademisk Boghandel.

McIntosh, A. 1963: *As You Like It*: a grammatical clue to character. *Review of English Literature* 4, 68–81.

Mulholland, J. 1967: 'Thou' and 'You' in Shakespeare: a study in the second person pronoun. *English Studies* 48, 34–43.

Ong, W. J. 1944: Historical backgrounds of Elizabethan and Jacobean punctuation theory. *Publications of the Modern Language Association of America* 59, 349–60.

Partridge, A. C. 1953: *Studies in the syntax of Ben Jonson's plays*. Cambridge: Bowes and Bowes.

Rydén, M. 1966: *Relative constructions in early sixteenth-century English*. Stockholm: Almqvist & Wiksell.

Salmon, V, 1965: Sentence structures in colloquial Shakespearian English. *Transactions of the Philological Society*, 105–40.

—1979: *The study of language in 17th-century England*. Amsterdam: Benjamin.

Simpson, E. M. 1928: A note on Donne's punctuation. *Review of English Studies* 4, 295–300.

Simpson, P. 1911: *Shakespearian punctuation*. Oxford: Clarendon Press.

Sørensen, K. 1957: Latin influence on English syntax. *Travaux du cercle linguistique de Copenhague* 11, 131–55.

Sugden, 1936.

Treip, 1970.

Trnka, B. 1930: *On the syntax of the English verb from Caxton to Dryden*. Prague: *Travaux du cercle linguistique de Prague*.

Van Der Gaaf, W. 1904: *The transition from the impersonal to the personal construction in Middle English*. Heidelberg: Carl Winter.

Vickers, B. 1968: *The artistry of Shakespeare's prose*. London: Methuen.

Visser, F. T. 1946, 1952, 1956: *A syntax of the English language of Sir Thomas More*. (3 vols.) Louvain: Libraire Universitaire.

—1963, 1966, 1969, 1973: *An historical syntax of the English language*. (4 vols.) Leiden: Brill.

Weida, G. 1975: *Der Gebrauch von shall/should und will/would in englischer Prosa am Ende des 16. Jahrhunderts*. Ph.D. dissertation: Ludwig-Maximilians-Universität, Munich.

Rhetoric, Humanism and Renaissance ideas. (For classical and Renaissance works, see Section 2 above). *Useful introductions to the subject:*

Bush, D. 1939: *The Renaissance and English Humanism*. Toronto: University of Toronto Press.

Clark, 1922.

Cockcroft, R. and Cockcroft, S. 1991: *Rhetoric: a study of persuasive techniques in English*. London: Macmillan.

Corbett, 1990.

Dixon, P. 1971: *Rhetoric*. London: Methuen.

Joseph, 1947.

Vickers, B. 1970: *Classical rhetoric in English poetry*. London: Macmillan.

—1988.

The following are just a few of a more specialized nature:

Buxton, J. 1954: *Sir Philip Sidney and the English Renaissance.* London: Macmillan.

Calder, A. C. 1989: *The dramatic language of Shakespeare's 'Henry VI': a stylistic and theatrical study.* Ph.D. dissertation: University of Aberdeen.

Crane, W. G. 1937: *Wit and rhetoric in the Renaissance: the formal basis of Elizabethan prose style.* New York: Columbia University Press.

Gilman, W. M. 1939: *Milton's rhetoric: studies in his defense of liberty.* Columbia: University of Missouri Press.

Goldsmith, U. K. 1950: Words out of a hat? Alliteration and assonance in Shakespeare's sonnets. *Journal of English and Germanic Philology* 49, 33–48.

Harrison, 1968.

Koller, 1964.

Lanham, R. A. 1968: *A handlist of rhetorical terms.* Berkeley and Los Angeles: University of California Press.

McKeon, 1942.

Mahood, M. M. 1957: *Shakespeare's wordplay.* London: Methuen.

Murphy, J. J. (ed.) 1978: *Medieval eloquence: studies in the theory and practice of medieval rhetoric.* Berkeley: University of California Press.

—(ed.) 1983a: *Renaissance eloquence: studies in the theory and practice of Renaissance rhetoric.* Berkeley: University of California Press.

—(ed.) 1983b: *A synoptic history of classical rhetoric.* Davis, California: Hermagoras Press.

Nowottny, W. M. T. 1976: Some features of Shakespeare's poetic language considered in the light of Quintilian and Thomas Wilson. *Hebrew University Studies in Literature* 4.2., 125–37.

Sackton, A. H. 1948: *Rhetoric as a dramatic language in Ben Jonson.* New York: Columbia University Press.

Sonnino, 1968.

Vickers, B. 1981: Rhetorical and anti-rhetorical tropes: on writing the history of *elocutio*. *Comparative Criticism* 3, 105–32.

Wilcock, G. D. 1943: Shakespeare and rhetoric. *Essays and Studies* 29, 50–61.

Index

Index

Index

Index